ENVIRONMENTAL DAMAGE COSTS

Record of a Seminar held at the OECD
in August 1972

ORGANISATION FOR ECONOMIC
CO-OPERATION AND DEVELOPMENT

The Organisation for Economic Co-operation and Development (OECD) was set up under a Convention signed in Paris on 14th December, 1960, which provides that the OECD shall promote policies designed :

- *to achieve the highest sustainable economic growth and employment and a rising standard of living in Member countries, while maintaining financial stability, and thus to contribute to the development of the world economy;*
- *to contribute to sound economic expansion in Member as well as non-member countries in the process of economic development;*
- *to contribute to the expansion of world trade on a multilateral, non-discriminatory basis in accordance with international obligations.*

The Members of OECD are Australia, Austria, Belgium, Canada, Denmark, Finland, France, the Federal Republic of Germany, Greece, Iceland, Ireland, Italy, Japan, Luxembourg, the Netherlands, New Zealand, Norway, Portugal, Spain, Sweden, Switzerland, Turkey, the United Kingdom and the United States.

*
**

FOREWORD

During the summer of 1972, the OECD Environment Directorate organised a Seminar on damage costs to the environment. The Seminar was held at the Paris headquarters of the OECD, and experts from seven Member countries attended. The goal of the seminar was to evaluate the extent to which the existing work on environmental damage costs and the knowledge of the probability of this damage can help the decision-maker set environmental policy objectives.

In effect, a better knowledge of environmental damage costs should, at least in theory, permit the decision-maker to rationalize his actions in relating the costs of prevention measures to the expected damage, while at the same time permitting him to determine environmental policy objectives whose social advantages outweigh, or at least balance, the social costs of their implementation.

In their papers, as well as in their discussions of these papers, the participants of the seminar reviewed existing work in their countries in an effort to identify the principal strengths and weaknesses of damage costs in order to develop some guidelines for future work.

*

* *

The analyses, undertaken by the participants, distinguished between two types of damage, or rather damage functions: monetary damage functions and non-monetary damage functions. A non-monetary damage function relates specific levels of pollution, noise, or environmental deterioration to adverse biological, physical, and/or psychological effects which occur at those levels. A monetary damage function relates levels of pollution to the amount of compensation that would be needed in order that society is not worse off than before the deterioration of the environment. This concept of damage includes loss in income, direct expenditure for reparation and replacement, and psychic costs. These two types of functions should not be considered separately as some knowledge about non-monetary damage functions is a necessary prerequisite for the development of monetary damage functions.

In the case of monetary damage, there are several methods which yield estimates: direct estimates of losses and expenditures (as of lost income and the cost of medical treatment), property value and other market response models, questionnaire surveys, legal estimates, and the study of individual responses to substitutes. No one method appears to be superior to all of the others.

Very little empirical work has emerged in which true monetary functions have been developed. To the knowledge of the participants, estimates of monetary damage functions have been made only in studies which relate property values to pollution and noise levels. For the remaining work, damage estimates are, in general, associated with only one level of pollution; the resulting estimates of the damage functions are based on arbitrary interpolation or extrapolation.

The comparison of empirical results from various countries is, in the aggregate, very difficult, even when similar methodologies have been used. At least two factors contribute to this variation: uncertainties and lack of agreement on the biological and environmental effects of pollution, and on the assignment of monetary values to these effects.

Finally this comparison is generally hampered because the concept of damage and its relationship to the general welfare economics framework have not been clearly defined. Most empirical studies have not included psychic costs and have thus underestimated the total damage.

The discussions of this seminar indicate that the knowledge of monetary and non-monetary damage functions is a useful element in decision-making. However, it is necessary to specify the operational context of their use and the assumed value judgments underlying their use for two essential reasons:

    i)   monetary estimates of real loss can reflect the existing or some assumed distribution of income and wealth;

ii)   the perception of damage and risk may differ depending on
whether it is that of the public (victims) or that of experts and
scientists.

*

*   *

Finally, through presenting an inventory of our current knowledge
in this area and in launching an inquiry on the utility of damage
functions for decision-making, this seminar has contributed towards
encouraging international cooperation in a difficult area by promoting,
within the Environment Committee, an important work programme on
environmental damage costs.

In particular, the Central Analysis and Evaluation Unit of the
Secretariat and the Sub-Committee of Economic Experts are undertaking a critical analysis of the various existing studies and are in the
process of preparing a handbook which will provide some useful
guidelines to Member countries desiring to evaluate damage to their
environments.

CONTENTS

ASCERTAINING ENVIRONMENTAL COSTS AND BENEFITS [1]

by

Serge Christophe Kolm
Professor,
School of Higher Studies, (Sorbonne),
Paris

1. THE NATURE OF THE PROBLEM

As soon as we try to formulate an environment policy, we are faced on every side with problems of knowledge. If we want to lay down prohibitions or to introduce regulations, how can we be certain of making the right choice, and what standards should we adopt? If we want to make the polluters pay the external social cost of their acts, how can we ascertain that cost, particularly if their action affects human health, natural beauty, the conservation of species or posterity?

In practice, it is just this question of knowledge which will guide our choice of one instrument rather than another to deal with a given environmental problem, or which will at least be a major factor in that choice. Assume, for example, that we are fully conversant with the external cost of the nuisance. This sometimes happens; one example is the pollution of water subsequently used by industries which need pure water and which therefore have to purify their supplies at a cost which is easily ascertained and which is the cost we seek. It is then sufficient to charge the polluters (or the creators of the nuisance) with this external cost of their action to make them fully conscious of its harmful effects when they decide to pursue it. The public authorities therefore no longer have the slightest need, in order to attain social effectiveness, to know the problems of the polluters and, in particular, the benefit to them of the right to pollute and the cost of abstaining. It follows that if it is hard for the authorities to know these latter elements, but easy for them to know the external cost, making the polluters pay seems the best instrument, since it eliminates the need for information which is difficult and even impossible to attain. In contrast, regulations restricting the nuisance or the activity which creates it cannot be imposed without comparing the external cost with the cost to the polluters of abstaining, which must therefore be estimated. Obviously, for our present purposes, paying the polluters the value of the benefit to their victims of their abstention from pollution is as effective as making them pay, and the same applies to the sale to or purchase from, the polluters, of the right to pollute at a price equivalent to the external cost and without restriction.

The knowledge we are talking about here is knowledge by the authorities responsible for dealing with the relevant environmental question. That obviously does not exhaust all the problems of knowledge raised by questions of environment. For example, the victims of air or water pollution or of noise may not know how far their health has been endangered. Or the polluters may not know the relation between their action and the nuisance they create, and so forth. This ignorance will nevertheless be an obstacle to the assessment of costs and benefits by the authorities since they cannot in these circumstances rely on what those directly concerned may think or therefore on what they disclose by their words and deeds.

In the absence of the knowledge needed to make a choice the first thing to do is to try to fill the information gaps. In the case of environmental problems, this information can be acquired in various ways, which we shall describe below. But there may be obstacles in the way of complete, or even sufficient knowledge. The information may be obtainable only at prohibitive cost; the costs of inquiries, experiments, etc., being additional to the cost of the effects of this process of acquiring information on the events about which the information is sought. And both the impossibilities and the costs of acquiring knowledge must be regarded as dynamic in the sense that it may be impossible or too costly to acquire such information within a specified time; if there is a cost attached to the postponement of decision until the information is acquired, this is part of the cost of acquiring knowledge, and if the decision has to be taken before the knowledge is acquired, or if it is finally found more profitable to act in this way, then the choice is made in a state of uncertainty.

Ultimately, by force or by choice, we are bound to take decisions with an imperfect knowledge of the elements of the problem. This is extremely frequent in environment policy. But this should on no account discourage us or resign us to an arbitrary choice. For this situation is in no way novel to the economist; the science of choices in a state of uncertainty is one of the most trodden paths of economic analysis (2).

These two ways of coping with ignorance - information and rational choice in a state of uncertainty - are obviously not mutually exclusive. Uncertainty at the moment of choice will become less, the greater the amount of information collected before the choice has

10

to be made. And just as there is a cost attached to information, an uninformed choice involves a loss since the decision taken is not the optimum decision which would have been made with perfect knowledge. Now, this loss decreases with the increase of information; but this increase of information involves the cost of acquiring knowledge. Knowledge must therefore be optimized prior to a decision taken in a state of uncertainty but allowing for the expected loss involved in such decision; this optimization will be the best compromise between the cost of acquiring more knowledge and the loss of having to choose with too much uncertainty. If the information can be acquired with time, but delay in decision is harmful, this optimization will include, in particular, choosing the optimum date of decision.

It will be obvious to the reader that this general problem of the relations between knowledge and decision is encountered in nearly all environment questions.

Finally, the seriousness of the problem of knowledge and the current possibility of revising a policy often means that the optimum strategy is a sequential decision. For example, the polluters are made to pay, and it is then ascertained whether the resultant level of pollution - which could not be exactly foreseen - is "acceptable" or whether it is still too high; in the latter event, the rate of charge is increased. If, on the other hand, the pollution disappears and there is some fear of having been too hard on the polluters, then the rate of charge can be reduced; convergence towards the "good" state by this method depends on structural properties which we analyse below.

The knowledge or ignorance we are discussing here relates to two factors, first, the external cost of the nuisance and, secondly, the benefit to the polluters of the right to create a nuisance - or the cost of abstention. It is in fact the comparison between these two factors which determines the optimum. In not very precise terms, it can be said that the optimum level of the nuisance is that which minimizes the "sum" of these two costs. At the optimum and in general, the marginal external cost and the marginal cost of abstention should be equal. But if the authority which should attain this optimum by its actions is ignorant of these factors, these conditions cannot be achieved in practice, even if the policy chosen is the best in the light of the existing uncertainty.

2. GOOD BEHAVIOUR

It is in no way surprising that difficulties of knowledge should be central to environment economics. Indeed, all economic problems are

11

basically problems of knowledge once it is agreed that questions of distribution are a matter for political science and ethics; the theory of prices and the theory of "perfect competition" are no more than information systems, and their maladies and crises (especially as explained by Keynes) and their externalities and collective concerns are merely defects in the mechanism for the transmission of information. This is clear in the case of external effects and public goods when it is realized that the heart of the difficulty is the "revelation problem". And the problems of the environment fall into this category. It is because, and in so far as, the markets and the price and competition systems fail to transmit among the interested parties information about the costs and benefits of these phenomena that there is a public problem. Questions of distribution are another matter, but even the question of what is a sound distribution can be regarded as a problem of knowledge.

In environmental matters everyone is fully conscious of the difficulties of knowledge, especially knowledge of external costs.

But, as noted above, while these difficulties are often real, and sometimes extreme (health, aesthetics, conservation of species, taste of future generations), they are, on the other hand, frequently minimal (cost of cleaning up pollution, loss of profit, etc.).

Furthermore, it must be recognized that the problem is inescapable. It is for example not a valid answer to say that regulations imposing a quantitative obligation will be preferred to charging the external cost because the level of the obligation cannot be determined without estimating the external cost of the nuisance; this also requires an estimate of the cost of the polluters of abstention, a factor which need not be known for the purposes of charging. Estimates of costs and benefits are implicit in every measure taken. Any action which is even moderately free - and inaction itself is merely a special form of action - automatically implies a certain judgment of costs and benefits and makes the actor responsible for it. Now, etymologically speaking, "implicit" means "hypocritical". It would certainly be better to bring underlying estimates into the light of day; their comparison with what is known of the facts cannot fail to improve them and therefore help towards a better choice. Furthermore, the publication of implicit estimates may set off reactions which themselves provide the information needed.

Finally the assertion that some particular cost (such as the psychological cost) or benefit is "unknowable" often merely betrays a lack of imagination or reflection. It is not unusual to find that in apparently very difficult situations there are ways and means of estimating these elements and of improving, if not of perfecting, our knowledge of them, but that these ways and means demand practical imagination to conceive

12

them, reflection to elaborate them and ingenuity and hard work to put them into practice. We suggest some examples below. But since "movement is proved by walking", we may cite some studies which have been made along these lines in the field of environment or allied fields.

One is Ridker's work, The Economic Cost of Air Pollution (3) where the estimate takes account of the cost of purification and illness and of the difference in site and property values between zones with varying degrees of air pollution. An excellent method, described below, devised by Harold Hotelling and applied by Marion Clawson, J. Knetsch, P. Davidson, F. Adams and J. Seneca has made it possible by observation of the transport costs accepted by visitors to assess the benefits of the use of national parks and open waters for recreational purposes, and consequently the social cost of the pollution of that water (4). The same method was applied to estimate the intensity of the desire for peace in Vietnam as revealed by the transport and loss-of- time costs accepted by mass demonstrators in Washington (5). Krutilla and his associates were able to estimate the amenity value of Hell's Canyon (State of Washington) which it was proposed to flood in order to make a hydro-electric reservoir (6). It has also been possible to assess the value of leisure spent in fishing (Sweden, Netherlands, United States) or riding (Netherlands) and therefore of the corresponding developments (7). Several other estimates of the value of recreation in natural parks or open waters (and therefore of the cost of their pollution) have been attempted in the United States (8).

A very skilful study of an estimate of the same type as that encountered in many environment problems is that of Herbert Mohring (9) who arrives at the benefit of time for road carriers by observing the speed they choose and calculating how a slight change would modify their costs for fuel and wear and tear of equipment (in this way he obtains the marginal benefit of time which is precisely the information most needed). In Sweden, Peter Bohm has estimated the benefit of a television programme as felt and assessed in monetary equivalent by spectators, by asking a sample of them in the course of a series of experiments differing in the financial implications of the reply for the person who makes it, thus making allowance for his temptation to prevaricate (10). It has been possible to apply this very subtle work to all public goods and community facilities, and therefore to nearly all environment questions. In the United Kingdom, the Roskill Commission, in analysing the social aspects of the selection of a site for London's third airport, made some remarkable estimates of the social cost of noise by estimating the monetary equivalent for the interested parties on the basis of very finely interpreted differences in the value of sites subjected to different noise intensities (11); this method of assessing

13

the social cost of noise has been applied in other cases in different
countries (12). Reference should also be made to the estimates of the
benefit of human life to society made by French engineers with a view
to selecting road schemes with a higher safety factor (13); these
results also apply to environment problems, since pollution, too, can
be fatal. There have been several attempts at a similar estimate of the
cost of disease, which also apply where the disease is caused by pollution. Finally, the imperfect distribution of incomes has been taken
into account by Robert Haveman and by a Netherlands study on the
development of a leisure zone (fishermen and riders do not come from
the same income groups), by inferring the coefficients of weighting
from the marginal rates of income tax (14).

None of these studies is above all criticism, and most of them
must be regarded as incomplete. They are, however, enough to show
that the proper attitude towards questions of knowledge in environmental
matters is neither abdication, scepticism nor despair, but the attitude
described by Lo Kuan-chung in the San Kuo Yen Yi, often cited by
Mao Tse-tung: "He knits his brows and a stratagem comes into his
mind".

3. KNOWLEDGE BY SOCIETY AND ITS DISTRIBUTION

A first distinction should be drawn between knowledge by society,
that is to say by any of its members, and the distribution of this
knowledge among the various members of society.

The first question is one of science and technology and progress
is achieved by scientific and technical research. For example, the
dispersion and biological effects of DDT and other pesticides and
weedkillers are not known with certainty. It is not very clear how
certain forms of air pollution spread or how far they are a cause of
cancer. The effects on climate of the destruction of a particular forest
may be open to question. The cost of purifying air or water of some
particular product is still unknown, and so forth.

The second kind of ignorance, however, is that of the relevant
public authorities who are unfamiliar with factors which are well known,
or better known, to other members of society directly concerned.
Examples are the cost to a given industry of accepting a particular
form of pollution, or of eliminating it or even of refraining from
creating it, which the industrialists concerned often have no difficulty
in ascertaining precisely. This category includes most of the effects
which are felt by individuals directly (i. e.: otherwise than through the

medium of the market, prices, etc.). In particular, individuals know their own preferences (if not "what is good for them") better than the authorities in question, on subjects such as aesthetics, nuisance from noise and smells, the disadvantages of illness, the joys of contact with nature and so forth. It is in connection with this second category of knowledge that the "revelation problem" arises.

4. PECUNIARY AND NON-PECUNIARY EFFECTS

A second distinction is that between pecuniary and non-pecuniary effects. Pecuniary effects are those which take the form of the gain or loss of money or which can be directly expressed in terms of money; money costs, financial losses or loss of income, or, on the other hand, money gains or financial benefits. Non-pecuniary effects are those which cannot be expressed in terms of money: psychic costs and benefits, various pleasures and displeasures, etc. This distinction differs from that referred to in the previous paragraph, although the knowledge of non-pecuniary effects falls fundamentally into the category of information where the problem is its distribution among the members of society (although, in speaking of the future, the authorities might say to the individual "I know you will be happier, or unhappier, in such a state, even though you think differently now, and, obviously, in your own judgment when the time comes. Psychology teaches me this, and observation and experience have shown me that 100% of subjects have been happier, or unhappier in that state"); pecuniary effects, on the other hand, may belong to both categories, but their knowledge requires information not only about technique, but also about the economy (prices).

The great merit of pecuniary effects is obviously that they are already measured in terms of money, which is the form in which we need them to assess costs and benefits. The measuring rod we need for non-pecuniary effects is their monetary equivalent for the person concerned, in other words, the amount of money which, given to or taken from that person would exactly compensate the advantage or disadvantage to him.

The pecuniary effects of environmental matters are extremely far-reaching. Pollution costs money and its elimination saves money: water filtering and purification, air filtering and ventilation, cleaning house fronts, cleaning clothes and motor cars, cleaning, restoring and improving public sites, disinfection and vaccination against infectious diseases or epidemics, medical treatment and medicaments to deal with them, soundproofing of residential or business

15

or cultural premises, anti-noise screens on motorways and so forth. These pecuniary costs and benefits often take the form of income or loss of income; loss of income due to physical or mental illness caused by lack of hygiene, noise or lack of environmental amenities, loss of income to fishermen when water pollution kills off the fish, or to huntsmen when crowds chase away the wildlife, gains or losses by hotelkeepers, shopkeepers, houseowners or landowners according to the state of the neighbouring forest, beach, river or lake, or because the construction of a highway or an airfield makes the place too noisy, and so forth. But monetary effects are still more frequent in the case of abstention from creating a nuisance; the extra cost of manufacturing less noisy engines or machines, of built-in sound-proofing, the extra wear on engines from the use of leadfree petrol (lead tetraethyl being a dangerous air pollutant), of the removal of dust and sulphur from fumes, the use of less polluting but more costly processes - in many fields - the evacuation, transport, burial or incineration of waste or refuse, or again, the loss to a hotelkeeper whose guests can no longer visit a neighbouring site, which is temporarily closed for protection or restoration (such as the Lascaux Caves), etc. Many of the monetary effects of environmental questions are due to location; loss from choosing a house or dwelling in a quieter or cleaner spot but which is more expensive or further from the workplace (thus causing travelling costs, in particular), or loss on the carriage of a product or the transport of labour resulting from the prohibition of the installation of a pollutant factory in a centre of population or a protected site, etc.

In addition to these direct monetary effects, the general inter-dependence of markets is the cause of a number of indirect monetary effects. But these are normally merely effects of redistribution; for example, when a price goes up, the buyers lose what the sellers gain; fundamentally, the end effect is a redistribution of income between the owners of the factors of production; these effects are what the economists call "Pareto-irrelevant" externalities; in imperfect markets, however, these differences may also have an influence on effectiveness ("Pareto-relevant" effects). The effects on the distribution of income should be taken into account only if the question of distribution in society is not settled elsewhere by other instruments.

Monetary effects can be measured directly by observation of the markets and of what economic transactors buy or sell on the market. This is not necessarily easy, and the difficulty is the same as that of ascertaining the basis of assessment of income tax or expenditure. But the difficulty of estimating non-monetary effects is quite a different matter and calls for different procedures.

5. THE DISCLOSURE OF BENEFITS

Fortunately, there are other ways of estimating the benefits we need to know. They are designed to acquire knowledge which is initially essentially in the possession of the transactors directly concerned. This information relates mainly to the non-monetary and non-technical effects (which might therefore be called "psychic") but it may also relate to monetary effects which are difficult to ascertain in any other way, or to technical data (for example the effect in a particular factory of submitting to pollution, or of having to refrain from creating a specific nuisance).

What we are looking for in every case is the monetary equivalent of the effect for the transactors concerned, a result which is given directly in the case of a monetary effect. This monetary equivalent is precisely the maximum sum which the transactor would pay to avoid an unfavourable effect or to bring about a favourable effect, or the minimum sum which would have to be paid to him in consideration of his willingly accepting an unfavourable effect or forgoing a favourable effect.

The most direct way of obtaining this information is to ask the person concerned. But there may be many difficulties about this. In addition to the cost, which may be very substantial where the transactors concerned are very numerous, and which may compel the use of estimates by sample, there are two obstacles to this form of inquiry.

The first is that the transactors concerned may themselves have difficulty in estimating the monetary equivalent to them of certain effects.

This may be due to their overlooking or imperfectly estimating certain costs or consequences of the phenomenon in question, or certain circumstances which affect their estimate. They may, for example, not know whether air pollution may affect their health, which is a matter of technical ignorance. Or they may not know what may be their future needs for quiet or "green spaces" or their own tastes in these matters.

But above all, giving a monetary equivalent for non-monetary effects, even for oneself, is an unaccustomed and troublesome operation. None of us can say without reflection what is the exact money value to us of a specific aesthetic pleasure, or of the enjoyment of better health (15). This does not indicate that the question is meaningless; if one had to pay for this pleasure or for this better health, provided it is

17

nothing too serious, there is a price limit beyond which we should not go. The need to reflect already prevents a certain number of people from answering. Others, however, who have the necessary intelligence to appreciate the question, can do so. The question can even be put in the form of "conceptual experience" to people who are not concerned but who are capable of answering, by asking them to "put themselves in the place" of those concerned, by empathy. To start with, the inquirer might interrogate himself and see what his own answer would be, by way of preparing the ground and helping towards a good formulation of the question. The answers obtained could be extended to the people who do not reply, or could at least serve as a basis for estimating the benefit to them.

The second difficulty is that some transactors might deliberately wish to say something untrue about the benefit of the phenomenon to themselves. This is the "problem of disclosure" in the strict sense.

Let us take the example of an improvement in the quality of the environment, and let us ask a beneficiary what it is worth to him. If he thinks that his answer will have no influence on the charges or prices which he pays, but has some chance of being taken into account in estimating the social benefit of the project, a benefit which will determine whether it is adopted or not, he will declare a benefit higher than the true benefit to him. He will even tend to declare the highest benefit which he thinks the questioner is likely to accept as credible. It is only if he is indifferent to the improvement that he will speak his mind freely, even if it means telling the truth.

But this improvement is generally a collective consumption, a "public good". And if the beneficiaries interested in the same degree as the one considered are numerous, its benefit to each of them is only a small part of the aggregate benefit. Even if he exaggerates a great deal, if the others do the same, the benefit he discloses is only a small part of the aggregate benefits disclosed. The gain from this untruth is therefore minimal and tends towards zero as the number of people interested to the same degree increases. In the extreme case it is no longer in his interest to prevaricate.

Obviously, if this person thinks that what he says will be used to charge him according to the benefit to him, in order to finance the operation, he will tend, on the contrary, to put forward a figure below the truth if the improvement is a public good, and even in the extreme case, nil, when there are a great many people similarly concerned, if this is credible. In practice, since what he says has little or no influence on the creation of the public good, he expects to be able to profit from it in this way at little or no cost. This is Samuelson and Buchanan's phenomenon of the free-rider. But this is not our present problem, which is purely that of estimating costs and benefits. For this purpose, the effect of the mass of collective consumption, instead of being an unfavourable phenomenon, is, on the contrary favourable to the truthfulness of the disclosure.

This is, however, true, only on two conditions. In the first place, there must be no collusion or understanding between the beneficiaries of this improvement. But if they are very numerous this will be very difficult to ensure, and, what is more, it will be known. It is also necessary that the person questioned should not think that his answer will be used as representative of that of a great many people in the same situation. Furthermore, it is often easy to tell whether a reply is truthful (if some one takes the trouble to estimate a precise answer, it is somewhat difficult for him to cheat at the same time).

The same analysis can be repeated for the cost of a deterioration of the environment, for the disadvantages of having to restrict an activity which is harmful to others, and the benefits, on the other hand, of being less constrained in this respect. For example, the victim of a deterioration will overstate the true cost to him if he thinks that his answer will be used to decide to avoid or correct this effect without his being asked to contribute to the cost, or will be used to compensate or indemnify him (16). But if this deterioration is a "collective concern" in which a great many people are concerned to the same degree as the person questioned, the first motive for over-valuation disappears (but the second, indemnification, continues where it exists), at least in the absence of collusion and the belief that this answer will be taken as representative. In the case of deterioration of environmental quality, collective concern also often exists among transactors affected in the same degree and has the same consequences, although it is of a special nature, as noted elsewhere (17): it arises out of subjection to a common regulation, and is a sort of "man-made" common concern, rather than "in the nature of things"; for example this phenomenon is met when one tries to ascertain the cost to motorists of a particular restriction on noisy or polluting motor traffic.

The following table summarizes the consequences of the inter- actions of concern and payment on the possibilities of knowledge and the achievement of the optimum (efficiency). Exclusive concern accompanied by related payment leads to a deal. Collective concern accompanied by related payment leads to the failure of the revelation of the free-rider. Exclusive concern unaccompanied by related payment imposes a blind and therefore certainly inefficient quantitative allocation. Collective concern unaccompanied by related payment removes the incentive to prevaricate. The failure of the free-rider and the removal of the incentive to prevaricate will be all the greater, the greater the mass of collective concern.

		CONCERN	
		EXCLUSIVE	COLLECTIVE
RELATED PAYMENT	YES	GOOD (market)	FAILURE (free-rider)
	NO	FAILURE (quantitative arbitrary)	GOOD (no incentive to prevaricate)

6. DISCLOSURE BY ECONOMIC CHOICE

But the most promising method of estimating non-monetary values is to observe the choice made by the transactors in question, which depends on the strength of their feeling about the phenomenon in question. It is in this field that the ingenuity of the researcher is particularly necessary to ascertain these observable and if possible measurable data, to assess what they disclose about the preferences it is desired to discover and to determine whether this information is necessary or sufficient for the selection of the environment policy which is the aim of the whole operation.

The behaviour observed is generally that of economic choices. Either the individual behaviour of transactors or the results of the choice of a number of transactors, sometimes a large number, such as market prices, may be recorded. The following are a few examples.

We are inquiring into the real nuisance from noise for the residents in a certain zone. We find that they soundproof their houses. But soundproofing is not absolute, and the more complete it is, the more it costs. Technical and economic data enable us to say that one decibel less inside the house costs an additional x francs in soundproofing, at the level of soundproofing actually installed. Now, in selecting this level, the residents disclose that, in their opinion, gaining another decibel is not worth the cost, but that the last decibel they succeeded in excluding was worth the cost. In other words, x is the marginal value of the monetary equivalent of the psychological cost of noise, or the marginal cost of the psychological effect of noise or the marginal monetary value of silence.

Similarly, if we are inquiring into the psychological cost of dirt in houses caused by air pollution, the observation of the marginal monetary cost of painting, washing and cleaning, gives the marginal cost, in monetary terms, of the psychological discomfort in question. Or again, if a town-dweller buys a car in order to go into the country on Sundays, that provides a measure of his estimate of the value to him of green spaces in the town. And so forth.

We need not stress the obvious precision which should be introduced into all these analyses. Thus, benefits differ from one individual to another, house cleaning has external effects since neighbours and passers-by also benefit from it as well as the owner, the acquisition of a car is a discontinuous choice in which a number of motives are generally mixed, and urban and rural greenery are not the same product, and so forth. There is one remarkable point which should be brought out. In our first example we have found only the marginal value of the estimate we are looking for. But this marginal cost is exactly what is necessary and sufficient to know to choose the optimum policy (subject to the exceptions discussed below)(18).

One of the most important applications of the method considered is to compare the price or rent of land in conditions which differ only in the quality of the relevant environment. For example, these prices are compared in two places which differ in respect of noise (proximity of an airfield, a highway or a factory) or of air pollution or of proximity to a park, beach, forest or landscape, but are otherwise comparable. Or prices are compared at two different dates between which the quality in question has changed. This difference in price discloses the value of the difference in environmental quality. And when the land is bought for residential purposes, it is essentially the psychological advantages or disadvantages whose monetary equivalent is obtained in this way.

Any other form of consumption whatsoever connected with the benefit of the environment can be used in the same way. One could think, for example, of various open air facilities, or of houses (prices, rents, hotel prices). But the disclosure sought, being here a value of demand, is all the better the less elastic is the supply. For example if the supply of open air facilities is perfectly elastic, these goods will continue to be sold at cost (thanks to competition) and the price will not change since the demand in question is relatively feeble in relation to that of all the factors which enter into their production, with the result that this price can disclose nothing about the value of installing camping grounds or sports grounds or a natural park or stretch of water in the neighbourhood. But land is the classical example of a good with inelastic supply; in a given environment, with given facilities and regulations, its value depends purely on demand. Buildings and

21

houses are also good choices because land may represent a substantial part of their price (19).

If there are only two places with different qualities of environment the difference in site values merely indicates a lower limit of the total value of this difference, since if someone agrees to pay more for improved quality, it is because he values it at least as highly as the extra price he pays. But in order to arrive at the optimum level of improvement or prevention of deterioration, it is necessary to estimate the marginal value in relation to an index of quality or to the variables which influence it. When there is a continuum of quality, this can be done by observing prices in the following way.

Let E be this index of the quality of the environment. In the case of noise, for example, E is an inverse function of the number of decibels (the structure of the nuisance could obviously be specified in greater detail). Let us assume that there are sites with every possible value of E (for example, in a town, with every conceivable level of noise, which is plausible) and let us assume for the moment that this is the only characteristic in which they differ. Let us assume that each individual buys a single plot of relatively small dimensions and therefore subject to a given value of E. Let $p(E)$ be the price of land subject to index E, and $s(E)$ the area of land whose quality lies between E and E + dE. The function $p(E)$ is progressive (E has been chosen as identifying a desired quality). An owner of land of quality E will find himself faced with this function and has therefore preferred E to any other level of quality. Figure 1 shows this choice; it plots

Figure 1

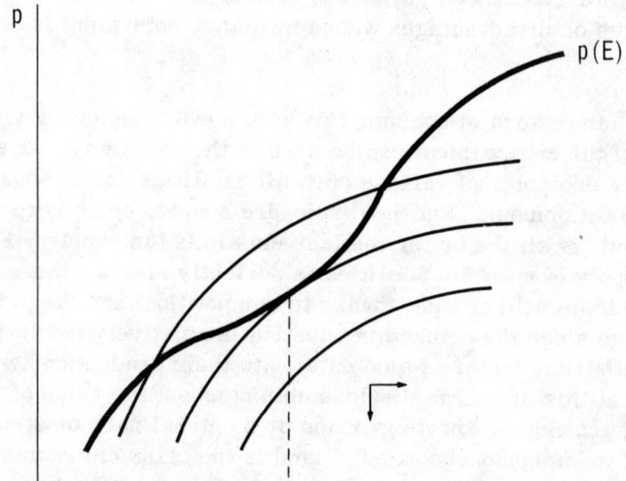

22

the curve p(E) and the curves of indifference of this transactor (who
prefers the highest E and the lowest p) including the tangent to the
curve p(E) which corresponds to his choice. It can be inferred from
this that the marginal monetary value of E for this transactor (or his
marginal propensity to pay for E, or the marginal rate of substitution
of money for E) in the state chosen is equal to the derivative p'(E)
of p(E), assumed to be existing and definite. Let us now take the
variations of an instrumental parameter of improvement or regulation
X, upon which the value of E at different places may depend. The
marginal social value of X expressed in money is:

$$V'(X) \quad = \quad \int p'(E) . \frac{dE}{dX} . \ s(E) . \ d \ E$$

if the distribution between the transactors concerned is correct. This
value makes it possible to determine the optimum value of X in
comparison with the marginal cost of X (almost nil if X is the parameter
of a regulation) and with the usual precautions.

Obviously, the price variations observable between different places
or different dates are rarely due solely to the cause whose value it is
desired to estimate. For example, the value of a site depends at the
same time on transport and trading facilities, neighbourhood, noise,
proximity of gardens, etc. And variation in time depends on the trend
both of the environment and of demand. But, in the first place, it is
sometimes possible to select the elements which are mainly differentiated by the characteristic studied. And, in the second place, the
estimate of the distribution of responsibilities among the various factors
of a variation is a classical problem in statistical analysis (20).

The best example of estimating the user value of a public environment asset by observation of related consumption is no doubt the
method devised by Harold Hotelling and applied to measure the
recreational value of a natural park, stretch of water, etc. or even
the intensity of public desire revealed by mass demonstration (21).
The related private consumption is that of transport from home to the
place in question; it is made up of miscellaneous expenditure and
cost of travelling time. The only thing it is necessary to observe is
the origin of the visitors. This is translated in terms of the distance
they have to come to get there. We therefore know that f(n). d n come
from between n and n + d n miles. It is easy to ascertain the total
population P(n). d n living in this zone. The transport cost (round
trip) per person corresponding to these n miles, p(n) is also calculated,
the inverse function being n(p). It is inferred from this that the
fraction f(n)/P(n) of the population is prepared to pay at least p(n) per
person to profit from this public asset. Finally, it is assumed that the

23

distribution of this taste for the public asset is the same everywhere. Thus, for every place of origin, the fraction:

$$g(p) = \frac{f[n(p)]}{P[n(p)]}$$

is prepared to pay at least p to "consume" this public asset. In consequence, the surplus which this visit affords to $P(n)$. d n residents in the zone of distance lying between n and n + d n is:

$$\int_{p=p(n)}^{\infty} [P(n) . dn] . g(p) . dp =$$

$$\left[\int_{p=p(n)}^{\infty} g(p) . dp \right] . P(n) . dn .$$

and the total social utility of this public asset is therefore:

$$\int_{n=o}^{\infty} \left[\int_{p=p(n)}^{\infty} g(p) . dp \right] P(n) . dn.$$

This analysis is, of course, open to the obvious improvements which it may require: imperfection of distribution among individuals, lack of regional uniformity in the taste for this asset, the existence of substitute public assets of the same kind elsewhere, and therefore with a cost of access varying according to the place of residence, allowing for other consumptions and general equilibrium, etc.

7. NECESSARY AND SUFFICIENT KNOWLEDGE

The first sign of skill in the matter of information is not to complain about not knowing what it is not necessary to know, and not to waste a lot of effort in acquiring useless knowledge. When we want to estimate costs or benefits, therefore, the first thing to do is to delimit what we really need to know about them. The harder it is to measure them, the more inept it is to try to learn more than is necessary. The following comments can be made in this connection, which we refrain from elaborating in detail or from expounding in full because consideration of them is very classical in economic analysis and their application

24

to the questions in which we are interested here affords no new conceptual difficulty.

The following are the elements which it is necessary to know:

- The marginal costs and benefits in the zone where it is known that the optimum will be, in order to determine or to ensure the choice of the exactly right levels. For a policy designed to impose the optimum by regulation, these elements must be known both for the external cost and for the cost or benefit specific to the creator of the externality, whereas for a policy of charging or subsidizing this creator, or for the sale or purchase of the relevant rights, only the marginal external cost is necessary, unless this action has to be at a constant rate or price within this zone, whereas the marginal external cost within the zone is not constant, since in this event, it is necessary to start by determining the optimum in order to find the right rate or price.

- A condition as to the relative variations of marginal costs and benefits within the same zone in order to ensure that the state obtained really is at least a local optimum. There is no need to know this condition in the case of charging or subsidization when the marginal rate may depend on the level chosen and may therefore follow the external cost.

- A condition as to the relations between costs and benefits over the whole field of variation of the variables in order to make certain that the optimum does not lie elsewhere. If there is no discontinuity in these costs and benefits an inequality in the marginal magnitudes valid over the whole field of variation may be sufficient.

- Special mention should be made of the origin, i. e. the zero value of magnitudes, since discontinuities known as fixed costs often come into play there which may determine whether it is desirable to continue the activity in question even in the smallest degree or whether it should be completely forbidden. There again a condition of inequality between global costs and benefits is necessary.

- The imposition of a charge or the grant of bonuses also makes it possible to do without the knowledge of these more global structures for the polluters in so far as the flexibility of these instruments and the knowledge of the external cost enables the amount of the charge or bonus to follow continuous or discontinuous variations in that cost.

- The considerations set out above also extend to cases where there are a number of interdependent variables and necessitate the classic conditions of economic analysis.

- In all these cases, the usual conditions of convexity are sufficient. Unfortunately, they are often not satisfied in the matter of external cost (35). But they are not necessary. The absence of this structure, however, obviously makes the analysis of conditions other than marginal conditions of the first order more difficult and less classical.

- In situations known as "second best" (22), certain information about the rest of the economy must also be estimated.

- Finally, it is not unusual for statistical conditions to make it possible to do without a great deal of information. One is the law of large numbers. For example, there may be a large number of polluters each of whom is responsible only for a small fraction of the quantity x of pollution, deterioration or harmful activity (production, input, number of uses, etc.). Or, there may be a large number of victims of the nuisance collectively concerned by x so that the marginal external cost of x for each of them is a small fraction of the sum of these costs for all of them. In these circumstances, with suitable assumptions of independence, the x corresponding to each cost of abstention by the polluters or the marginal external cost for each x are determined, even if the costs for each of these transactors are not. And the averages of these elements for each transactor are all that we need to know about them.

8. POLITICAL REVELATION

Faced with the difficulties of estimating the optimum level of an environmental quality or of an external cost, a common attitude is to have this level defined by government. In this spirit, the authorities issue regulations, standards to be observed or not to be exceeded, critical thresholds, etc. These authorities may be administrations, governments or assemblies, and they may be national or local (regional, municipal, etc.) or supra-national. They may have more or less general functions or they may be created ad hoc. There is an abundance of instances and cases.

This mode of determining the levels to be attained is independent of the method of enforcement. This is usually, but not necessarily, a mandatory regulation. The French River Basin authorities (agences de bassin) for example, regulate water pollution by charging the polluters but fixing the levies in such a way that pollution is at a level selected by the River Basin Councils (conseils de bassin) on which the transactors concerned are represented. Similarly, Dales proposes (23) that the "right to pollute" should be sold to polluters, but only at levels determined by the government.

The obvious objection to this mode of determination is the question how can we be sure that the choice is a sound one? If it were not, it would not be the first time that an administration, a government or an assembly made a mistake! It is indeed in these terms that the question arises for an administrator or statesman who wants to attain the optimum, and he then has to rely on all the considerations present-ed in this work. But the interesting situation arises when this choice is a forced one and determined in the last analysis by the political process which selects or directs the government which itself issues orders to the officials.

This choice is therefore the right one if, and only if, the political process which determines it is perfect, at any rate so far as concerns this decision. This implies a set of conditions which even the most advanced political science is still far from having completely analysed. A necessary, but not sufficient, condition is that both the victims and the authors of the nuisance and not one single category alone, influence the decision directly or indirectly - this is an application of the principle that "every person concerned in a choice must be able to influence it" (24). It would carry us too far here to pursue the presentation of these conditions for the optimum of the political process (25). We will merely say that no real process is perfect. But in practice it is sufficient to know whether it is good enough to yield better results than other modes of choice which are equally imperfect, particularly because of information difficulties.

In some cases, too, one can or should choose the political structure to which the choice is referred. This often happens today in environ-mental matters, since the problems which arise are new ones. This determination of the best political structure to handle a specific problem is a vast and absorbing subject which can be broken down into a number of sub-questions. One is the specific character of the political body which makes the decision; will it be constituted for this sole purpose or will this responsibility be assigned to a body responsible for other questions too? As an example of the first alternative, the level of pollution of French rivers is determined by the River Basin Councils (conseils des agences de bassin) consisting of all the interested parties in each catchment basin or their representatives (the extreme case would be a committee which met once only for a single decision whereas the Councils in question are standing bodies). Under the second alternative, the competence of the decision-making body may be sectoral but with a wider geographical basis (this would be the case, for example if it dealt with air pollution for the whole of France), but

it is more often inter-sectoral; it is often a body with more or less
general political competence (municipal, national, United Nations,
etc.). An allied question is that of representation: from the point of
view of problems, a referendum is specific, but the election of a
Member of Parliament, a Mayor, or the President of a Republic is not.
Among the criteria which determine this choice, the distribution of
knowledge and the costs of information take first place; the more
specific the decision-making body, the better, in general, is its knowledge of the problems; representatives are generally less familiar
with their constituents' problems than the constituents themselves,
but on general technical questions they are usually in a better position
to inform themselves and their knowledge is an advantage for the
whole body of their constituents. The costs of decision and of the
political process (votes, etc.) are another important criterion; it may
be extremely costly in decision time for the whole of society to
multiply decisions and decision-making bodies. Finally, questions of
distribution, especially through the public budgets, are another
essential criterion.

9. INDIRECT POLITICAL REVELATION

The cases considered in the last two paragraphs are not symmet-
rical, one in the field of market economy and the other in the field of
politics. In fact the disclosure analysed by economic choice was
indirect, that analysed by political choice was direct; the second bears
directly on the question of environment under consideration, while the
first gave us the value we were looking for indirectly through the
observation of the choice of other elements. The reason is obvious:
it is precisely because the economy does not deal spontaneously and
properly with the aspect of environmental quality under study.

But indirect disclosure can also be obtained from the observation
of political choices. For example, if the choice is to limit pollution
in a given place to a given level and if another place is in no way
distinguishable in any relevant respect, the analyst can infer from this
that pollution in this second place should also be limited to the same
level. The many regulations, charges and bonuses could be used in
the same way. This procedure simply amounts to ensuring the
coherence of activities affecting society and of public choices.

This method raises two questions. First of all: why has the
political process not declared itself on the question in issue since it
has done so on a similar question? There may be many reasons for
this; for example, the problem in question may be a new one which

has not yet been the subject of any political action, or it may be beyond the competence of the authority which has taken the decision, or the costs of the political process (votes, election campaigns, sessions of assemblies, organisation of referendums, costs of taking part in an election or more generally in politics) may mean that it is not easy to repeat the choice in the field in question. Furthermore, the procedure is sound only if and so far as the political process whose decision is observed is itself sound and we are thus brought back to the comments in the last paragraph.

10. THE QUESTION OF "ECONOMIC AGENTS"

These comments on the non-market processes of social choice also call into question some of the procedures described above. We have considered monetary effects and "monetary equivalents" for "economic agents". These may include entities of a political type - communes, municipalities, provinces, States, etc. - or of a "proto-political" type, such as associations with common interests, trade unions, employers' associations, etc. For example it is often their budget which bears the cost of water purification, sewage, garbage collection and disposal or incineration, cleaning, maintenance and improvement of streets, parks, monuments, beaches, forests and other public places, and of preventive or curative medical treatment, as well as the loss in value of collective or public property and administrative, police and legal costs in enforcing regulations for the protection of the environment, etc. And improvements in environmental quality may reduce some of these costs. But what interests us from the normative and ethical point of view is fundamentally the benefits for the individual. It follows that these costs or savings give a correct measurement of what we want to know only if they are themselves optimum for the whole community of interested parties, or in other words if the political process or collective choice which determines them is perfect.

But then we must go further. Some of these costs and benefits are those of enterprises. In theory this amounts to counting "at source" the effects felt by their proprietors. But in fact the real processes of decision within the enterprise are not always such as to allow this identification. It is no doubt valid for a "sole proprietor". But it must be challenged prima facie for a big firm where the decisions are taken by the managers of the "technostructure" whose interests may differ from those of the proprietors and who may pursue objectives other than the profit of the firm, such as the increase of its turnover or its share of the market (though in this case profit may again be sought as a source of self-financing and this may bring the real choice into line with those which would be justified if the costs and benefits of the firm were assimilated to the values for society).

Finally, the last remaining agents are "households" which are also centres of relevant choices and decisions. But most "households" are families and the process of decision within a family is also very often remote from the optimum. The division of family authority between men and women should be mentioned here. But the most serious thing is that half of the interested parties have very little voice in the conclave, namely the children. It is true that the feelings of love and empathy which generally reign within families raise the problem in a particular way. But in the purely environmental choices which interest us here what millions of sometimes scandalous divergences there are between the decisions or behaviour of the parents and the interests of their children !

I certainly do not advocate that all these problems should be disentangled before the costs and benefits for society are estimated! The wise course is to take these values, and in particular the monetary effects, as they come, except when it is manifest that they misdescribe the advantages and damage for individuals.

11. GENERATIONS TO COME

Among the citizens concerned but who have no voice in the conclave are those who are yet unborn. While some qualities of the environment can be improved fairly quickly, as is often the case with pollution, for other aspects, on the contrary, decisions taken today have only long term, and often very long term effects. This applies particularly to the destruction or protection of sites or historical monuments, of forests which take tens of years to grow, of rare species, of ecological or eco-human equilibrium which it would be impossible or very costly to reconstitute. The generations to come are then those who are primarily interested. But they cannot, by their money or their votes, influence a decision taken today, or disclose what they think by their economic or political behaviour or answer an inquiry.

It might be hoped in the first place that people now living would show proper concern for the environment of their descendants, in the same way that they leave them the inheritance of private wealth. Family feelings of this kind, however, rarely go beyond one generation, whereas the effects of decisions may last much longer, and even for direct descendants what has been said above about the attention paid by

parents to the interests of their children leaves it doubtful whether
the problem can be properly solved in this way.

It is often thought that since future generations do not manifest
their preferences by buying or selling on existing markets, it is a
matter for the State to take present account of their future needs. But
governments are concerned with their re-election in a much shorter
term. They therefore try to please present electors and if these
electors are unconcerned about future generations, so are governments.
And this is all the more marked the more democratic is the political
process.

But the fact that an individual is not greatly concerned for his own
remote descendants, his line, his lineage or his "house" does not
necessarily mean that he has little interest in future generations as a
whole. The fate of these generations is thus a collective concern for
people now alive. Moreover, the further one advances into remote
generations, the more ancestors each of them has in the present
generation, and the more his fate becomes a present collective concern
even if everyone is concerned only with his own posterity. In the last
analysis, this collective concern for future generations is the best
hope. Its very character of a general collective concern justifies the
State in taking up the question. It then becomes in the interests of
governments to do so, precisely because the subject interests the
electors.

In fact, however, citizens rarely think in these terms. They are
invited to reason about impersonal and timeless entities, such as
"safeguarding the heritage of France". But if a man concerns
himself with capital beyond the enjoyment he derives from it for
himself and particularly beyond his own life-span, it is certainly
because he is interested in the benefits to be derived from it by other
people, and especially by future generations.

Obviously, since children are in no position to defend, or even to
voice, the adult interests they will have in later life, they, too, must
be counted among the "future generations". If the truth were told,
even today's adults are often ill able to foretell the needs, tastes and
desires which they will experience in a few years' time. It is in the
interests of the grasshoppers themselves that they should be compelled
to garner a few grains "while the sun shines". This raises a similar
problem, which is both less acute, because after all people are fairly
well able to look forward to their own future, and more delicate,
because they protest against usurpation and dictatorship if anyone
professes to know better than themselves what they will want in a little
time to come.

However, even if society concerns itself more or less adequately with future consumption, that does not solve the problem, since those who are concerned at the present moment do not necessarily know the preferences of these future consumers. The problem of assessing costs and benefits remains untouched. Objective estimates can, of course, help, as can forecasts of population growth, exhaustion of natural resources, saturation of certain needs and so forth. But we still do not know the tastes of the future.

Now this raises a highly delicate and also highly disturbing problem. For the tastes of the future depend on the present; for young people already living they depend on education, advertising, propaganda, or the results of experience in the form of habit or custom, or conversely, distaste, boredom or the desire for change, and for generations yet unborn they depend on the chain of successive education. Future tastes are therefore not independent of what is done today. They can be modified. They are not wholly "given". This fact cannot fail to shake the foundations of the whole philosophy of "consumer sovereignty" which underlies the whole attempt to estimate social benefits in the light of individual preferences. And this doubt about future benefits could even extend to present benefits, since they themselves are the fruit of past actions and particularly of education, propaganda and the like inflicted on the interested party by other people. This challenge to the legitimacy of present benefits is, however, different in kind. It is hard to carry it to its extreme conclusion, since our genetic stock itself is imposed upon us by past society. And if we did so, what kind of legitimacy would we cling to? The idea of accepting the past as "given" is not indefensible! The problem of future tastes, however, arises in a different way, because they can be modified. And even if skilfully applied normative economics afford a theoretical answer to this problem, the fact remains that people are not prepared to accept it when they find out what it involves.

The guiding principle of normative economics is the search for individual happiness. We shall say nothing here about the distribution of the material bases of happiness among individuals and in time. The future happiness of an individual will depend both on his consumption, his situation and his environment and so forth, and on his tastes and preferences at the moment. If these latter elements can be influenced the aggregate of instrumental variables of happiness includes both these consumptions and so forth, and whatever makes it possible to influence these tastes. And one is "in duty bound" to handle these instruments to ensure the greatest possible happiness.

And yet the consequences of this course of action may be extremely disturbing. For example, instead of safeguarding with enormous trouble and at enormous cost the environment of our grandchildren,

it may be more "beneficial" for their own happiness to condition them
to enjoy the rich diversity of garbage piles, the music of internal
combustion engines or jets, the perfume of exhaust gas (just as many
Parisians find a certain pleasure in the distinctive smell of the Métro)
and on the contrary to inspire them with a hatred of trees, an
anguished fear of silence, such as most of our ancestors felt for the
horrors of the mountain-tops, and a feeling of ridicule for that heap
of grotesque old stones, Notre-Dame de Paris. Of course, a lot of
people will say that it is impossible, that men will be happier with
quiet, nature and beautiful buildings, even at the cost of making
substantial sacrifices in other respects to safeguard them or improve
them. Plato and John Stuart Mill declared that it was enough for
men to be <u>informed</u> - and not necessarily <u>educated</u> - for them
to prefer quality spontaneously, to wish to be a questioning Socrates
rather than an unquestioning beast of the field. But in the present
state of our knowledge this is a pious hope rather than a proven fact.
In practice, people do not only want future generations to be as happy
as possible (apart from distribution in time). They also have
preferences for the consumption, in the broad sense, of these future
generations, and even for their prospective tastes. This is a special
case of the "vicarious desires" which we shall now consider.

12. VICARIOUS DESIRE

A "vicarious desire" ("désirs tutélaires") is defined as the desire,
preference or taste of an individual relating to the consumption or to an
aspect of the situation or state of another person not arising out of any material effect (physical or monetary) involving the first individual. The
cause of such desire may, for example, be of an ethical or aesthetic
type, or may arise from a feeling of jealousy or envy or so forth.

Vicarious desires abound in environmental matters. People want
other people to live in healthy, clean and agreeable surroundings
(to their own taste, or even to the taste of the other people). These
desires extend not only to consumption, but also to the tastes of the
people concerned: not only do I want them to profit from nature, I
want them to love it. These preferences for the preferences of
another person are the raison d'être for education in the sense of the
formation (or deformation) of tastes as distinct from education in
the sense of the transmission of knowledge.

A vicarious desire whose subject matter depends on individual
choice is, in effect, a particular external effect for the person who
feels it. It is a collective concern between the person who feels it and

the person directly interested (it belongs to the category which we have elsewhere called "heterogeneous collective concerns")(26). The collectivity concerned is even larger if a number of people have vicarious desires on the same subject. Vicarious desires can therefore theoretically be treated like any other external effect or collective concern. Furthermore, the modes of social realization are the same. Thus, there may be a direct understanding (I can pay my neighbour not to read a book which the mere thought of his reading pains me, or I can buy him a tie, and so forth) but the political-public way is more common; countless regulations, charges or bonuses are designed to satisfy the vicarious desires of the citizens (27).

It may be thought that these vicarious desires should not be taken into account because those who experience them are meddling in something which is no business of theirs. It would therefore be an infringement of the principles of normative economics in relation to externalities and public goods. What is the right attitude? In the last analysis, it is the general recommendation of normative economics provided it is applied properly, that is to say, without omitting the compensatory redistribution which enables everyone to profit from any specific measure which it proposes. For example, if someone does not like my reading a particular book, that is no reason for prohibiting its sale, but if he prefers to give me 10 francs rather than that I should read it and I prefer to receive 10 francs rather than read it, this deal makes everyone happy. Similarly if people are prepared to pay for others to enjoy bigger parks, their desire should be met, but, if the initial distribution was correct, only by making them share in the cost.

Account must therefore be taken of the psychological costs and benefits arising out of vicarious desires. The estimate of the corresponding monetary equivalents is not conceptually distinguished from that of other monetary equivalents, except perhaps that it is one of the most difficult examples. Disclosures by the market are hardly available, either directly or indirectly. On the other hand, inquiries and political disclosures take the same form as that analysed above, with the same problems. It should, however, be noted that political decision is reflected less exclusively in the imposition of quantities or qualities, prohibitions or regulations and it is not rare for the vicarious desires thus manifested to take the form of taxes, bonuses or special public prices (28).

With regard to the situation of future generations, vicarious desires are the only ones which exist at present and which can therefore be assessed by disclosure techniques.

13. THE IGNORANCE OF THE INTERESTED PARTIES

There is a phenomenon which is often confused with vicarious desires and which is often manifested in the same forms, but which is nevertheless fundamentally different. It results from the fact that conditions affecting some people are better known to others than to themselves. For example, the effects of pollution on somebody's health are generally better foreseen by a doctor. In particular, the government, with all the scientific assistance available to it, may be better informed than the interested parties about something which affects them directly. This is a "perverse" distribution of information compared with that described above. It is true that the knowledge in question is technical, and even more precisely, that it requires scientific knowledge which is not possessed by every citizen. This state of affairs manifests itself from time to time in environmental questions, for example, in the case cited above, either in forecasting the fairly long term trend of environmental resources, or in estimating the economic market effects (especially on prices) of environmental parameters.

The fact that the interested parties know less about their own situation than the specialists or the government is often relied upon to justify the authorities choosing in their place and substituting their decisions for those of the parties directly concerned. In fact the acquisition of this central knowledge and its use in the interests of the parties concerned may be one of the tasks assigned by the whole citizen body to their government.

But this method has one grave danger: that members of the government or the administration may use this disparity of knowledge, or even claim it falsely, to impose their own preferences on the consumption or situation of the governed. This would be an instance of vicarious desires prevailing entirely over the desires of those directly interested, which is very different from saying that proper account should be taken of those desires.

To avoid this, decision in the place of the interested party may be replaced by giving him the information and then leaving him to choose with full knowledge of the circumstances or assuming his informed preferences by the methods described in this Chapter. For example, cigarette packets in America carry the statement that tobacco is bad for the health and the bars announce that alcohol kills slowly. Similar information can be given about the effects of air pollution on physical health or of noise on psychological health before assessing their evaluation by individuals.

But this method has its limits. The transmission of information may be costly in time, effort or material resources. One cannot, for example, make everybody study medicine. There is some information which quite simply cannot be communicated because it is too complicated. However, useful it may be to me to know that "smoking may endanger my health" it does not tell me much about the gravity of the danger!

There is therefore room for the replacement of private choice by public decision. But this public act must be an honest one. For that purpose, an estimate must be made of the costs and benefits which enter into its determination, on the basis of an estimate of what the interested parties would prefer if they had all the available information.

14. DISTRIBUTION

The value of the costs and benefits considered to the individuals and transactors concerned having been estimated, they must then be compared with each other so that conclusions can be drawn. But can one man's cash be compared with that of another? Can they be added up to give the social benefit of a public good, at any rate for marginal evaluations? In theory the marginal monetary benefit for each individual should be weighted by the marginal social benefit of his income   This weighting would in practice disappear only when the distribution of income is optimal, which is a bold assumption.

This is an extremely difficult problem, but not a new or original one. In fact the discovery of these optimum inter-individual weightings is the crux of normative economics; the question is a very tough one, almost omnipresent and inevitable. The elements of an answer are, however, by no means lacking.

At action level the pressure of the problem can be lessened, first by recommending that the policy envisaged should be associated with transfers for the redistribution of income which make the whole operation profitable for everybody. But in addition to the political or institutional obstacles (which are not necessarily unjustifiable), this procedure may come up against built-in snags. Suppose, for example, that for the sake of efficiency it is desired to deal with an environmental problem by charging the polluters (let us take a case where we can hardly subsidize them if they refrain because in this event a number of transactors would profess to want to undertake this harmful activity in order to gain the bonus, without it being possible to detect the fraud). Let us further assume that this charge amounts

36

to an undesirable redistribution of income. Can these effects be compensated by an <u>ad hoc</u> transfer? No, because the pre-condition for benefiting from it is to have paid the charge and therefore this compensation cancels out the other. And in particular, it wipes out its effectiveness.

Similarly, a common state of affairs is that "problems of distribution" are "settled elsewhere", for example by general taxation and transfers designed to achieve distributive justice, which makes it possible to disregard weighting. It has the great merit of relieving the analyst of a difficult problem which raises questions of a different kind from the field under consideration. But it is its ethical validity which is of prime importance. That these problems should be settled elsewhere is a well-warranted proposition. But what counts is that they should be settled. And if it is asserted that they are settled, one must be able to prove it, which is not too easy. To say that they must be settled elsewhere, and to infer from that that they can be disregarded, is to mistake the problem; the problem is not the distribution of responsibilities among public authorities, but the achievement of the social optimum.

One is therefore often constrained not to stop short of these weightings. But where are they to be found? As a very general rule, two elements must be known. The first is the overall situation of the people as to their wealth, their condition and even their tastes, in order finally to estimate the bases of their well-being. It is very difficult, but it is at least a well-defined question of fact, unlike the second element, the criterion of justice itself. Having written at length on this point elsewhere, we shall not dwell on it here (29).

These difficulties call for a less ambitious practice. For example, a responsible politician, deemed to be duly elected, might be asked to provide these weightings. Or the coherence of public decisions can be ensured by estimating them in the light of the inter-individual weight implicit in other public choices, such as fiscal structure, public expenditure, transfers, subsidies and public concession prices, etc. (but sometimes the defects of the political process result in injustices precisely in these other fields which should not be repeated in the field in question, and should perhaps even be corrected by compensation) (30). Obviously a great many simplifications in the work are called for, such as considering only similar classes of people affected in the same way and not each individual in particular. But the political process often directly reveals its distribution choices in the sector considered by imposing quantities, qualities, charges or bonuses. These measures are general and apply identically to all the members of one of the groups (authors or victims of the nuisance) if they are aimed at distribution between the members of the group on the

one hand and the rest of society on the other, while they include
exemptions, favours and special treatment if they are also aimed at
redistribution within the group among its members.

15. SECOND BEST AND THE REST OF THE ECONOMY

Since there is no analysis which embodies the whole of society in
all its details, any normative conclusion involves some suppositions
about what is not explicitly taken into account and is not completely
independent of it. In particular it implies assumptions about the rest
of the economy. Traditionally, the assumption is that of what is
called the "perfection" of the economy, that is to say, not necessarily
"perfect competition" but much more generally, social efficiency.
When this condition is not satisfied in a field related to that under
consideration, one finds oneself faced with a problem known as "second
best". These questions are studied more particularly elsewhere (31).
The only aspect which concerns us here is the fact that the solution
calls for even more information, such as the differences between
prices and marginal costs in other parts of the economy and elasticities
of substitution. This is knowledge of a "technical" kind, but particular
in that it applies to economic data. But estimating these elements
is a classical feature of economic analysis and we need not dwell on it
here.

16. STATISTICAL KNOWLEDGE

Nor is there any need, since they, too, are classical, to dwell on
the consequences of the fact that the impossibility or high cost of
exhaustive knowledge compels the resort to statistical estimation. This
applies to nearly all the modes of information described in this Chapter.
For example, inquiry and interrogation refer to the theory of samples,
the use of stochastic costs and benefits refer to the theory of probability
and so forth.

17. TRIAL AND ERROR

Any action by the authorities arouses reactions on the part of the
transactors concerned. These reactions disclose, and the study of
them teaches us, something about the conditions of the transactors

within this particular field of action; preferences, needs, production possibilities, etc. This new information may make it possible to improve action. This new form of action again discloses something about the relevant elements. And so forth. The action selected may thus ultimately tend towards the optimum.

This sequential process is an iterative method, by trial and error, of solving the problem raised. It may be called the method of trial and error ("tâtonnement") by extension of the name given by Léon Walras to his theory of markets, which is of this kind. It is generally a very fruitful technique for overcoming ignorance of important elements.

More precisely, this method is designed to solve the question of the inadequate distribution of knowledge throughout society, and more precisely of the ignorance by the "central" authorities of the conditions of the transactors concerned which it needs to know in order to follow the optimum policy; it assumes that each of these transactors knows best the elements concerned which affect him directly.

Let us start by considering the possibilities afforded by this idea in the simplest context. There is an activity at the level x which causes an external cost; x may, for example, be a quantity of pollutant discharged, or of a product or factor which causes a nuisance, or a number of uses (assumed to be a large number since it can be treated as a continuous variate), etc. The marginal external cost is $c(x)$. The marginal value to the polluters of being able to carry on this activity at level x, that is to say the marginal cost to them of having to limit it to x, is $w(x)$. Let x^* be the optimum x. We find that:

$$c(x^*) = w(x^*)$$

and $c(x)$ does not increase more slowly than $w(x)$ to $x = x^*$, which means that:

$$c'(x^*) \geqslant w'(x^*)$$

a condition which is satisfied in particular in the standard case where $c' > 0$ and $w' < 0$. We again disregard the effects of income and distribution and discontinuities of costs and aggregate values.

We distinguish two types of trial and error which differ in the instrument used by the authority. In one case it is the rate of a charge (or bonus) at a constant rate (i.e. independent of x). In the second, it is a level of x which will be attained by the purchase or sale of the right to pollute in this given quantity. Referring to the dynamics of supply and demand described by Léon Walras and

Alfred Marshall respectively, we shall call the first <u>Walrasian trial and error</u> and the second <u>Marshall trial and error</u>. But this terminology should not conceal the fact that the problem of externality studied here differs considerably from the supply and demand of a private good which they study. The difference is that the x attained here does not result from exchange between the authors and the victims of the nuisance but solely from the choice of the former subject to the environment policy measure, the latter having to put up with the result (that is indeed the whole definition of externality).

That is why the <u>achievement</u> of the optimum for the variable x merely requires action in respect of the polluters, who choose it on their own, and not in respect of their victims. But the choice of this optimum public action calls for knowledge covering <u>a priori</u> both the cost of abstention by the polluters and the external cost suffered by the victims. Now information on these two factors may be disclosed by the reactions of these two categories of transactors to the public measures which affect them. In particular, this reason confers utility on measures affecting the victims of the nuisance.

Let us look first at the case where the marginal external cost $c(x)$ is known with certainty, but the marginal cost of abstention $w(x)$ is not. Assume we are in a situation where a charge on or bonus to the polluters must be at the constant rate t (32), but $c(x)$ is not constant in the field of utility (otherwise it would be enough to take a t equal to this constant and the optimum would be attained straight away). This charge or bonus may also be a sale to or purchase from the polluters of the right to pollute at a given price equal to t, these transactors buying or selling the quantity they please at that price. "Walrasian trial and error" operates as follows (Figure 2). Let us fix a level t. The polluters choose an x which is expressed as x_1 and which gives $w(x_1) = t_1$. Observing this x_1 and knowing the function $c(x)$, we calculate $c(x_1)$. Then we compare $c(x_1)$ with $t_1 = w(x_1)$. If $c(x_1) < t_1$, we start again with t at a different level t_2, verifying that $t_2 < t_1$. If, on the contrary $c(x_1) > t_1$, we start again with t at a level t_2 verifying that $t_2 > t_1$. And so on, taking smaller t where t has had to be reduced and higher t where it has had to be increased. Subject to certain conditions, the t_i and x_i tend towards the optimum where the values of t and x and of t* and x* confirm that:

$$t^* = w(x^*) = c(x^*)$$

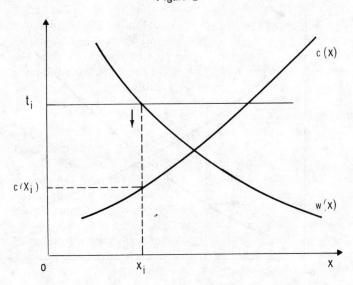

Figure 2

Still in the case where c(x) is known, a "Marshall trial and error" is conducted by buying from or selling to the polluters rights to pollute in a fixed quantity x. (Figure 3). Let us assume that the number of polluters and the other conditions are such that a competitive market in these rights is established among polluters, which can be deemed to be a market of perfect competition. The observation of the price p established on this market discloses the information sought as to w, since p = w(x). The process then is as follows. x is fixed at a level x_1. The value p_1 of the corresponding market price p is observed. A calculation is also made of $c(x_1)$. If $p_1 > c(x_1)$, we start again with a new level of x, x_2, such that $x_2 > x_1$. If, on the contrary, $p_1 < c(x_1)$, we start again with a new level of x, x_2 such that $x_2 < x_1$. And so on, taking smaller x where x has had to be reduced and higher x where it has had to be increased. Subject to certain conditions recalled below, the x_1 and p_1 thus tend towards the optimum at which the values of x and p, x* and p* confirm that:

$$p^* = w(x^*) = c(x^*).$$

In both cases, if c(x) is not exactly known but is merely estimated, if this estimate can be made by a probability distribution, the whole of the reasoning can be maintained by replacing c(x) by the mathematical expectation of c for each x, $\bar{c}(x) = E(x)$.

41

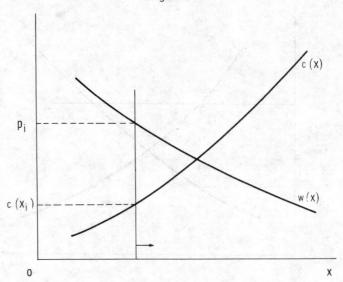

Figure 3

But if $c(x)$ is unknown, we can also try to make up for this lack of information by iterative trial and error. In this case, it is easy to construct the equivalents of the two preceding procedures, $w(x)$ being known or replaced by its expectation for each x, $\overline{w}(x)$. But, as we have seen above, the application becomes difficult if there is more than one victim of the nuisance considered, since x is then most frequently a collective concern among them and problems of disclosure arise in their full gravity. If x is divisible and exhaustive in relation both to the users and to its external effects (this condition is satisfied for one of these categories of transactors if it consists of a single member only) it is possible, without knowing all the costs and benefits, to conduct an iterative process on $c(x)$ and $w(x)$ simultaneously. It may be of either of the types considered and these trial and error processes will then become exactly the dynamics of adjustment envisaged respectively by Léon Walras and Alfred Marshall in the case of markets (33). But in this case, moreover, a market may in fact determine the optimum x without the public authorities intervening in the process.

In every case a necessary condition of the convergence of the process is that $c(x)$ grows faster than $w(x)$ in the domain considered. When the optimum is unique this is nothing other than the necessary condition of the optimum described above. The classic convexities satisfy this condition (34), but they are not the only cases in which this happens. This is fortunate since externalities display serious sui generis convexity diseases (35).

42

In all these examples the stages of the iteration were states actually achieved. Since they are not at the optimum (except where they hit it direct by accident) the result is social losses. Now, another type of iterative determination of the optimum can be tried in which all the stages are fictitious. For example, the polluters could be asked what level of activity they would choose if they were charged at rate t and the corresponding overall x could be obtained by adding up the answers. But problems of disclosure may arise, depending on what these transactors think about the financial transactions affecting them which will in fact be made.

Such a purely informative iterative process may serve to determine the optimum in the frequent case where the externality is a collective concern among its victims. Since this method is analysed in detail for a "public good" in l'Etat et le système des prix, we shall not describe it more fully here (36).

18. THE MEASURE OF ALL THINGS

One thing remains to be said. However diverse the considerations set out above, they are all inspired by the same guiding principle, namely, that in determining the costs and benefits relevant to an environmental policy choice, the ultimate criterion is to be found in the desires of individuals. In other words, we equate the value of things with the happiness of man.

It is, of course, conceivable that this attitude might be open to criticism. Some people think that places or nature should be respected for their own sake and not because of what human beings think of them. This view seems to have a stronghold in the matter of conservation. It is difficult to justify by hedonism alone, even the most subtle, even allowing for the possible desires of future generations, the safeguard of species or of the cultural or monumental heritage of past societies. Man's burden seems to include a sort of responsibility towards "nature" or towards his "ancestors" to protect or conserve what cannot be re-created. It seems difficult to justify these acts by the mere fact, however,important, that men can enjoy the spectacle of a beautiful or strange animal or cultural creation. People desire, for example, to conserve, at great cost, a particular species of insect, even though it is virtually invisible (37). Neither does the desire to satisfy future curiosity, even scientific curiosity, suffice. We are, in fact, faced with a position similar to that of knowledge for the sake of knowledge, science for the sake of science, art for art's sake.

This outlook is, to say the least of it, hardly in line with the thinking of economists. It would be child's play for them to challenge its legitimacy as a matter of faith rather than of reason, defended all the more obstinately since it lacks argument, hostile to compromise and thus scarcely affording any criteria for compromise in the frequent cases where compromise is inescapable. Using the conceptual wealth of their tools of thought, they reduce these hopes to the desires and tastes of those who express them; perhaps they even accuse them of disguising as absolute what is only the chemical composition of their hormones.

For my part, I believe that even if these economists miss something - but if they recognize it, the danger is not too great - their point of view embodies the greater part of the truth for most of the choices which concern us here, provided it is applied with all the finesse required by the difficulties referred to in this text. This philosophy ultimately comes down to relating everything to man, "the measure of all things" and to postulating that man is responsible only to man and is accountable only to man. Perhaps, after all, that is the true humanism.

NOTES

1. A part of the research on which this paper is based was funded by CORDES.

2. Cf. "Politiques anti-pollution optimales en présence d'incertitude", Kyklos, 1971, I.

3. Ed. Praeger, New York, 1971. See also Ronald B. Ridker and John A. Hennin, "The Determinants of Residential Property Values with Special Reference to Air Pollution", The Review of Economics and Statistics, 49 (May,1967), pp. 246-257, and A. Myrick Freeman III, "Air Pollution and Property Values: A Methodological Comment", The Review of Economics and Statistics, Nov. 1971, pp. 415-416.

4. Cf. Marion Clawson and J. L. Knetsch: Economics of Outdoor Recreation, Baltimore, 1966: J. Knetsch: "Demands and Benefits", P. Davidson, F. Adams and J. Seneca: "The Social Value of Water Recreation Facilities Resulting from an Improvement in Water Quality: the Delaware Estuary", in A. Kneese and C. Stephen, editors, Water Research, Resources for the Future, Inc. , Washington, D. C. , Johns Hopkins Press, 1966.

5. Charles J. Cicchetti, A. Myrick Freeman III, Robert Haveman and Jack L. Knetsch: "On the Economics of Mass Demonstration: a Case Study of the November, 1969, March on Washington", The American Economic Review, Sept. 1971.

6. Fischer, A. C. , J. V. Krutilla, et C. J. Cicchetti, "The Economics of Environmental Preservation. A Theoretical and Empirical Analysis", The American Economic Review, Sept. 1972.

7.   See, for example, Brown, W. G. , A. Singh and E. N. Castle,
     "An Economic Evaluation of the Oregon Salmon and Steelhead
     Sport Fishery", Technical Bulletin 78, Agricultural Experiment
     Station, Oregon State University, Corvallis, Oregon, September
     1964.

8.   See, for example, J. Stevens: "Recreation Benefits from Water
     Pollution Control", Water Resources Research, Vol. 2, 2nd
     Quarter, 1966, and Robert Dorfman. (Measuring Benefits of
     Government Investments, Brookings Institution, Washington,
     April 1965.

9.   Mohring, W. D. and M. Harwitz, Highway Benefits, An
     Analytical Framework, Northwestern University Press, 1962.

10. P. Bohm, Estimating Demand for Public Goods: An Experiment,
     University of Stockholm, stencilled.

11. The fate of this study is so instructive from the point of view of
     the social use of economic calculation that it is worth mentioning.
     Let us say at the outset that this was the most elaborate cost-
     benefit analysis ever made.   Furthermore, and this is not so
     frequent in this field, its conclusion was perfectly clear-cut; one
     of the contemplated sites was unquestionably better than the
     others in the interests of society as a whole.   But it was in a
     well-to-do residential area, and the influence of the residents
     with the British government was such that a different choice was
     finally made!

12. The references will be found in David Pearce, "The Economic
     Evaluation of noise-generating Abatement Projects", in
     Problems of Environmental Economics, OECD, Paris, 1972.

13. Abraham and Thédié: "Le prix d'une vie humaine dans les
     décisions économiques", Revue Française de Recherche Opéra-
     tionnelle, Third quarter, 1960, N° 16.

     Although this pioneer study (preceded, however, by the book
     by Lotka and Galton, The Money Value of Man in the nineteen-
     thirties, and even the calculations of Sir William Petty two
     hundred years ago) is very interesting, I disagree with its basic
     principle.   This is to measure the "cost of death" to the
     community by the discounted value of the prospective production
     of the dead man if he had lived.   It would also be possible to
     infer the discounted value of his prospective consumption. But
     then, for someone who leaves no estate, this value cannot be
     positive (it is nil if, in addition, he has no capital at the time of

death) - at any rate with perfect markets. And if he leaves an estate, why make the calculation for an individual and not for him and his descendants (some of whom might be born after the date of an accident which is prevented). Even if we confine ourselves to this individual, the heirs in general would usually prefer him not to die and not to leave them his estate. And so, if allowance is made for their grief, the value is still negative. Furthermore, by this measuring-rod, the value of old people who are no longer productive is always negative. But society manifestly has no desire to kill off its old people. This indicates to us, moreover, that the greatest absolute value of these negative sums is a lower limit of what society is prepared to pay to keep these people (and perhaps all people) alive from pure benevolence (that is to say, apart from any material interest). Furthermore, perhaps only a person's minimum survival consumption should be taken into account, since any surplus above this gives him pleasure. But then allowance would also have to be made for the fact that the dead man's wages would usually and largely be a reward for the hardness of his work, and its value would in turn have to be deducted from the cost since death has relieved him of it!

But these remarks lead us to consider the utility of life to the dead man himself. This loss seems to us to be the major social cost of death. The material costs to the rest of society are an accessory detail and not the essence of the problem. Of course it is meaningless to ask how much a person would pay to escape death, since he would give at least all that he could. But in fact the problem arises not in these terms but in terms of risk. The object is to lessen the probability of death. Now, the risk of death is a variable with which everyone is very familiar, and with which we are constantly making compromises, by accepting higher risks to gain money, time or pleasure or to avoid loss and effort, for example by riding in a car, by not fastening the safety belt, by taking an airplace, by smoking and so forth. And the various methods based on the principle of observed preferences can be used to estimate the value which everybody attaches to lessening the risk of death. The fact that we are dealing with very slight probabilities of very dramatic events and with people who are ill-informed, makes the exercise somewhat delicate but perfectly feasible.

The immediately succeeding factor in the scale of importance is people's "vicarious desire" (see below) for other people's lives. It is very strong for our nearest and dearest, and much less strong for other people - who are, however, very numerous. Engineers have thought of it for those who are nearest (and also

for other people in their discussions - if not in their calculations -
about mass accidents). But they seem to have forgotten that
we all die sooner or later; early death merely advances the date
of that sorrow. With a positive (subjective) discount rate, it is
indeed, a loss; but very often the people who suffer it are not
the same (children, other deaths, etc.). Nevertheless, in fact,
the legal pretium doloris adopted by the engineers no doubt
succeeds in representing this advancement of sorrow, rather
than the sorrow itself.

It is only subsequently that material losses obviously come into
play. Among these, the American economist, Lave, in a study
on the costs of air pollution, has allowed for the advancement
of funeral costs: it took an American to think of that; in response,
Ezra Mishan noted if one dies at a younger age, the casket
(may) be smaller: it took an Englishman to give that response.

The criticism that I put forth here seems to have been already
given a long time ago by Jacques Drèze. And I have just learn-
ed that an economist from Chicago is at present applying a
method of market revealed preferences in order to estimate the
value to an individual of the probability of escaping a fatal
accident. His method is the analysis of salaries given for
professions more or less exposed to this danger.

14. R. Haveman: "The Measurement of Economic Welfare: An
     Empirical Experiment", in Water Resources Investment and the
     Public Interest, Vanderbilt University Press, Nashville, 1965.
     But their method strikes me as wrong.

15. One remarkable result of Peter Bohm's experiment on the value
     of television programmes referred to above is that those
     questioned accepted all the questions put as significant and
     gave nearly all their answers in a minute or less. Very few of
     them found the questions unreasonable or difficult.

16. The equivalent of this indemnification for an improvement would
     be indemnification for abstention: this seems infrequent.

17. Cf. "Possibilités et limites de la régulation des problèmes
     d'environnement par entente directe entre les intéressés".
     Revue Consommation, July-September 1971, No. 3.

18. In these exceptions it is generally necessary to know the total
     cost to the individual in order to make a choice which is not the
     exact level of the nuisance or its limitation, but its existence
     or its complete prohibition. This total cost is, with the correct

definitions, the sum of the psychological cost and the monetary cost (cleaning, soundproofing), which does not rule out the fact that the marginal cost is not the sum of the corresponding marginal costs but one or other of them (they are equal) because these two disadvantages are alternative to each other.

19. A detailed analysis of the reasons why differences in the prices of immovable property may not accurately represent environment benefits, with special reference to nuisance by noise, will be found in the article by David Pearce cited above.

20. Estate agents are very well aware of the exact number of francs by which the market price of a flat varies as the result of a given exposure to noise or the given proximity of a park or garden, etc.

21. References cited above.

22. Cf. "Le moindre mal en politique d'environnement", CEPREMAP, stencilled.

23. Pollution and Prices, op. cit.

24. Cf. "Le niveau optimal de décision collective", Le Monde.

25. Some elements of this analysis will be found in l'Etat et le système des prix (op. cit. Part I, Chap. 4 and Annex).

26. Cf. "Concernements et décisions collectifs ; Analyse et Prévision", June 1967.

27. Richard Musgrave in The Theory of Public Finance uses the term "merit wants" to describe the desires of governments as to the consumption of citizens. This is different from a vicarious desire which is the desire of an individual. The weakness of Musgrave's concept is that the government is not an individual. But a citizen and a member of the government may have vicarious desires. These are the origin of the phenomenon described by Musgrave, but taking them into account would certainly lead to a much wider view. It is nevertheless interesting to pay special attention to the desires of a politician for the consumption or situation of individuals, not so much because they represent his personal opinion, but because they are the vicarious desires of his electors.

28. Housing subsidies and taxes on luxury goods may fall into this class (see "La taxation de la consommation ostentatoire", Revue d'Economie Politique, 1972, I).

29. Cf. "La production optimale de justice sociale", in Economie Publique ; CNRS, Paris, 1968. "La théorie démocratique de la justice sociale", Revue d'Economie Politique, March 1969, and Justice et équité, CNRS, monograph, Paris, 1972.

30. They should not be corrected when this compensation serves as an excuse for not correcting them more completely (starting direct with the reform of the unfair structure itself).

31. See above.

32. Cf. "Optimum anti-pollution policies in the presence of uncertainty", op. cit.

33. Other iterative processes are conceivable, such as, in this case a "Cobweb" where the authority fixes alternately a price or rate and a quantity x; the condition of convergence is then different.

34. This is no longer true if we try simultaneously to determine several variables of the type x; this phenomenon is well known with Walrasian trial and error.

35. Cf. "La non-convexité d'externalité", stencilled, CEPREMAP, and the literature quoted there.

36. Op. cit. : Part I, Section II. This method was already suggested in our work Introduction à la théorie du rôle économique de l'Etat : les fondements de l'économie publique (IFP 1964-1965). Various articles by E. Malinvaud: "Procédures pour la détermination d'un programme de consommation collective" (paper presented to the Econometrics Congress in Brussels in September,1969), "A Planning Approach to the Public Good Problem", The Swedish Journal of Economics, Special Issue, N° 1, 1971 and an article by J. H. Drèze and D. de La Vallée Poussin: "A Tatonnement process for public goods", Review of Economic Studies, April 1971, 38(2), analyse various other interesting aspects of this method.

37. In the discussions on the passage of the South Highway through the Forest of Fontainebleau it was mentioned that this would exterminate a species of insect neither useful nor harmful and extremely small. It is hard to put in a utility function something which can be neither seen, heard, touched nor felt.

A SURVEY
OF ENVIRONMENTAL DAMAGE FUNCTIONS

by

R.E. Wyzga,*
Environment Directorate,
OECD, Paris

We are at the first stages of estimating environmental damage in economic terms. Several studies in the area of environmental damage functions have been launched, but they have had to contend with a number of difficulties, none of which have been solved definitively. An imperfect knowledge of the effects of pollutants, the difficulty of distinguishing the effects of different pollutants, non-uniform definitions and appreciation of damage, as well as the difficulty of attaching monetary values to "damage", confront attempts to quantify monetarily environmental damage.

This paper presents a survey of existing environmental damage functions. It gives special attention to the methodologies used in making estimates of environmental damage. Those studies which attempt to measure _direct_ damage in monetary terms are given principal attention; the measurement of disamenities such as recreational and aesthetic losses, are covered only superficially. The results of the various studies are then compared in an effort to judge their compatibility. It is necessary to consider output separately from methodology as the lack of adequate data can detract from the results of a study with a sound methodology.

I. AIR POLLUTION

Most of the economic estimates of direct damage have treated the effects of air pollution, and most of these studies have limited themselves to a specific area such as health, materials, vegetation, or property. There have been some attempts to find overall national estimates of air pollution damage. We shall briefly examine them before going on to consider specific types of damage.

*   The opinions expressed in this paper reflect the author's views and not necessarily those of the OECD Secretariat.

The report of the RECAT Committee (1) made some damage estimates of pollution from motor vehicles in the United States as part of a cost-benefit analysis of the Clean Air Act regulations for motor vehicles. The damage estimates are taken principally from a study by Barrett and Waddell (2), which in turn uses results from a wide variety of studies, most of which shall be discussed below. A summary of the damage estimates from this overall study is presented in Table A. Table A-1 presents the estimated damage from all sources of pollution and Table A-2 gives damage estimates from motor vehicle sources. In each of these two tables two estimates are given depending upon the assumptions made about the health effects of CO, HC, and NO_x. These assumptions will be discussed later in the paper. An earlier estimate of the total US damage from air pollution was made by Ridker (3), and his most important results have been incorporated into the damage estimates of the RECAT report.

In addition to the United States national estimate, national estimates of air pollution damage exist for at least three other countries. Zerbe has calculated air pollution damage estimates for Canada, Ontario and Toronto. These are presented in Table B. Unfortunately no description of his methodology is available. If we calculate the US per capita air pollution damage from the RECAT Report, we obtain $ 95-126 per capita estimate which is larger than the Zerbe estimates, but could be explained by differences in costs between the two countries and by the three-year time-difference. More serious is the difference in the share of damage among various categories in the two countries. Health sustains the largest share of damage in the US (47-63% of the total damage or $44-76 per capita), whereas in Canada, health sustains only 4.5% of the total damage or $2.38 per capita. On the other hand, damage to materials represents 93% of total damage in Canada or $48.83 in yearly per capita costs; this category represents only 19-25% of US total damage and $24 per capita yearly damage. These large differences imply that dissimiliar methodologies were used and that the two estimates are not comparable.

The Beaver Committee (4) was the first to make a national estimate of economic damage resulting from air pollution, making such an estimate for Great Britain in 1953. Table C presents the estimated damage costs of this study. Health damage was not considered. The per capita damage costs are from £5.68-6.17, far less than the American and Canadian per capita estimates after one has excluded health costs and updated the British costs by fifteen years.

A more recent national estimate of damage from air pollution was prepared by the Programmes Analysis Unit (5). The study defines two types of costs, social and economic. The latter are defined to be the

Table A

1. ESTIMATE OF NATIONAL TOTAL DAMAGE COSTS OF POLLUTION IN UNITED STATES 1968

(million dollars)

EFFECTS	1968 COSTS		
	SO_x AND PARTICULATES ONLY	INCLUDING CO, HC, AND NO_x	
		ESTIMATE A	ESTIMATE B
Residential Property	5,200	5,200	5,200
Materials	4,752	4,752	4,752
Health	6,060	15,169	8,886
Vegetation	120	120	120
TOTAL	16,132	25,241	18,958

2. ESTIMATED NATIONAL ANNUAL COSTS OF POLLUTION IN 1969 DUE TO GASOLINE MOTOR VEHICLES ONLY, INCLUDING ESTIMATED HEALTH EFFECTS OF CO, HC, AND NO_x

(million dollars)

EFFECTS	AUTOMOBILES ONLY	
	ESTIMATE A	ESTIMATE B
Residential Property ...	39	39
Materials	587	587
Health	4,550	1,305
Vegetation	24	24
TOTAL in 1968 (dollars)	5,200	1,955
TOTAL in 1970 (dollars)	5,720	2,150

Adapted from: Cumulative Regulatory Effects on the Cost of Automotive Transportation (RECAT), Final Report of the Ad Hoc Committee, February 28, 1972, Office of Science and Technology.

Table B

TOTAL COST ESTIMATES PER CAPITA FOR CANADA, ONTARIO,
AND TORONTO FOR 1965

(Canadian dollars)

		CANADA	ONTARIO	TORONTO
1.	Housing, Painting and Repair	7.04	9.75	12.34
2.	Corrosion Inhibiting Paint	0.11	0.15	0.20
3.	Commercial and Industrial Painting and Repair	26.76	35.70	45.20
4.	Stone and Brick Cleaning	0.70	0.96	1.14
5.	Depreciation of Building	0.61	0.86	1.08
6.	Contract Building Maintenance Service	1.35	1.87	2.37
7.	Metal Corrosion Losses	3.62	4.60	4.47
8.	Commercial and Home Laundry and Dry Cleaning	3.51	4.85	8.63
9.	Shelf Goods	0.28	0.36	0.54
10.	Clothing and Furnishing	5.59	7.16	10.81
11.	Mortality and Morbidity	2.38	3.04	2.94
12.	Rubber Depreciation	0.22	0.31	0.39
13.	Leather Depreciation	0.03	0.05	0.06
14.	Nursery Plants	0.00	0.00	0.00
15.	Air Filtering Equipment	0.02	0.02	0.03
16.	Crops	0.32	0.16	0.00
17.	Animals	0.09	0.12	0.00
18.	Additional Lighting	0.43	0.48	0.63
19.	Additional Transportation	0.39	0.50	0.49
	TOTAL	52.46	70.94	93.98

SOURCE: Richard Zerbe Jr., The Economics of Air Pollution: A Cost-Benefit Approach, unpublished manuscript
1969, p. 108-109.

FROM: Damage Functions, EQM Working Paper No. 15, Systems Research Group.

Table C

ECONOMIC DAMAGE RESULTING FROM
AIR POLLUTION IN GREAT BRITAIN IN 1953,
ACCORDING TO THE BEAVER REPORT ESTIMATES

(million pounds)

Direct Costs	
Laundry	25.0
Painting and decoration	30.0
Cleaning and depreciation of buildings	20.0
Metal corrosion	25.0
Damage to textiles, etc., and other assets	52.5
TOTAL	152.5
Indirect Costs	
Agriculture	10.0
Losses in work efficiency in industry	
Losses in work efficiency in other fields	100.0
TOTAL	110.0
Value of fuel lost in badly functioning plants	25-50
GENERAL TOTAL	287.5-312.5

SOURCE: Ente Nazionale Idrocarburi, Economic Costs and Benefits of an Antipollution
Project in Italy, Special Issue for the U.N. Conference in the Human Environment, Stockholm, June 5-16, 1972.

the monetary equivalent of physical damage effects and of recognisable
effects other than physical damage which are reflected in market behaviour. This category includes the costs of premature replacement,
increased maintenance costs, reduced crop yields, medical expenses,
reduced wages, and lower property values, etc. The former category
(social costs) includes recognisable effects which produce physical

55

damage, but not wholly reflected in expenditure patterns or markets, and it includes effects that are not usually expressed in monetary terms and have no defined values. Examples of effects in this category include suffering from pollution-induced diseases and the subjection to less attractive buildings because of pollution effects.

The methodology used in this study is basically one which sought to divide the country into "clean" or "polluted" areas, and estimates of the difference per capita in costs in these areas, are then used to calculate the national "marginal" costs of air pollution. These produce the estimates of marginal damage given in Table D. Assuming that damage costs are linearly related to mean urban pollution levels, estimates of the total national costs of pollution are calculated and given in Table E.

The total economic costs in Table E are those which are comparable with the US and Canadian estimates of total air pollution damage. The 1970 per capita estimated economic costs of air pollution in the UK were £7.36, a noticeably smaller quantity than the estimated costs to US and Canadian individuals. It is also worthwhile to note the important contribution to agriculture in the UK estimate. Despite the smaller overall estimated costs of air pollution in the UK, the agricultural damage there is far greater than the per capita agricultural damage in Canada and in the US. This could be due to differences in estimation methodology or to the fact that the United Kingdom is a much more densely populated country, a large amount of whose agricultural areas are near to polluted conurbations.

An Italian estimate has been made by Mammarella (6), and its results are presented in Table F. The estimate is considered to be a "subjective appreciation" rather than based on a "scientific hypothesis"; nevertheless the results are of interest. The per capita costs are approximately $12, which is considerably less than the estimated American and Canadian estimate costs.

For an explanation of the methodology used and the detailed results of this study, see the paper by Muraro in this volume.

A.   HUMAN HEALTH

At least four detailed studies have tried to attach economic values to the health effects of air pollution:

1.   Ridker, Economic Costs of Air Pollution, Praeger, 1967.

Table D

ESTIMATED 1970 MARGINAL COSTS[a]

(million pounds per annum)

CATEGORY	ECONOMIC COSTS		SOCIAL COSTS		TOTAL
	MEAN	STANDARD DEVIATION	MEAN	STANDARD DEVIATION	MEAN
Painting	–	–	6.3	2.5	6.3
Laundry and Household Goods (including car cleaning)	0.5	0.1	164	60	164.5
Exterior Cleaning of Buildings	–	–	1.5	2	1.5
Window and Office Cleaning	5.0	0.2	–	–	5.0
Corrosion and Protection of Metal Structures	10	5.5	–	–	10
Damage to Textiles, Paper, Leather, etc.	33	4.5	–	–	33
Agricultural Production	39	11	–	–	39
Health	40	7.5	140	29	180
Amenity – Point Sources	–	–	100	33	100
Motor Vehicles	–	–	3	1	3
Total Costs	130	15	410	75	540

a. The economic costs are the excess of costs in conurbations over costs in non-conurbations, i.e. "polluted" as opposed to "clean" areas, except for agricultural costs which refer to costs in rural areas. The social costs are not truly marginal costs.

SOURCE: Programmes Analysis Unit, An Economic and Technical Appraisal of Air Pollution in the United Kingdom, Chilton, Didcot, Berks, 1971.

Table E

1970 TOTAL DAMAGE COSTS

(million pounds per annum)

| CATEGORY | ECONOMIC COSTS | | SOCIAL COSTS | | TOTAL |
	MEAN	STANDARD DEVIATION	MEAN	STANDARD DEVIATION	MEAN
Painting	–	–	6.3	2.5	6.3
Laundry and Household Goods (including car cleaning)	0.5	0.1	164	60	164.5
Exterior Cleaning of Buildings	–	–	1.5	0.2	1.5
Window and Office Cleaning	5.0	0.2	–	–	5.0
Corrosion and Protection of Metal Structures	42	28	–	–	42
Damage to Textiles, Paper, Leather, etc.	33	4.5	–	–	33
Agricultural Production	195	110	–	–	195
Health	130	63	510	243	640
Amenity – Point Sources	–	–	100	33	100
Motor Vehicles	–	–	3	1	3
Total Costs (rounded)	410	130	780	252	1 190

SOURCE: Programmes Analysis Unit, An Economical and Technical Appraisal of Air Pollution in the United Kingdom, Chilton, Didcot, Berks, 1971.

Table F

ESTIMATE OF ANNUAL AIR POLLUTION
DAMAGES IN ITALY IN 1968

(billion lire)

Direct Costs	
Damage to human health	60
Laundry expenses	20
Damage to various materials (textiles, plastics, rubber, paper, leather, etc.)	50
Deterioration of varnishes, paints, wall decorations, etc., pictures, paintings, etc.	50
Deterioration of buildings, monuments, works of art, etc.	70
Corrosion of metals and metal structures generally	30
TOTAL	260
Indirect Costs	
Damage to agriculture and forests	5
Work efficiency losses (sick leave, time off, longer travelling time, etc.)	20
Loss of efficiency in other fields (increased electricity consumption, fuel losses due to bad plant functioning, lost tourist trade, etc.)	50
Various losses not included in the previous headings	15
TOTAL	90
GENERAL TOTAL	350

SOURCE: Ente Nazionale Idrocarburi, Economic Costs and Benefits of an Antipollution Project in Italy, Special Issue for the U.N. Conference on the Human Environment, Stockholm, June 5-16, 1972.

2.   Lave and Seskin, "Air Pollution and Human Health", Science, 169, 723.

3.   Riggan, "Cost to Federal Government of Health Effects," mimeographed, Chapel Hill, N.C.

4.   "The Effect on Health", Section IV G, An Economic and Technical Appraisal of Air Pollution in the United Kingdom, Programmes Analysis Unit, Chilton, Didcot, Berks, 1971.

Ridker restricts himself to six categories of disease: cancer of the respiratory system, chronic and acute bronchitis, pneumonia, emphysema, asthma, and the common cold. At least one important disease category (cardio-vascular) is omitted. Ridker defines four types of costs: those due to premature death, those associated with morbidity, treatment costs, and prevention or avoidance costs. Because of data limitations he considers neither the prevention nor the psychic costs associated with illness and death. He thus believes his measures of costs to be underestimates.

There are two important steps in the estimation of pollution damage. The first is the attribution of given effects to a certain level of pollution and the second is the placing of an economic value on these estimated effects. The approach taken by Ridker is to estimate the total costs of a specific disease and then to attribute some percentage of these costs to air pollution. Ridker chooses 20% because the difference between urban and rural death rates adjusted for smoking, age, sex and race for the above categories of death in the USA in 1949 was about 20%. A Pennsylvania study of urban-rural differences corroborates this result for lung cancer.

There are two problems with this type of damage estimate, both of which are due to a lack of data and information. The urban-rural difference estimate is a crude one, subject to much debate, and this difference varies greatly from disease category to disease category. Moreover, this method of estimation ignores the more specific aspects of the pollution-effects relationship. The type of estimate presented is valuable only for a national or area estimate of the damage due to pollution. The basic assumption is that if urban levels of "air pollution" could be reduced to rural levels, then 20% of the urban effects could be eliminated (Weighed against this value, the total national (or regional) expenditure for pollution control could be presented in a cost-benefit analysis.) But there are difficulties in defining urban and rural pollution levels. Instead of a simple dichotomy, there is a continuous scale of pollution intensity with the generally higher levels for most pollutants present in urban areas. If one were to wish to evaluate some specific policy or to consider assessing damage, more detailed information would be essential. One would need to have some idea of the effects

60

associated with a particular level of each individual pollutant. One could perhaps avoid this objection by assuming all pollutants to be equally culpable and by assuming a linear pollution-response curve between the two defined points (urban pollution, urban mortality and rural pollution, rural mortality).

Ridker computes the loss of output, burial costs, treatment costs, and absenteeism costs and sums them to obtain the total costs of a particular disease. He then supposes 20% of these total costs are due to pollution. Ridker defines the total costs of premature death due to a disease as the output a person would have produced had he not died prematurely, rather than the difference between output and consumption. This cost is calculated as the sum of an individual's expected earnings discounted for each additional productive year of life had he not died prematurely. The following formula from Ridker best defines his calculation:

$$V_a = \sum_{n=a}^{\infty} \frac{P_{a_1}^n \cdot P_{a_2}^n \cdot P_{a_3}^n \cdot Y_n}{(1+r)^{n-a}}$$

where: V_a is the present value of the future earnings of an individual at age a;

        $P_{a_1}^n$ is the probability that an individual of age a will live to age n;

        $P_{a_2}^n$ is the probability that an individual of age a living at age n will be in the labour force at age n;

        $P_{a_3}^n$ is the probability that an individual of age a living and in the labour force at age n will be employed at age n;

        Y_n is the earnings at age n; and

        r is the rate of interest.

Ridker obtains estimates of $P_{a_1}^n$, $P_{a_2}^n$, and $P_{a_3}^n$ from existing demographic sources, aggregated over all occupations. Y_n is the average

61

wage earnings of an individual of age n aggregated over all occupations. This figure does not include non-market wages or services; thus for example, the values of housewife services are not included. Ridker calculates V_a for two rates of interest 5% and 10%.

Ridker defines burial costs associated with premature death as "the difference between the present cost of burial and the present value of the future expected cost of burial". The following formula shows his method of calculation:

$$C_a = C_o \left[1 - \sum_{n=a}^{\infty} \left(\frac{P_{a_1}^n}{(1+r)^{n-a}} \right) \right]$$

where: C_o is the cost of burial;

C_a is the present value of the net expected gain from delaying burial at age a; and

$P_{a_1}^n$ and r are as above.

In an effort to determine the treatment costs of the six disease categories, Ridker gathers estimates from other sources. He emphasises the lack of adequate treatment cost data presently available. Absenteeism costs are also taken from other sources which give estimates of the time lost from work due to a specific disease. It is interesting to note that Ridker uses the total unadjusted treatment costs for terminal care; he does not use the difference between the actual treatment costs and the present value of expected terminal care costs.

Ridker assumes that 20% of the total deaths and cases of the diseases he considers are due to air pollution. His estimates of the costs due to air pollution are presented below in Table G.

Lave and Seskin examine several air pollution-health studies in an effort to fix a quantitative relationship between these two variables. They then determine the relative decrease in morbidity and mortality for several disease categories if urban air pollution levels were to be abated 50%. They consider bronchitis, other respiratory diseases, lung cancer, other cancers, and cardiovascular diseases. They do not consider the common cold, a category to which Ridker attributes considerable costs.

To calculate the damage due to air pollution in the United States, Lave and Seskin take the costs of disease from Dorothy Rice's Estimating

62

Table G

RESOURCE COSTS OF DISEASES ATTRIBUTED TO AIR POLLUTION (1958)

(million dollars)

TYPE OF COST	COSTS ASSOCIATED WITH SELECTED DISEASES[a]							
	CANCER OF THE RESPIRATORY SYSTEM	CHRONIC BRONCHITIS	ACUTE BRONCHITIS	COMMON COLD	PNEUMONIA	EMPHYSEMA	ASTHMA	TOTAL
Premature Death	103.6	3.6	1.2	n.a.	65.8	12.4	11.8	198.4
Premature Burial	3.0	0.1	< 0.1	n.a.	2.6	0.4	0.4	6.5
Treatment	7.0	17.8	n.a.	40.0	14.6	n.a.	27.6	107.0
Absenteeism	22.4	10.4	n.a.	26.2	15.0	n.a.	12.0	86.0
Total	136.0	31.9	1.2	66.2	98.0	12.8	51.8	397.9

a) Using a discount rate of 5%.

Adapted from: R. G. Ridker, Economic Costs of Air Pollution, Frederick A. Praeger, New York 1967.

the Cost of Illness (7) and attribute percentages of these costs to air
pollution. Included in these costs are direct disease costs comprising
expenditures for hospital and nursing home care, services of physicians
and other health professions and indirect costs calculated in terms of
the wages foregone by those who are ill or prematurely dead. Not
included are other direct health costs such as drugs, appliances, industrial inplant health services, medical research, administrative
health costs, etc., which Lave and Seskin believe could be as large as
50% of the other direct costs. The premature burial costs of Ridker
are not included either. Table H gives damage estimates for the US
in 1963 due to "excess" air pollution, the base level of pollution defined
as being 50% lower than the current urban levels. Lave and Seskin
believe that these are gross underestimates of "the amount society is
willing to pay to lessen pain and premature death caused by disease",
but that there exist no sufficient data to allow such a calculation.

The Riggan paper limits itself to the consideration of pollution from
motor vehicles and considers four disease categories: lung cancer,
bronchitis, arteriosclerotic heart disease, and motor vehicle accidents.
For lung cancer, Riggan searches the literature to arrive at a percentage of 50% of those cases due to an urban factor of which he attributes
one-half, or 25% of the total cases to air pollution. (He further deflates
this percentage in considering pollution only from motor vehicles sources.)
For the other disease categories, Riggan only presents percentages of
cases which he attributes to motor vehicle pollution. It is of interest
to note that he attributes 10% of motor vehicle accidents (and hence
injuries and deaths) to air pollution.

Riggan considers only costs to the federal US government. His
method of calculating income tax losses is an adaptation of Ridker's
method for calculating lost income, but Riggan uses a 6% discount rate
and distinguishes between males and females. In addition Riggan uses
his attributed percentages to estimate the amount of Social Security
disability payments due to motor vehicle pollution.

For the sake of completeness, the additions made by the RECAT
Report to the Barrett and Waddell estimates should be mentioned. To
compensate for the fact that the costs of CO, HC, and NO_x damages
are not included in the health costs of the earlier studies, the RECAT
Committee attempts to estimate these costs. They calculate the ratios
between the air quality standards for CO, HC and NO_x and that for SO_x
to arrive at "severity factors". These factors were multiplied by the
total tonnages of CO, HC, and NO_x emitted. The sum of these products
is then compared with the sum of similarly calculated products for SO_x
and particulate matter and the ratio of these two sums is multiplied by

Table H

RESOURCE COSTS OF DISEASES ATTRIBUTED TO AIR POLLUTION (1963)

(million dollars)

| | BRONCHITIS | RESPIRATORY | COSTS ASSOCIATED WITH SELECTED DISEASES | | CARDIO-VASCULAR DISEASES | TOTAL |
			LUNG CANCER	OTHER CANCER		
Estimated Costs ..	250–500	972	33	357	468	2 080

the estimated damage of SO_x and of particulate matter to health to arrive at an estimate of the damage costs to health from CO, HC, and NO_x. Because the ratios of air quality standards differ (according to place and by time units used to form averages), the estimated total damage costs vary. This explains why there are two estimates, A. and B. in Table A.

The method puts much faith in air quality standards. The fact that estimates A. and B. differ by so great an amount, even under the assumption that air quality standards for specific pollutants are set relative to their damage to health, suggests that this method is not at present a very profitable one.

A comparison of the methodologies and results of Ridker, Lave and Seskin, and Riggan shows that the basic methodologies are the same. Total national costs are estimated for specific diseases and a percentage of these costs is attributed to pollution. There is an implicit assumption that the average costs of pollution-induced cases are the same as those of all cases. This assumption could lead to underestimates of the total costs, if, for example, pollution-induced cases are younger than other cases, more potential income being lost. But, in the absence of further data it seems as if this assumption must be kept.

The various authors did not use the same information sources in deriving the percentages of cases attributed to pollution, although all looked at the differences between urban and rural disease and/or mortality rates. Table I presents the percentages used by the various authors for those disease categories examined by two or more authors. Despite the lack of detailed information, it is encouraging to see the general agreement among the authors on the proportion of cases attributable to air pollution. (It is possible that since the authors of the later studies were acquainted with the earlier estimates, they were thereby influenced by them in making their own estimates.) It should also be noted that Lave and Seskin consider the percentage of total cases attributed to incremental urban pollution, whereas the others consider the total of cases attributed to pollution. But since all three studies choose their percents of cases attributed to pollution from urban-rural differences, it appears as if the greatest difference in the definitions of pollution-attributed cases is a semantic one.

Apparently the lack of suitable data prevented all of the authors from trying to construct a more detailed damage function which would associate proportions of cases with specific levels of pollution. There is some hope that such a curve can be constructed in the near future as more data become available. The results of the USEPA's CHESS programme will be particularly valuable in the construction of a dose-

Table I

PERCENT CASES ATTRIBUTED TO AIR POLLUTION

DISEASE	STUDY		
	RIDKER 1958	LAVE AND SESKIN 1963	RIGGAN 1970
Lung Cancer	20%	25%	25%
Bronchitis	20%	25-50%	-
Total Respiratory ..	20%	25%	-

response curve. This study has applied the same methodology in several US communities with differing degrees of air pollution and seeks to define a dose-response curve.

Agreement on the cost assessment is not as uniform, despite the fact that similar cost categories are considered. Ridker is the only one to consider premature burial, but this category contributes only about 1.5% of his total costs. All of the authors believe their costs to be underestimates because of lack of data although they do not always cite the same omissions. Because Riggan's cost estimates are highly specific we can only compare those of Lave and Seskin with Ridker's. Unfortunately the methods used to calculate Lave and Seskin's costs were not specified, hence only the results and not the methods can be compared. Table J presents the costs associated with selected diseases as given by Ridker and by Lave and Seskin. The costs include those due to premature death, absenteeism, and treatment of disease. The Ridker data are for 1958 and those of Lave and Seskin for 1963. Ridker uses a 5% discount rate; that for Lave and Seskin is unknown. If one adjusted for inflation and population increase, one would expect the 1963 costs to be about 20% higher. Changes in disease rates within this period have not been very great except for possibly the total respiratory disease category, as there was an influenza epidemic in 1963.

The comparable cost estimates do not appear to conform. Ridker's lung cancer cost estimate is far greater than that of Lave and Seskin, although one would expect the Lave and Seskin estimate to be larger because of the larger number of cases of lung cancer they attribute to pollution. The bronchitis cost estimate of Lave and Seskin is more

Table J

COSTS ASSOCIATED WITH SELECTED DISEASES

(million dollars)

DISEASE CATEGORY	RIDKER 1958	LAVE AND SESKIN 1963
Lung Cancer	665	132
Bronchitis[a]	227	930
Total Respiratory[b]	1 957	4 887

a. Includes the Ridker categories of chronic bronchitis, acute bronchitis, and emphysema.
b. Includes the Ridker categories of cancer of the respiratory system, chronic bronchitis, acute bronchitis, common cold, pneumonia, emphysema, and asthma.

than three times as great as Ridker's estimate; one would expect it to be only one and a half times as large if the estimates were conformable. Similarly the Lave and Seskin cost estimates for total respiratory deaths are far greater than those of Ridker. It thus appears that the methodologies used to estimate costs in these two studies are not comparable.

The British study uses a methodology similar to those of the American studies, but it limits itself to two disease categories, bronchitis and lung cancer. The British study considers three major categories of cost: (a) economic costs incurred by the nation; (b) economic costs which are not reflected in GNP; and (c) social costs. The first category can itself be broken down into costs due to loss of production, costs of treatment, and costs of premature death. An outline of the methodology used to estimate the loss of production from pollution-induced bronchitis will illustrate the general methodology. First of all, the total national loss of production from bronchitis is estimated for men and for women. The Department of Health and Social Security data indicate that 32 million man-days and 45 million women-days per year are lost through absence from work due to bronchitis. After adjusting these figures for possible non-reporting, total lost production through bronchitis to men in 1970 is estimated to be in the range of from £128 million to £200 million with a midpoint of £164 million. (E = £164 million). It is further assumed that bronchitis prevalence differs in urban areas from rural areas by a factor of from 1.0 to 1.5. (F the ratio of per person damage in polluted areas to unpolluted areas is estimated to be 1.25). Finally R, the ratio of the number of persons living in urban areas to those living in rural areas is assumed to be 1.5. These estimates allow one to attribute about 15% of total bronchitis to excess air pollution in urban areas. From these estimates the total excess costs (C) in conurbations over non-conurbations due to bronchitis in males is estimated to be £14.8 million, from the formula:

$$C = E \ \frac{(F - 1)}{(F + R)}$$

A similar estimate of £1.4 million is made for lost production due to bronchitis in females. For lung cancer, a total estimate of excess loss of production in urban areas over non-urban areas of £0.4 million is obtained for 1970. In reaching this estimate, the ratio of incidence in urban areas to that in rural areas is assumed to be 1.125, thus attributing about 5% of the cases of lung cancer to excess urban pollution.

The second category considered in estimating the costs of bronchitis and lung cancer from excess urban air pollution is treatment costs. The national yearly costs for treating bronchitis are assumed to be from £93.5 million to £200 million and those for treating lung cancer are assumed to be between six and ten million pounds. Attributing some 15 and 5% of the cases of these respective disease categories to excess urban air pollution, point estimates of the national treatment costs due to urban pollution of £14 million and £0.4 million are obtained for bronchitis and lung cancer respectively.

The last category of costs considered under national economic costs of pollution-induced diseases is the cost of premature death. For an individual, this is defined to be his gross income minus total consumption. Since most people who die of bronchitis do so after they have completed their working life, this cost is assumed to be very small for pollution-induced bronchitis cases. In the case of lung cancer this cost is estimated to be £13 million, of which £0.6 million is assumed due to excess urban air pollution. This is estimated by tabulating the number of lung cancer deaths for each age category, calculating the total number of earning years lost, assuming the loss of a foregone working year through premature death to be £260 per person, and discounting foregone income at an annual rate of 10%.

As economic non-GNP costs for these diseases, lost production from illnesses of housewives, of uninsured working women and of students is calculated. For bronchitis these losses are estimated to

69

be £7.46 million, and for lung cancer they are estimated to be £0.3 million.

As social costs of pollution-induced ill-health, the study includes disamenity of illness and the non-economic value of avoiding premature death. An arbitrary value of £1000 is allocated per annum for disamenity. The ranges of legal compensations for similar disamenities and of the per case amounts of monies spent on ameliorating or overcoming the effects of similar disamenities include the value chosen for this study. For bronchitis the social cost of disamenity of pollution-induced urban cases is estimated to be £70 million, and for lung cancer this cost is estimated to be £1.3 million.

The social cost of premature death is assumed to be £1,000 per year of life lost, as it is reasonably in accord with the evidence from social expenditure. With this assumption, the social cost of premature death from pollution-induced urban bronchitis cases is estimated to be £30 million per annum, and the similar social cost related to lung cancer deaths is given at £19 million per annum.

Table K presents a summary of all of the estimated health costs of excess pollution in conurbations over non-conurbations. To arrive at an estimate of the total pollution costs, the damage costs are assumed to be zero at background levels. The total damage costs are then assumed to be approximately four times marginal costs. The total national health cost of air pollution in 1970 in the UK is estimated to be £160 million in economic costs and £480 million in social costs.

The methodology of the British study suffers from many of the same weaknesses as the American studies. Many assumptions need to be made, and the final results give damage estimates for but two levels of pollution, background levels and existing national levels which cannot be easily characterized. The novel feature of this study is that it attempts to present social costs, in addition to economic costs. These estimates require even more contestable assumptions than the economic estimates, but the estimates of these costs are three times greater than the economic costs. This fact indicates that despite the speculative nature of these estimates, they are probably indicative of the fact that social costs of pollution-induced disease are much greater than the economic costs; hence in any complete accounting, social costs need to be considered.

B. MATERIALS

Among the adverse effects of air pollution on materials are the corrosion of metals, the deterioration of rubber, the discolouration

70

Table K

EXCESS COSTS OF THE EFFECT
OF AIR POLLUTION ON HEALTH

(million pounds per annum)

COST CATEGORY	BRONCHITIS		LUNG CANCER	
	MEAN	STANDARD DEVIATION	MEAN	STANDARD DEVIATION
Economic (GNP)				
Loss of production .	16	5.0	0.4	0.2
Treatment	14	5.0	0.4	0.2
Premature death ..	–	–	0.6	0.4
Economic (Non–GNP)				
Loss of housewives' services	4.1	1.4	0.3	0.2
Loss of women not recorded as receiving sick payments .	3.2	1.1	–	–
Students	0.2	0.1	–	–
Total economic costs	37.5		1.7	
Social				
Premature death ...	30	10	19	11
Disamenity of illness	70	24	1.3	0.8
Total social costs	100		20.3	

SOURCE: Programmes Analysis Unit, An Economic and Technical Appraisal of Air Pollution in the United Kingdom, Chilton, Didcot, Berks, 1971.

71

of paint, and soiling. Several studies estimate air pollution damage
to various materials. Four are examined here for their methodology
and results:

1. Stickney, Mueller, and Spence, "Pollution vs. Rubber",
Rubber Age, 45, September 1971.

2. Midwest Research Institute, Systems Analysis of the Effects
of Air Pollution on Materials; January 1970.

3. Ridker, Economic Costs of Air Pollution; Praeger, 1967.

4. Sections IV B, IV D, IV E, and IV C: An Economic and
Technical Appraisal of Air Pollution in the United Kingdom;
Programmes Analysis Unit, Chilton, Didcot, Berks, 1971.

The Stickney et al paper is highly specific, restricting itself to one
product area, but its methodology and results can be compared with
those of the Midwest Research Institute study. Two general factors
comprise the damage to rubber products (elastomers) by air pollution.
These are increased costs in providing products that are resistent to
pollutants and the costs of the early replacement of damaged products.

Two alternative methods are used to determine the first set of costs.
A questionnaire was sent to 60 representative companies asking the
estimated yearly cost of protection against air pollution for specific
products. The results, from 30 companies, are used to calculate the
total US protection costs for 1970, estimated at $54 million. From the
information given in the paper, it appears as if the estimated protection
costs from the firms are relatively consistent with each other, but more
information would be desirable to check carefully for consistency. The
second methodological approach consists in calculating the added costs
for various protective finishes. Companies were asked to what extent
these finishes are used to protect against air pollution. This percentage
is multiplied against total value to obtain a total cost of $59.7 million
for 1970 in the US. The difference between the two estimates is small
and the average of the two, $57 million, is multiplied by three, a
"reasonable" ratio of retail to manufacturing costs in the rubber industry, to obtain a total added cost of $171 million to the consumer.

Using information from rubber producers, consumers, and Battelle
Columbus Laboratories, the authors produced estimates for determining
the cost of the early replacement of rubber products necessitated because
of pollution. They first estimate the percentage of products which have
a shortened life due to pollution, and they then assess the average percent of life lost to calculate the value lost. The estimated total replacement cost to US consumers in 1970 is $227 million.

The sum of the two costs above is $398 million, but it ignores labour costs required by early replacement and by the replacement of an entire subassembly because a rubber component has failed. To compensate for these omissions the authors raise the total cost of rubber deterioration from air pollution to $500 million to US consumers in 1970. No attempt is made to construct a function relating pollution concentrations to amounts of damage; but since apparently only one pollutant (ozone) adversely affects rubber products, a knowledge of the threshold effect value would allow an approximate function to be constructed.

The MRI (Midwest Research Institute) Report presents the results of a systematic analysis of all of the physical and chemical interactions between materials, pollutants and environmental parameters needed to assess the economic damage to materials from air pollution. Because there is almost an infinite number of materials, the study limits itself to the fifty-odd most economically important, which represent about forty per cent of the economic value of all materials exposed to air pollution. The study tries, where possible, to determine the pollutant dosage - material response relationship and to transpose this relationship into a pollutant dosage - monetary damage function.

First a matrix of pollutant-material pairs is constructed for special study. After an intensive literature search (8), attempts are made to satisfy the matrix, to assess the quantity and quality of information and data available for each cell, to form dosage-response relationships, and to establish the more significant economic effects.

The MRI study first calculates the economic value of the material and then applies the rate of deterioration to this value to estimate the economic loss from material deterioration. The economic value of material exposed to air pollution Q is calculated through use of the following formula:

$$Q = P \times N \times F \times R$$

where $P =$ product of the annual dollar production volume;

           $N =$ economic life of the material based on usage;

           $F =$ weighted average factor for the percentage of the material exposed to air pollution;

           $R =$ labour factor reflecting the in-place or as-used value of the material.

The rate of deterioration or interaction V is then calculated by estimating the difference between the deterioration rates in polluted and unpolluted environments divided by the average thickness of the material. (For some materials the lack of available information reduces the estimate of V to a subjective guess.) This rate (V) is multiplied by Q to obtain the estimated yearly cost of deterioration for each material.

The results are found in Table L. The costs of protecting a material against deterioration and the costs of replacing deteriorated materials are not included. The total deterioration costs of synthetic rubber and natural rubber products are $194 million which is comparable with the total replacement costs of $227 million estimated by Stickney, Mueller, and Spence, especially when one considers that the MRI study applies to an earlier period (9). The total costs of deterioration, $3.8 billion, represent damage costs to only 40% of the total value of materials which are exposed to air pollution. If one were to extrapolate the same average rate of damage to the remaining 60%, the total costs of deterioration would be $9.5 billion.

The MRI study also estimates the costs due to soiling. It mentions three possible approaches to obtain an estimate of these costs:

1. survey consumers;

2. survey the cleaning industry;

3. assign an economic value to the aesthetic loss suffered by a material through soiling.

The MRI study uses the third approach, estimating the soiling damage cost, L by Q x V where Q is the value of the exposed material as defined above, and V is the soiling interaction value per year. The calculation of V is complex and differs for fibres and non-fibres:

$$V_{fibres} = \frac{0.10\,\Delta f}{Rw}$$

$$V_{non\text{-}fibres} = \frac{0.10\,\Delta f}{Rw\rho t}$$

where

w is the material price per pound,

R the labour factor,

ρ the density,

74

Table L

DETERIORATION

RANK	MATERIAL	VALUE OF (yr^{-1}) INTERACTION	IN-PLACE VALUE OF MATERIALS EXPOSED (BILLION $)	VALUE ECONOMIC LOSS (MILLION $)
1.	Paint	0.50×10^{-1}	23.9	1,195.0
2.	Zinc	0.29×10^{-1}	26.83	778.0
3.	Cement and concrete materials	0.10×10^{-2}	316.21	316.0
4.	Nickel	0.25×10^{-1}	10.40	260.0
5.	Cotton (fiber)	0.40×10^{-1}	3.80	152.0
6.	Tin	0.26×10^{-1}	5.53	144.0
7.	Synthetic rubber	0.10×10^{0}	14.00	140.0
8.	Aluminium	0.21×10^{-2}	54.08	114.0
9.	Copper	0.20×10^{-2}	54.88	110.0
10.	Wool (fiber)	0.40×10^{-1}	2.48	99.2
11.	Natural rubber	0.10×10^{0}	0.54	54.0
12.	Carbon steel	0.50×10^{-2}	10.76	53.8
13.	Nylon (fiber)	0.40×10^{-1}	0.95	38.0
14.	Cellulose ester (fiber)	0.40×10^{-1}	0.82	32.8
15.	Building brick	0.10×10^{-2}	24.15	24.2
16.	Urea and melamine (plastic)	0.10×10^{-1}	2.27	22.7
17.	Paper	0.30×10^{-2}	7.53	22.6
18.	Leather	0.40×10^{-2}	5.15	20.6
19.	Phenolics (plastic)	0.10×10^{-1}	1.98	19.8
20.	Wood	0.10×10^{-2}	17.61	17.6
21.	Building stone	0.23×10^{-2}	7.65	17.6
22.	PVC (plastic)	0.10×10^{-1}	1.54	15.4
23.	Brass and bronze	0.42×10^{-3}	33.12	13.9
24.	Polyesters (plastic)	0.10×10^{-1}	1.37	13.7
25.	Rayon (fiber)	0.40×10^{-1}	0.33	13.2
26.	Magnesium	0.20×10^{-2}	6.50	13.0
27.	Polyethylene (plastic)	0.10×10^{-1}	1.17	11.7
28.	Acrylics (plastic)	0.10×10^{-1}	1.00	10.0
29.	Alloy steel	0.40×10^{-2}	2.18	8.7
30.	Polystyrene (plastic)	0.10×10^{-1}	0.85	8.5
31.	Acrylics (fiber)	0.40×10^{-1}	0.19	7.6
32.	Acetate (fiber)	0.40×10^{-1}	0.19	7.6
33.	Polyesters (fiber)	0.40×10^{-1}	0.16	6.4
34.	Polypropylene (plastic)	0.10×10^{-1}	0.64	6.4
35.	ABS (plastic)	0.10×10^{-1}	0.61	6.1
36.	Epoxies (plastic)	0.10×10^{-1}	0.47	4.7
37.	Cellulosics (plastic)	0.10×10^{-1}	0.40	4.0
38.	Bituminous materials	0.10×10^{-3}	22.45	2.2
39.	Gray iron	0.50×10^{-3}	3.86	1.9
40.	Nylon (plastic)	0.10×10^{-1}	0.17	1.7
41.	Polyolefins (fiber)	0.40×10^{-1}	0.04	1.6
42.	Stainless steel	0.85×10^{-4}	18.90	1.6
43.	Clay pipe	0.10×10^{-2}	1.44	1.4
44.	Acetate (plastic)	0.10×10^{-1}	0.12	1.2
45.	Malleable iron	0.16×10^{-2}	0.58	0.9
46.	Chromium	0.75×10^{-3}	1.08	0.8
47.	Silver	0.12×10^{-2}	0.57	0.7
48.	Gold	0.10×10^{-3}	5.80	0.6
49.	Flat glass	0.10×10^{-4}	28.59	0.3
50.	Lead	0.11×10^{-3}	2.18	0.2
51.	Molybdenum	0.25×10^{-3}	0.51	0.1
52.	Refractory ceramics	0.10×10^{-4}	1.93	0.02
53.	Carbon and graphite	0.10×10^{-5}	0.30	0.00

TOTAL 3,800

SOURCE: Midwest Research Institute, Systems Analysis of the Effects of Air Pollution on Materials, January 1970.

t   the average thickness, and

$\triangle$f   the increased frequency of cleaning due to pollution;

i.e., the cost for cleaning fibres is taken to be $0.10 per pound, and for non-fibres $0.10 per square foot. On the basis of some previous work and of subjective opinions, the authors define values of $\triangle$f for different classes of materials and for an urban suspended particulate level of $100\,\mu g/m^3$ as opposed to a rural one of $40\,\mu g/m^3$. The resulting cost estimates of soiling damage are presented in Table M. They represent the soiling costs for only 40% of the total value of materials exposed to air pollution. These costs are about 25 times higher than the total deterioration costs to the same materials. It is difficult to judge the method used because no similar results are available with which to compare these. These results depend upon the reasonableness of the estimates of V, which are highly subjective.

Ridker attempts to estimate both soiling and deterioration damage, but fails to find any reasonable estimates. His approaches are essentially the first two suggested by the MRI study. He tries to correlate air pollution levels with per capita receipts from laundry and dry cleaning establishments. Even after adjusting for climate, per capita income, and interurban price differentials, his findings are negative. Similar negative results occur when Ridker tries to correlate air pollution levels with office and apartment building interior cleaning costs, performance frequencies by a contract cleaning firm, supermarket sales of cleaning supplies, and frequencies of commercial cleaning and maintenance procedures. Ridker further examines data of the frequency of repainting of electric transmission tower and household survey data, but again with negative results. Possible reasons for his negative results could be inaccurate or inappropriate pollution measures, but Ridker suspects the principal reason to be that there are too many intervening variables for whose effects one cannot properly adjust. Ridker is able to calculate some costs due to a specific air pollution episode through a household and institution survey, but the episode was a rather spectacular one.

The British study assesses the damage caused by air pollution to paints, metals and textiles, as well as the effects of soiling. Its results are summarized in Table N. The methodology used is very similar to that used in assessing health costs. The total value of annual paint consumption and the labor costs of applying it are calculated. This monetary result is multiplied by the fraction of paint used in "polluted" areas of the UK and by the relative extra costs incurred to maintain paint in a polluted area. There appears to be no increase in the frequency of painting in the more polluted areas of the UK; other factors such as surface preparation, sunlight, and financial situation are much

76

Table M

SOILING

RANK	MATERIAL	SOILING INTERACTION FACTOR (yr^{-1})	IN-PLACE UNPROTECTED MATERIALS VALUE (BILLION \$)	SOILING COST (BILLION \$)
1.	Paint	$0.15 \times 10^{+1}$	23.9	35.0
2.	Zinc	0.90×10^{0}	26.8	24.0
3.	Flat glass	0.66×10^{0}	28.6	19.0
4.	Cement and concrete	0.17×10^{-1}	316.2	5.4
5.	Aluminium	0.90×10^{0}	54.1	4.9
6.	Leather	$0.48 \times 10^{+1}$	5.15	2.5
7.	Polystyrene (plastic)	$0.26 \times 10^{+1}$	0.85	2.2
8.	PVC (plastic)	$0.10 \times 10^{+1}$	1.54	1.54
9.	Paper	0.15×10^{-1}	7.53	1.12
10.	Nickel	0.96×10^{0}	10.40	1.00
11.	Polyethylene (plastic)	0.50×10^{-1}	1.17	0.59
12.	Cotton (fiber)	0.90×10^{-2}	3.80	0.34
13.	Copper	0.35×10^{-2}	54.90	0.19
14.	Brass and Bronze	0.50×10^{0}	33.12	0.17
15.	Chromium	0.15×10^{-2}	1.08	0.16
16.	Stainless steel	0.72×10^{-2}	18.90	0.14
17.	Building brick	0.47×10^{0}	24.15	0.11
18.	Polypropylene (plastic)	0.14×10^{0}	0.64	0.090
19.	ABS (plastic)	0.14×10^{0}	0.61	0.085
20.	Synthetic rubber	0.50×10^{-2}	14.00	0.070
21.	Building stone	0.90×10^{-1}	7.65	0.069
22.	Lead	0.30×10^{-1}	2.18	0.065
23.	Urea and Melamine (plastic)	0.27×10^{-1}	2.27	0.061
24.	Wool	0.22×10^{-2}	2.48	0.055
25.	Tin	0.96×10^{-1}	5.53	0.053
26.	Cellulose ester (fiber)	0.54×10^{-1}	0.82	0.044
27.	Polyesters (plastic)	0.30×10^{-1}	1.37	0.041
28.	Phenolics	0.20×10^{0}	1.98	0.040
29.	Rayon (fiber)	0.10×10^{-1}	0.33	0.033
30.	Nylon (plastic)	0.17×10^{-2}	0.17	0.029
31.	Bituminous materials	0.12×10^{-1}	22.45	0.027
32.	Acrylics (plastic)	0.26×10^{-3}	1.00	0.026
33.	Wood	0.14×10^{-1}	17.61	0.025
34.	Acetate (fiber)	0.78×10^{-1}	0.19	0.015
35.	Nylon (fiber)	0.15×10^{-1}	0.95	0.014
36.	Epoxies (plastic)	0.24×10^{-1}	0.47	0.011
37.	Cellulosics (plastic)	0.25×10^{-1}	0.40	0.010
38.	Acrylics (fiber)	0.26×10^{-1}	0.19	0.005
39.	Polyesters (fiber)	0.21×10^{-3}	0.16	0.003
40.	Magnesium	0.26×10^{-1}	6.50	0.002
41.	Acetate (plastic)	0.10×10^{-1}	0.12	0.001
42.	Polyolefin (fiber)	0.35×10^{-3}	0.04	0.001
43.	Gold	0.13×10^{-3}	5.80	< 0.001
44.	Silver	0.72×10^{-3}	0.57	< 0.001
45.	Gray iron	No effect		
46.	Malleable iron	No effect		
47.	Alloy steel	No effect		
48.	Molybdenum	No effect		
49.	Clay pipe	No effect		
50.	Refractory ceramics	No effect		
51.	Carbon and graphite	No effect		
52.	Natural rubber	No effect		
53.	Carbon steel	No effect		

TOTAL 100.0

SOURCE: Midwest Research Institute, Systems Analysis of the Effects of Air Pollution on Materials, January 1970.

Table N

ESTIMATED DAMAGE COSTS OF AIR POLLUTION
IN THE UNITED KINGDOM, 1970

(million pounds)

ITEM	MARGINAL DAMAGE		TOTAL DAMAGE	
	ECO-NOMIC COST	SOCIAL COST	ECO-NOMIC COST	SOCIAL COST
Painting	–	6.3	–	6.3
Corrosion and protection of metal structures	10	–	42	–
Textiles	33	–	33	–
Leather, paper, wood, rubber	–	–	–	–
Damage costs	43	6.3	75	6.3
Laundry and household goods (including car cleaning)	.5	164	.5	164
Exterior cleaning of building	–	1.5	–	1.5
Window and office cleaning	5.0	–	5.0	–
Soiling costs	5.5	165.5	5.5	165.5
TOTAL damage and soiling costs	48.5	171.8	80.5	171.8

SOURCE: Programmes Analysis Unit, An Economic and Technical Appraisal of Air Pollution in the United Kingdom, Chilton, Didcot, Berks., 1971.

more important determinants of the frequency of painting. The study group believes, however, that there is a social cost of enduring pollution-damaged paint, and they calculate the cost of renewing this paint as a social cost of pollution. The excess social cost of urban areas over non-urban areas is estimated to be £ 6.3 million.

The corrosion damage to metals is calculated in much the same way as paint damage. Estimates of the quantity of total exposed metal are multiplied by the differential extra incurred costs due to repainting, replacement, cleaning, and other maintenance procedures for three types of environments and by the relative amount of exposed metal in each of these three environments. One difference in this procedure from that used in determining paint damage is that three environments are considered (rural, industrial, and severe industrial) rather than two (urban and non-urban). The estimated marginal damage (excess industrial and severe industrial over rural) of metal corrosion is £ 10 million, practically all of which is in the form of damage to iron and steel. (Stainless steel, aluminium, and copper are damaged very slightly.) The total national damage of metal corrosion from air pollution is estimated to be £ 42 million.

The British study also estimates the damage and soiling costs of air pollution to textiles. The study notes that for most textiles, life is determined by sunlight exposure, humidity levels, and fashion, rather than by air pollution. Nevertheless, it estimates the excess and total damage to textiles to be £ 33 million per year. Air pollution damage to paper, leather, wood and rubber appears to be negligible.

The last category the British study considers is the cost of extra cleaning due to air pollution. Surveys indicate that there is no difference between urban and rural areas in frequency of cleaning laundry and household goods, and of motor vehicles. But there is certainly more soiling in urban areas. Hence social costs of enduring this extra soiling are calculated to be the material and labour costs needed to maintain rural levels of cleanliness. For laundry and household goods and for car cleaning, the economic costs of air pollution (marginal and total) are estimated to be £ 0.5 million and the social costs £ 164 million. For the exterior cleaning of buildings the excess and total social costs of air pollution are estimated to be £ 1.5 million, and for window and office cleaning economic costs (total and excess urban over rural) of £ 5.0 million are given.

The above results indicate that one can obtain estimates of material damage from air pollution. The data and methodology which relate this damage to specific pollution concentrations appear to be lacking for most materials, although the MRI study reports that good quantitative data are available for several metals. Thus for some specific materials, damage functions which relate degree of damage to pollutant concentration may be possible.

Estimates of soiling effects are much more difficult to ascertain. Ridker failed to obtain them through a direct estimation procedure, and the MRI type of approach assumes that a material is cleaned because it is dirty or that it suffers an aesthetic loss equal to the cleaning costs. British survey results are similar to those of Ridker; the Programmes Analysis Unit solved this problem, however, by distinguishing between two types of costs, economic and social, and the latter are estimated to be much greater than the former.

C. VEGETATION

Damage to vegetation from air pollution is believed to be significant. Wide-scale studies of this damage have been reported in the following:

1.   Benedict, Miller and Olson, Economic Impact of Air Pollutants on Plants in the United States, Stanford Research Institute, November 1971.

2.   Millecan, A Survey and Assessment of Air Pollution Damage to California Vegetation in 1970, California Department of Agriculture, Sacramento, California, June, 1971.

3.   "The Damage to Agriculture", Section IV F, An Economic and Technical Appraisal of Air Pollution in the United Kingdom, Programmes Analysis Unit, Chilton, Didcot, Berks, 1971.

In addition, Landau has examined several such studies and considers the overall problem of methodology in estimating vegetation damage:

Landau, "Statistical Aspects of Air Pollution as It Applies to Agriculture", presented at the 1971 Meeting of the Statistical Societies, Fort Collins, Colorado.

Landau gives an estimate of $120 million damage to US agriculture in 1968 in terms of prices paid to the farmer. The methodology behind this estimate reflects an informed judgement: although there is considerable knowledge on the physical effects of pollutants, Landau believes that there is no basis at present for quantifying the losses on a national scale in any scientifically acceptable manner. He feels there are serious limitations in using approaches based upon litigation or upon linear functions which relate reduction in yield to percentage of destroyed leaf

80

area and to sulfur dioxide. Sample surveys have been used in the past, but often unsuccessfully, as the demands upon the data collector are heavy and his individual judgement affects the results of the survey. The most successful type of survey is one in which trained crop survey reporters are used, such as was undertaken in California in 1955 and in Pennsylvania in 1969. A refinement of this approach would be to measure air pollution losses to sample crop populations and to extend the loss to the entire crop within that air basin, but the lack of trained observers prevents the gathering of wide-scale damage estimates at the present time.

Despite this scepticism, the Stanford Research Institute estimates that air pollution in 1964 cost US growers about $132 million in direct injury to crops and ornamental plants. This estimate is an underestimate as the growth-suppression factors of air pollution and the damage to the horticultural industry and home gardens are ignored.

The study begins by selecting those US counties where major pollutants (oxidants, SO_2, and fluorides) are expected to affect plants. A relative potential severity index of pollution is then assigned to each county based on emission rates of these pollutants per square kilometer. (It is important to note that concentration measures were not generally available, hence emission rates were derived from fuel consumption data, etc.). The dollar values of specific crops and of forests are then calculated for each county. The extensive literature available was then used to prepare tables showing the relative sensitivity of the specific plants to the three pollutant categories. From these tables, the study produces new tables giving estimates of the percentage loss of plant species for given different degrees of pollution. From the various tables, estimates are then made of losses on a crop by county basis. The results are summed up and are presented in Table O-A.

The authors admit to several potential sources of error in their study. Besides an inaccurate pollution measure, the measures of crop sensitivity to pollution are subject to controversy: plant strains and sensitivities vary greatly and preventive measures can be and have been taken. Moreover, pollution episodes may be more important than emission rate averages, and this importance, in turn, is dependent upon the occurrence of pollution episodes with respect to the crop cycle.

Data from the independent Californian survey are presented in Table O-B. The damage in these surveys is estimated by trained crop surveyers who visited agricultural areas throughout that state. The results indicate that crop damage from air pollution varies greatly from year to year, apparently dependent upon pollution, meteorological and growth cycle interactions. (Pennsylvania data indicate even greater

Table O

A.   ESTIMATED 1964 CROPS AND ORNAMENTAL PLANT VALUES OF THE US AND ESTIMATED LOSSES DUE TO AIR POLLUTION

TOTAL US	VALUE IN POLLUTED AREAS ($000)	LOSSES ($000) DUE TO			
		OXIDANTS	SO$_2$	FLUORIDES	TOTAL
Field crops	3,357,000	17,984	3,044	4,336	24,008
Seed crops	16,000	200	10	18	228
Fruit and nuts	334,000	10,541	17	265	10,822
Vegetables	170,000	3,341	5	2	3,348
Forest and nursery ..	425,000	18,494	134	566	19,194
Citrus	348,000	27,429	5	388	27,823
Crop total	4,650,000	77,989	3,225	4,209	85,423
Ornamentals	1,346,000	43,407	2,979	127	46,513
Total all plants	5,996,000	121,396	6,204	4,336	131,936

B.   COMPARISON WITH INDEPENDENT CALIFORNIAN ESTIMATES OF COMMERCIAL CROP LOSS DUE TO POLLUTANTS

(in dollars US)

	CALIFORNIA ESTIMATES		SRI ESTIMATE
	1969	1970	1963
Field crops	1,579,000	2,653,000	3,189,000
Citrus	33,565,000	19,553,000	20,969,000
Fruit and nuts	1,165,000	720,000	4,695,000
Vegetables	1,651,000	764,000	111,000

SOURCE: Benedict, Miller, and Olson, Economic Impact of Air Pollution on Plants in the United States, Stanford Research Institute, November 1971.

variability from year to year). A methodological approach as that of the Stanford Research Institute would not allow the year to year variation in damage estimates which apparently exists. The only parameters in the determination of the SRI estimate which can vary over time are total emitted pollution (by weight) and crop values, and these do not vary sufficiently to produce the type of yearly damage fluctuations existent in California and Pennsylvania.

The UK estimate of agricultural damage of excess pollution in urban areas over rural areas is based upon two assumptions: firstly, that productivity is 10% higher in cleaner areas; and secondly, that 25% of the cultivated land lies in polluted areas. Given these two assumptions, based on informed opinion, £ 39 million of damage per year is estimated as the result of excess urban air pollution over rural levels, and the total annual cost of air pollution damage to agriculture is given to be £ 195 million. It should be noted that this estimate like that of the Stanford Research Institute is derived from a procedure which allows no yearly variation. As such, this estimate suffers from many of the same weaknesses as the SRI estimate.

D. PROPERTY VALUES

Several studies have attempted to estimate the deleterious effects of air pollution on residential property values. If these values are indeed affected, then they reflect the public's perception of the detrimental effects of air pollution; as such, their inclusion in a damage estimate could introduce double-counting. Damage to property values is not absolute in the sense of the other damage described above as the supply demand market mechanism certainly interacts with any pollution effect on value. Additionally, there need be unrestricted mobility for this type of damage estimate to be unbiased. To estimate the total global loss of property values from pollution, estimates need be made in the framework of sophisticated general equilibrium models.

The types of estimates given in the following studies give some approximation of property losses within local areas:

1. Ridker, Economic Costs of Air Pollution; Praeger, 1967.

2. Anderson and Crocker, "Air Pollution and Residential Property Value", Urban Studies 3, 171-180, October 1971.

3. Crocker, Urban Air Pollution Damage Functions: Theory and Measurement, prepared for Environmental Protection Agency, June 15, 1971.

83

4. Wieand, "Property Values and the Demand for Clean Air: Cross Section Study for St. Louis" presented at the Committee on Urban Economics Research Conference, September 11-12, 1970.

Ridker considers two approaches to estimate market value losses for this problem: a cross-sectional approach and a time-series approach. In the cross-sectional approach Ridker regresses the median values of single-family residences by census tract in Metropolitan St. Louis on a set of social, economic, and physical variables which include a pollution variable. Ridker uses a stepwise linear regression procedure thus ensuring that all variables that are at least as important as the pollution variable are included in the analysis. The results suggest that residences lose $245 value for about each increase of 0.25 mg $SO_3/100$ cm^2/day in the annual geometric mean sulfation level.

The time-series analysis consists of comparing the average sale prices of residential units in a study area and in an adjacent control area over a nine-year period. At the midpoint of the study period a new firm moved into the study area and began emitting noxious odours which led to many complaints. The results of this study are more difficult to interpret: there is a divergence in property values between the two areas after the firm moved into the study area, but there were price divergences for two years before the relocation of the firm.

The Anderson and Crocker study is a cross-sectional approach to census tract data from three US metropolitan areas: Washington DC, Kansas City and St. Louis. They assume a multiplicative relationship, regressing the logarithms of dependent variables on those of the independent variables. Three different dependent variables are analysed: median property value, median gross rent, and median contract rent. Their list of independent variables is greatly abbreviated compared to that of Ridker (six vs. fourteen non-pollution variables), and they do not use a stepwise regression procedure. Two pollution variables are used: the sulfation index used by Ridker and a particulate index.

The results for the nine regressions (three dependent variables for each of the three cities) show at least one pollution variable coefficient to be significantly negative for each equation, and the only positive coefficient for a pollution variable is not statistically significant. The estimated coefficients suggest that an increase in pollution of 10 mg/m^3 day of suspended particulates and of 0.1 mg $SO_3/100$ cm^2/day leads to a $300-700 property loss or $2-4 monthly rent loss.

Since Ridker and Crocker and Anderson use similar data for at least part of their studies, some comparisons can be made. Crocker and Anderson obtain the best precision when natural logarithms of the variables are used, implying that the use of a simple linear model (as Ridker uses) is undesirable. Of the dependent variables, the median gross rent variable appears to be superior in that its regression has the largest multiple correlation coefficient (R^2). There exist two drawbacks of their study vis-à-vis that of Ridker. They use two highly-correlated pollution variables rather than one; this makes any effect of pollution more difficult to estimate and to detect. In their St. Louis regression, comparable to Ridker's, Anderson and Crocker do not find the pollution variables to be statistically significant; if they had restricted themselves to one pollution variable, that variable might have been statistically significant. Secondly, one can criticise their use of a small set of independent variables; many variables which are statistically significant in Ridker's study are not considered in the Anderson and Crocker study: percentage of recently built homes, housing density, highway accessibility, neighbourhood school quality, occupation ratio, persons per housing unit. It is better in studies of this nature to have a surplus of independent variables and to use step-wise regression techniques; the results are then more conservative and any statistically significant negative effect of pollution is more credible.

The Crocker study considers seven different dependent variables in regression analyses, but results are presented for only six: sale prices of housing units, FHA-estimated market prices of the site, FHA-warranted prices for the whole property, FHA-estimated yearly maintenance costs, annual property taxes, and median of owner-estimated value by census tract. The comparison of the results using each of these dependent variables can aid in the choice of such variables for future studies and can address itself specifically to any effects of aggregated dependent variables such as average or median census-tract values.

Crocker lists thirty-three independent variables including ten pollution variables, but his selection from them for the regression analyses is unclear. Instead of using step-wise regression techniques, he selects his independent variables for each regression in an unspecified manner. This fact weakens his results, subjecting them to criticisms of omitting variables correlated with the pollution variables, which could help explain the dependent variable. Among the types of variables he omits are variables describing the racial composition, population density, and the degree of industrialisation of a neighbourhood, all of which are correlated with the pollution variables.

Crocker actually considers multiplicative multiple regression models in which the natural logarithms of each variable are taken. The results suggest a negative pollution influence on property values.

At the original arithmetic means of all of the variables, Crocker calculates the marginal capitalised damage for a pollution increase in the
annual averages of 10 mg/m³/24 hr for suspended particulates and of
one part per billion/24 hr SO_2. The marginal damage for specific
dependent variables is given in Table P. The only dependent variable
whose results appear inconsistent with the others is the estimated maintenance cost variable: higher pollution levels are associated with lower
maintenance costs. It is difficult to choose an optimum dependent variable from the others. The independent variables in the respective
regression equations are not always the same, hence the multiple correlation coefficients are not comparable and the inclusion of two highly
correlated pollution variables makes any comparison of their coefficients
meaningless. Through the use of an analysis of covariance procedure,
Crocker compares the use of sale price data and of census tract median
estimated values as dependent variables to learn if aggregation biases
results. The results are mixed, but suggest that any aggregation bias
is of little or no importance. The same analysis of covariance tests
similarly indicate the relative unimportance of any difference between
the sale price and FHA estimated value; however, a third analysis
indicates that tax assessment "under-assesses" the effects of air
pollution.

Crocker is able to draw several conclusions from his study.
Because the ratio of marginal damage from air pollution to value is
greater for a site than for an entire property, he concludes that land
or site values are more sensitive to air pollution than are property
values. The author states that there exists evidence that there is
declining marginal damage associated with increased pollution levels;
however, the evidence is very weak and any statement about marginal
damage made from Crocker's results is speculative. There is evidence
that property values are more sensitive to minimum monthly pollution
variables rather than maximum monthly pollution variables, but this
could be because the minimum values tend to be more closely correlated
to average pollution values. Crocker also includes the second and third
moments of the pollution variables in some regression equations, and
the results suggest that skewness has some influence on damage with
greater disutility attached to those situations where more extreme
concentrations of air pollution are likely; (i.e., when the pollution-
concentration-probability- distribution function is skewed to the right).
In other words, this result demonstrates the existence of a risk-aversion
factor here.

The Wieand study uses the same St. Louis data as Ridker and
Anderson and Crocker, but his approach is different. He develops a
measure of land use intensity as a dependent variable by multiplying
average rentals plus 0.01 of owner estimated market values in each

Table P

MARGINAL CAPITALISED DAMAGE TO REPRESENTATIVE RESIDENTIAL PROPERTY

(dollars)

DEPENDENT VARIABLE		SALE PRICE	ESTIMATED VALUE OF SITE	FHA ESTIMATED PROPERTY VALUE	FHA ESTIMATED MAINTENANCE	PROPERTY TAXES	MEDIAN PROPERTY VALUE BY CENSUS TRACT
YEAR	POLLUTION VARIABLE						
65	......	344.12	167.00				426.19
66	......	601.45	323.85	505.75			604.64
67	......	191.09	399.12		negative	.44	418.73

87

census tract by the number of each type of unit. This total is then divided by residential land area to arrive at a measure of the monthly rent per acre. The natural logarith of this value is taken as the dependent variable in the regression equation. Wieand uses eleven non-pollution independent variables and one independent pollution variable in each regression equation, although he tries several pollution variables.

Wieand's results generally give negative coefficients to the pollution variables, but they are not statistically significant. When Wieand uses a measure of average rent and of market value (similar to the dependent variables of Anderson and Crocker, and of Ridker), he finds the pollution variable to be significant. He argues that this variable is unsuitable and that his results should caution against the acceptance of the others' results.

The study results generally indicate negative effects of pollution on property value, rent, land use intensity, etc., although these effects may not always be statistically significant, and they reflect damage to health, materials or vegetation. For this reason when overall estimates of damage from pollution are desired, property value losses cannot be added directly to estimates of loss to health, materials, vegetation or serious double-counting will result.

II. NOISE (10)

Several studies focus on the estimates of the damage due to noise either from aircraft or from motor vehicles. There appear to be no attempts to place cost estimates on the direct damage of noise, as loss of sleep, hearing impairment, etc. Most studies try to estimate damage from noise through its effect upon property values. Hence, many of the same fundamental questions which are raised in the analysis of the effects of air pollution upon property values are relevant here.

Results from the following are considered here:

1.   Diffey, "An Investigation into the Effect of High Traffic Noise on House Prices in a Homogeneous Sub-Market", presented at a Seminar on House Prices and the Micro-economics of Housing, London School of Economics, December 1971.

2.   Plowden, The Cost of Noise, Metra Consulting Group Ltd., London, 1970.

3.   Paik, "Impact of Transportation Noise on Urban Residential Property Values with Special Reference to Aircraft Noise" Consortium of Universities, Washington, D.C., August 1970.

4. The Economic Impact of Noise, USEPA, Washington, December 31, 1971.

The Diffey article illustrates the weakness of many of the studies which use regression techniques: the possibility of mis-specification. In this study the sale prices and time-adjusted sale prices of houses in a carefully selected area of Birmingham (UK) are regressed upon a series of independent variables which include one noise parameter. The differential noise in the study is motor vehicle-generated, and the parameter represents measurements of noise level and nearness to the motorway. Diffey uses a stepwise regression procedure. Contrary to expectation, he finds a statistically significant positive association between noise levels and sale prices implying that the good people of Birmingham prefer noisy houses, a doubtful finding. This result is probably due to the absence of some relevant independent variable which is highly correlated with noise or nearness to a motorway and to the fact that this variable has far greater influence on housing prices than noise at the levels present in this study.

The Plowden paper reports the results of a very different type of study which provides some justification for studying the effects of noise on property values. This study was carried out as part of the enquiry on the siting of the Third London Airport and seeks to find "the amount of money a person would have to be given upon the imposition of a noise nuisance alone, if he were, in his own estimation, to be as well off after as before the nuisance arose." The first part of this study consisted of a survey in which people were asked how much less a certain house in a noise-defined environment would have to be than an ordinary house before one would consider buying it. The results are given in Figure 1, and indicate that a majority of people would not accept payment for the inconvenience of high noise levels.

This study also seeks to estimate moving costs due to noise. These costs have three components: a possible decrease in the value of a house, removal expenses, and those costs associated with uprooting oneself, dislocation costs. To estimate the latter, survey techniques are used. Owner-occupants were asked if they could sell their homes and buy similar homes while making a profit of £100, would they consider moving. If not, what profit would they consider necessary. The results (Figure 2) indicated a surprisingly high number of respondents (38%) who would accept no (infinite) money; a resurvey with a reworded question found this percentage to be only 8%, but there is close agreement for the other figures. Decreases in housing values are estimated by polling two hundred real estate agents in the South East of England and asking them how much less a house of a certain value would sell for if it were in a "noisy" or "very noisy" area. From these results, the study gives linear equations relating selling price to value and noise level.

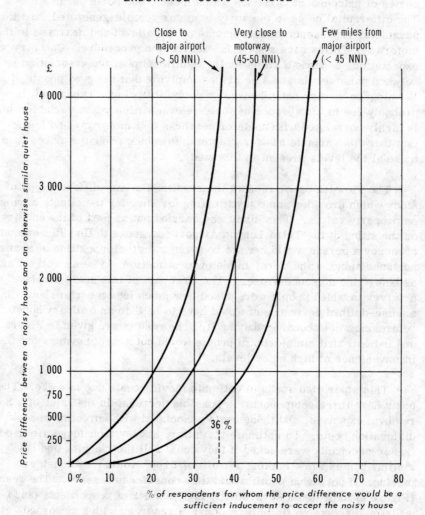

Figure 1
ENDURANCE COSTS OF NOISE

Close to
major airport
(> 50 NNI)

Very close to
motorway
(45-50 NNI)

Few miles from
major airport
(< 45 NNI)

£

Price difference between a noisy house and an otherwise similar quiet house

4 000

3 000

2 000

1 000

750

500

250

0

36 %

0 %   10   20   30   40   50   60   70   80

*% of respondents for whom the price difference would be a
sufficient inducement to accept the noisy house*

Source : Plowden, *The Cost of Noise*, Metra Consulting Group, Ltd., London, 1970.

Figure 2
DISLOCATION : COST OF MOVING TO ANOTHER AREA

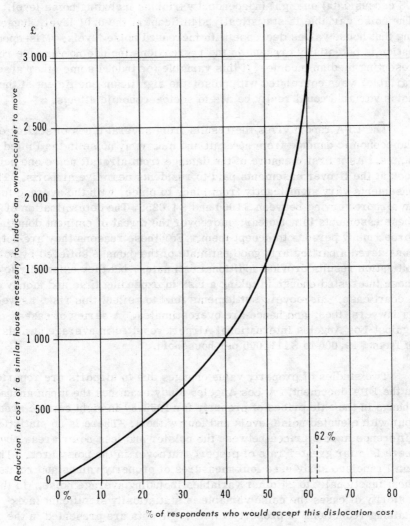

Source : Plowden, *The Cost of Noise*, Metra Consulting Group, Ltd., London 1970.

Using estimates for the above costs, Plowden presents estimates of the minimum social costs of noise which are presented in Table Q. To those individuals with supposedly infinite dislocation costs, Plowden assumes a dislocation cost equal to 50% of their property value.

The Paik study analyses the impact of noise on the values of single dwelling units near the John F. Kennedy Airport in New York. The author regresses median (self-appraised) residential values (taken from US census data) on eight independent variables including noise level. The noise variable is statistically significant at the 0.01 level, suggesting that house values decrease with increased noise levels. Mis-specification is potentially present as the regressions include no variable representing median income. If this variable (or indeed some other absent variable) were correlated with noise, the significant coefficient of the noise variable could really be due to socio-economic effects.

The EPA report gives the results from several types of studies of the economic damage from aircraft and motorway noise in the United States. As a first measure of the damage from aircraft noise one can look at the flyover easements paid to residents near five airports. The easements vary significantly from place to place, with the average for an airport varying between $1000 and $4,625. The determination of these easements is not clear; moreover the threat of eminent domain forces many persons to accept them. For these reasons they are not considered a particularly good estimate of the damage suffered by noise. Litigation results provide additional estimates, but they exist only for those interested enough in taking a risk in expending time and money on a court case. Moreover, settlements tend to reflect this risk, as well as lawyers' fees, and hence are overestimates. A series of cases against Los Angeles International Airport resulted in average awards of from $19,000 to $111,000 per household.

Two studies of property value changes due to airports are reported in the EPA document. A Los Angeles study examines the mean annual change in the sale prices of property for 1955-67 in eight sample areas, four with elevated noise levels and four without. There is no statistical difference in sale prices between the noisier and less noisy areas, but there is a far greater rate of property turnover in the noisy area. The San Francisco study uses four measures of property values and relates them functionally to 24 other variables including average noise. In the majority of cases the noise variable is statistically significant in explaining reductions in property values. No data are presented in the EPA report, however.

The report also notes some of the damage from noise experienced by schools. It notes that the Los Angeles Unified School District is seeking $95 million in damages against the airport. The costs of

Table Q

SOCIAL COSTS OF NOISE: OWNER-OCCUPIERS

TYPE OF SOCIAL COST	HOUSEHOLDS AFFECTED AND AMOUNT	PERCENTAGE OF HOUSEHOLDS FOR WHICH EACH TYPE OF SOCIAL COST IS THE SMALLEST	AVERAGE MINIMUM COSTS (£)
	over 50 NNI		
Endurance cost		37	951
Moving cost		35	2 599
Modified moving cost		28	4 396
TOTAL		100%	2 506
	Over 50 NNI		
Endurance cost		42	689
Moving cost		33	2 184
Modified moving cost		25	4 128
TOTAL		100%	2 028
	35-45 NNI		
Endurance cost		55	571
Moving cost		23	1 791
Modified moving cost		22	3 615
TOTAL		100%	1 508

Each section of the table permits an average minimum cost to be calculated for owner-occupiers in three levels of noise imposed on an area.

The results given in this section indicate that the total minimum cost associated with the imposition of a noise on owner-occupiers of houses when developments such as airports, roads or other sources of noise impinge on their environment is in the range of £1,500 to £2,500 depending on the NNI value.

SOURCE: Plowden, The Cost of Noise, Metra Consulting Group, Ltd., London 1970.

rebuilding or insulating twenty-eight noise-affected schools in Los Angeles was $9.08 million in 1968 prices.

With respect to motor vehicle noise, the EPA monograph reports the results from two studies. A study of Portland, Oregon, uses stepwise regressions of apartment rental values on several other variables including freeway noise. The general conclusion of this study, however, is that any disutility due to noise is not reflected in rents. A second study in Toledo, Ohio, first focused on the impact of freeway noise on residential property values for fifteen different areas. Their inconclusive result led them to restrict themselves to a detailed study of one lower-to-middle income area. There is no difference in the behavior of the property values one block from an expressway versus those three to five blocks away. Two questionnaires, one to realtors and one to residents, follow up this study. Both suggest that property near to freeways is undesirable, with realtors expressing the belief that property values decrease 20-30% if they are adjacent to a freeway.

The EPA monograph presents some estimates of the total relocation costs if people are required to move because of undesirable noise levels. A conservative estimate of the relocation of families subject to undesirable noise levels from highways in 1970 is $3.93 billion, of which $2.68 billion is for land purchases. The prices of land for highway and airport easements were not the same: $10,000 per acre was used in calculating the highway easements, and $20,000 per acre in calculating the airport easements. As an alternative to moving, the authors consider the possibility of insulating the homes affected by airport noise. These costs would vary from $10.7 billion to $35.7 billion depending upon the extent of the insulation measures taken.

It appears as if we are in a difficult position with the estimation of damage from noise. Theoretically from surveys, litigation, etc., it appears as if there is damage involved, which includes a decrease in property value, but the studies to date have been largely unsuccessful in uncovering any relationship between noise levels and property values. It could be that most of these studies have not properly adjusted for housing supply or the fact that some individuals are more sensitive to noise than others. These and other potential influences need be investigated, and more realistic models need be developed if we are to obtain reasonable estimates of the relationship between noise and property values.

III. WATER POLLUTION

The estimation of damage due to water pollution introduces a different kind of problem: one of putting damage estimates on the disamenities (11) due to pollution. Except in some special cases direct damage due to water pollution is rarely significant. Attempts to estimate the industrial damage from polluted water have shown them to be minimal; for many industrial processes (e.g. cooling), water of almost any quality is acceptable, and for other industrial uses (food processing, boilers) the necessary water quality is so high that practically all water needs to be treated, and the treatment costs are relatively insensitive to initial quality. The latter situation is the case for drinking water; hence municipal water supplies suffer little damage from polluted water. Direct damage from water pollution can be sustained by agriculture and the fishing industry, however. If sodium chloride or some other crop-damaging substance is added to irrigation water, that water must be treated or agricultural output will decline. There exist cases where polluted waters have affected agriculture and fishing output; however, no published studies of this damage are available.

The most usual losses associated with water pollution appear to be those associated with aesthetics and recreation. There are some case studies which attempt to assign monetary values to these disamenities, and other studies seek methodologies which can be used to obtain damage estimates. Most of these studies concern themselves only with the problem of measuring the recreational benefits independently of the water pollution problem or in conjunction with some specific water management or development project. One study which does, however, consider these benefits in the water pollution context is a study of Lake d'Annecy:

Deportes, J. P., Problèmes Economiques liés à l'Assainissement du Lac d'Annecy, Institut National de la Recherche Agronomique, Station d'Hydrobiologie Lacustre, Thonon, France, 1972.

This study seeks to relate water quality to tourist volume. It does this by extrapolating the current decrease in tourism associated with decreasing water quality. In the absence of any new water treatment, the water quality will decrease, and the accompanying decrease in the volume of tourist business is estimated. This estimated decrease in the number of tourist nights is multiplied by the average daily tourist expenditure for the expected lifetime of the pollution control facility and appropriately discounted to arrive at an estimate of the damage to the tourist industry of the lake. (This is compared with the costs of cleaning the lake in the framework of a traditional cost-benefit analysis.) It is of interest to note that lost tourist income, unsupplemented, is chosen as a measure of the pollution damage to the lake; hence, this lost expenditure is equated to the recreational benefits it would have bought.

A list of methods used to estimate recreational benefits is given in the book by:

Clawson and Knetsch, Economics of Outdoor Recreation, Resources for the Future, Inc., The Johns Hopkins Press, Baltimore and London, 1971.

The measure of total benefit of a recreational resource advocated by Clawson and Knetsch is an estimate of the sum of the maximum prices which various users would pay for the enjoyment of the resource. As a first step in determining this measure, the authors construct a demand curve for the use of the resource, and the area under the curve is determined through use of surveys estimating the total cost to parties visiting the resource and the number of parties visiting the resource at each level of cost. (It is interesting to note that in the authors' illustrative examples the principal component of this cost is travel expense.) The authors note that because of time limitations and other constraints, the above-suggested measure is an underestimate of total benefit. Nevertheless they assert the estimates remain, "(1) economically meaningful and (2) consistent with and comparable to the benefit estimates for other project services." As a supplement to the above measure, Clawson and Knetsch recommend that one estimate the values capitalized in land in the vicinity of the recreation area.

In their book, Clawson and Knetsch list several other measurement methods for evaluating recreation benefits:

a) Gross Expenditure Method estimates the total amount spent on recreation by the user. Included in this estimate are travel expenses, equipment costs and expenses incurred while in the recreation area. The authors argue against this method stating that gross values are not needed; "it is the net increase in the value of the recreation opportunities that is crucial; this represents a true net yield that can be compared with what the resource would yield if it were used to produce other services."

b) The Market Value of Fish Method is attacked by the authors as assuming the primary recreational objective is the catch and not the activity.

c) The Cost Method estimates the benefits to be equal to the cost of generating them, but this method could automatically justify all recreational projects.

d) The Market Value Method measures total benefit through multiplying attendance by some charge, which is usually related to prices charged at some privately-owned recreation areas. The authors note

96

that the prices of privately owned recreation areas may only reflect payments for marginal benefits over those available at free or less expensive areas. They also note that the length of visit also is a function of cost, and for this reason it may be unfair to extrapolate the amount paid daily at a private area for each day of visit at a public area.

e) The Direct Interview Method assesses directly the willingness-to-pay for a resource, but there can be problems of bias and of interpretation with these results.

Most of the estimates of recreational benefit have used one or more of the methods mentioned by Clawson and Knetsch, but variations on their preferred method of using demand curves appear to be the most widely used approach. Many of these studies have shown much ingenuity in applying this method to specific environmental and recreational resources. One important variation of this type of analysis is sensitivity analysis which provides benefit estimates of an action or resource for different assumed values of initial benefit, growth in demand, discount rate, etc. One can then compare the estimated benefits under these alternative hypotheses with the estimated costs in cost-benefit analyses or with the estimated benefits of alternative actions.

A good example of this type of analysis is:

Krutilla and Cicchetti, "Evaluating Benefits of Environmental Resources with Special Application to the Hells Canyon", Natural Resources Journal 12(1), 1-29, January 1972.

Krutilla and Cicchetti consider two alternative futures for the Hells Canyon: a hydroelectric alternative and a preservation alternative. For the latter alternative, the authors attempt to estimate the present and future benefits. The basic equation used to estimate the model is:

$$PV_p = \sum_{t=1}^{T} \frac{b_o (1+\alpha)^t}{(1+i)^t}$$

where PV_p is the present value of preservation,

b_o is the benefit in the initial year,

i is the discount rate,

α is the annual rate of change in the benefit, and

T is that time period in which the discounted value of benefit falls to zero.

Krutilla and Cicchetti alter this model slightly to make it more realistic, by making α, the growth rate in demand, a function (i) of the projected growth rate in real per capita income, (ii) of the rate of growth in the quantity demanded at zero price dampened to equal eventually only the rate of growth in population, and (iii) of the recreational capacity of the resource. For several combinations of the model parameters the authors then calculate the initial year's preservation benefits necessary in order to have the present value of preservation equal to development.

Lack of space and time prevent the description of further studies in which estimates of the damage to water quality or of the benefits of water-based recreational facilities are calculated. An abbreviated bibliography which could be helpful in a further consideration of the damage of water pollution is given below:

(1) Stevens, "Recreational Benefits from Water Pollution Control", Water Resources Research 2, 1966.

(2) Kavanaugh and Gibson, "Measurement of Fishing Benefits on the River Trent", presented at a symposium on the Trent Research Programme, the University of Nottingham, 15th-16th April 1971.

(3) Seneca, "Water Recreation, Demand, and Supply", Water Resources Research, 5(6), December, 1969.

(4) Cicchetti, Seneca, and Davidson, The Demand and Supply of Outdoor Recreation, Bureau of Economic Research, Rutgers University, March 1969.

(5) Brown et al, "Net Economic Value of the Oregon Salmon-Steelhead Sport Fishery, Journal of Wildlife Management, 29(2), April 1965.

(6) Scheftel, "An Economic Evaluation of the Sport Fishery in Minnesota", "Transactions of the 23rd North American Wildlife Conference, 3rd-5th March 1958."

(7) Wennergren, "Valuing Non-market Priced Recreational Resources", Land Economics, 40(3), 1964.

(8) Kieth and Wennergren, "Economic Evaluation of Stockwater Developments", Journal of Range Management, 18(3), 1965.

(9) Grimes, "Evaluation of Recreation and Aesthetic Uses of Water in an Urban Setting", Paper presented at the Urban Economics Workshop, University of Chicago, 27th February 1970.

(10) Mäler, "A Method of Estimating Social Benefits from Pollution Control", The Swedish Journal of Economics, 73(1), 1971.

(11) Bohm, "A Note on the Problem of Estimating Benefits from Pollution Control", in Problems of Environmental Economics, OECD, Paris, 1972.

(12) Cesario, "A Method for Estimating Recreation Benefits", Appendix E in Resource Management in the Great Lakes Basin, Butrico et al. editors, Heath, Lexington Books, Lexington, Mass.

NOTES

1. Cumulative Regulatory Effects on the Cost of Automotive Transportation (RECAT) Final Report of the ad hoc Committee, 28th February 1972, Office of Science and Technology.

2. Barrett and Waddell "The Cost of Air Pollution Damages - A Status
Report", Environmental Protection Agency, April 1971, Appendix
I-J of RECAT Report.

3. Ridker, Economic Effects of Air Pollution, Praeger, 1967.

4. Committee on Air Pollution, Report of the Parliament, London,
HMSO, 1954.

5. An Economic and Technical Appraisal of Air Pollution in the United
Kingdom, Programmes Analysis Unit, Chilton, Berks, 1971.

6. Mammarella, L'inquinamento dell'aria, ISVET Document No. 27,
Rome, 1970.

7. US Department of Health, Education, and Welfare, Washington
1966.

8. An important output of this study is the extensive bibliography.

9. The Stickney et al. study refers to 1970 costs whereas the MRI
study indicates no dates, but as it was written from 15th June 1969 -
14th January 1970, the costs are certainly pre-1970.

10. For another review of the use of damage functions of noise, see
Alexandre, A. and Barde, J. Ph., Le Temps du Bruit, Flamma-
rion, 1973.

11. Loss of amenity is probably included in property value losses.

ON ESTIMATING ENVIRONMENTAL DAMAGE:
A SURVEY OF RECENT RESEARCH
IN THE UNITED STATES

by

Robert H. Haveman
University of Wisconsin
USA

INTRODUCTION

In this paper, a survey will be made of the estimates of the damage imposed on society by the use of scarce environmental media — water courses, lakes, estuaries, the air mantle — for residuals disposal. This review will emphasize both conceptual and measurement issues. In relating the work undertaken in the US to estimate environmental damage, both the estimates released by government agencies and the more detailed estimates of basic researchers will be discussed.

The first section of the paper presents a view of the environment and its relationship to the economy which sets the concept of "environmental damage" into its proper economic perspective. This section is followed by a discussion of the concept of "environmental damage". The importance to public investment decisions of knowledge of the shape and level of functions which relate emission levels to damage is emphasized. The third section presents estimates of environmental damage which have been released by the Federal government. In some sense these estimates stand as "official". In the final section a number of research efforts designed to estimate regional and national damage functions are described and evaluated. It will be seen that, at the present time, firm estimates of the extent of environmental damage are for the most part unavailable. More important, basic research efforts to estimate such damage functions have been plagued with difficult data and measurement problems.

I. THE ENVIRONMENT AS A RESOURCE (1)

The standard definition of the term "environment" emphasizes the totality of natural external conditions and suggests that the state of these conditions affects the way things live and develop. To facilitate the discussion of environmental damage, a more rigorous analytical definition is required that will put the environment into the economist's usual frame of reference. An economic definition would, first of all, emphasize that changes in natural external influences are interesting only as they affect man directly or indirectly. Hence, an economic definition would note that deterioration in the quality of the air mantle is not important in and of itself. Rather it is important because it has, among other things, direct mortality and morbidity effects on man. As a first step, an economic definition of the environment makes man the measure of all things. Consistent with this, the evaluation of environmental changes must encompass not only the short-run and direct effects on man but also the indirect and long-run effects.

As a further refinement of the economic definition of environment, we could view the environment as a non-reproducible, capital asset which yields over time a stream of services for man. These services are tangible (such as flows of water or minerals), or functional (such as the removal, dispersal, storage and degradation of residuals), or intangible (such as a scenic view).

One of the most valuable services yielded by the environment involves the dispersing, storing, or assimilating of residuals which are generated as a by-product of economic activity. This service is most clearly portrayed in the Materials Balance Model and its corollary, the Principle of Materials Balance (2). In the Materials Balance Model, the environment is viewed as a large shell surrounding the economic system. Raw materials flow from the environment, are converted into consumer goods in the production sector and then — at least in part — passed on to the household sector. To be sure, not all of the raw material inputs are embodied in the produced consumption goods; some of them are wastes from production and are returned to the environment by producers. The produced consumption goods are used by households, and eventually, when their economic life has been exhausted, they are also returned to the environment as residuals.

All of these material flows obey the basic law of physics governing the conservation of matter. Thus, in an economy with no imports or exports and where there is no net accumulation of stocks, the mass of residuals returned to the natural environment will be equal to the mass of basic fuels, food, minerals, and other raw materials which enter the processing and production system. This equality in the flows of materials to and from the environment, measured by mass, is the Principle of Materials Balance.

A picture of the Materials Balance Model is shown in Figure 1 for a developed economy. In that figure, the production sector is divided into the energy conversion and materials processing sectors. Inputs into these sectors include minerals, the products of photosynthesis, air, and water. These two sectors supply the household sector with valuable goods and services, including food and metal products and useful energy. However, as a by-product of this activity, the production sector yields a variety of residuals, including slag, scrap, unrecovered chemicals, carbon dioxide, particulates and waste heat. In its turn, the consumption activities of the household sector yield residuals in the form of solids (trash), liquids (sewage), and gases (respiratory carbon dioxide and the combustion by-products of home heating).

As the diagram shows, the solid and waterborne wastes of both the production and consumption sectors may go through another stage of processing before being returned to the environment. This processing, however, only changes the form and perhaps the ultimate destination of the residuals flow; the mass of material to be returned to the environment is unaltered. In Table 1, some sketchy data is presented concerning the materials throughput for the United States economy for the years 1963-1965. The table shows that the total weight of materials input to the US economy was about 2.6 billion tons in 1965, of which about 5% came from the net importation of materials. For the entire US economy, inventory accumulation accounts for about 10-15%, so that the return of residuals back to the environment is smaller than the total material inputs — about 2.2 to 2.4 billion tons. Perhaps three-fourths of the total weight of the throughput is discharged back into the atmosphere as carbon and hydrogen in combination with atmospheric oxygen. This results largely from fuel combustion, food "combustion", and incineration. The remaining throughput is either in the form of other gases, dry solids, or "wet" solids carried in suspension or solution into water courses. Without better data on the outputs of all residuals, particularly atmospheric residuals, it is difficult to present a more accurate picture of the return flow side of the throughput process.

Two items in Table 1 deserve further comment. The first is the predominant contribution of mineral fuels to the material inputs to the economy. By implication, the combustion of these fuels is a major contributor to environmental pollution. The second important item is the throughput of pulpwood. The 56 million tons shown for 1965 represent the dry weight of pulp logs delivered to paper mills. About 60% of that weight emerges in the form of paper; the remaining 40% is residual organic material, most of which is released into water courses.

Figure 1

SCHEMATIC DEPICTION OF MATERIALS BALANCE MODEL

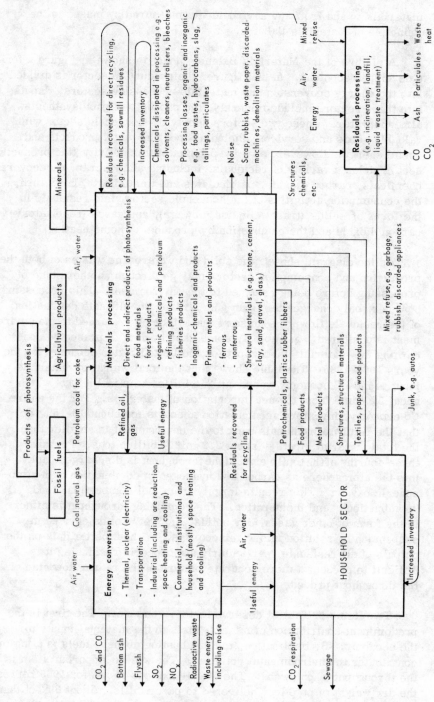

Reproduced by permission from Allen V. Kneese, Robert U. Ayres, and Ralph C. d'Arge, *Economics and Environment : A Materials Balance Approach*, Washington : Resources for the Future, Inc., 1970.

Table 1. WEIGHT OF BASIC MATERIALS PRODUCTION
IN THE UNITED STATES, PLUS NET IMPORTS,
1963-1965

(million tons)

	1963	1964	1965
Agricultural (incl. fishery, wildlife and forest) products			
Food and Fiber			
Crops	350	358	364
Livestock and dairy	23	24	23.5
Fishery	2	2	2
Forestry Products (85% dry wt. basis)			
Sawlogs	107	116	120
Pulpwood	53	55	56
Other	41	41	42
Total Agricultural	576	596	607.5
Mineral Fuels	1,337	1,399	1,448
Other Minerals			
Iron ore	204	237	245
Other metal ores	161	171	191
Other non-metals	125	133	149
Total Other Minerals	490	541	585
Grand Total[a]	2,403	2,536	2,640.5

a. Excluding construction materials, stone, sand, gravel, and other minerals used for structural purposes, ballast, fillers, insulation, etc. Gangue and mine tailings are also excluded from this total. These materials account for enormous tonnages but undergo essentially no chemical change. Hence, their use is more or less tantamount to physically moving them from one location to another. If these were to be included, there is no logical reason to exclude material shifted in highway cut-and-fill operations, harbor dredging, landfill plowing, and even silt moved by rivers. Since a line must be drawn somewhere, we chose to draw it as indicated above.

SOURCE: R.U. Ayres and A.V. Kneese, "Environmental Pollution," in Federal Programs for the Development of Human Resources, a Compendium of Papers submitted to the Subcommittee on Economic Progress of the Joint Economic Committee, United States Congress, Vol. 2 (Washington: Government Printing Office, 1968). Some revisions have been made in the original table.

One indication of the significance of materials throughput for the US economy can be gained by comparing the physical volume of throughput with the dollar value of the Gross National Product (GNP). For 1965 it is estimated that about 8 pounds of throughput were required for every dollar of GNP.

The ability of the environment to provide this service of dispersing, storing, or assimilating residuals stems from the action of natural environmental processes. Wind currents, for example, disperse potentially harmful concentrations of air pollutants. Rain and gravity remove some particulates from the air. Bacteria in water feed on and transform organic wastes into inorganic nutrients for algae, the first link in the aquatic food chain.

Clearly, if the environment had unlimited capacity to absorb or assimilate wastes, the release of residuals into the environment would not generate environmental costs or damages. However, the assimilative capacity of the environment is limited in several ways. For example, bacteria feeding on waterborne organic residuals employ oxygen. If oxygen supplies are depleted in the water course, other forms of aquatic life become adversely affected. For some substances, the environment has no assimilative capacity at all; mercury and some other heavy metals are cases in point. A relatively small amount of metallic mercury released into a water course is transformed into organic mercury compounds and eventually winds up in heavy concentrations in swordfish and tuna.

A second important class of environmental services involves the support of human life. The environment provides a hospitable habitat for man and other forms of life. However, and this is the important point, the life supportive services of the environment are threatened and in many cases reduced in volume as the residuals disposal services of the environment increase. As the processes of consumption and production release residual by-products into the environment, the concentration of residuals increases and the environment becomes less hospitable through the impairment in the life support services offered.

A third class of services provided by the environment can be called amenity services. People utilize these services largely through the pursuit of recreation activities. Although we know little about individual perceptions of environmental amenity services, we do know that the demand for outdoor recreation is rapidly growing on both sides of the Atlantic. We also know that the value of environmental recreation services are inversely related to the volume of residual absorptive services offered by the environment.

Finally, as the Materials Balance Model has demonstrated, the environment services as a source of material inputs to the economy. As with the non-residual absorptive services already discussed — life support services and amenity services — these material input flows can also be impaired in quality and quantity by increases in the flow of residuals absorptive services by the environment. Such impairment is also an environmental damage in that the cost of obtaining food and materials from the environment is raised.

Having delineated these forms of environmental services, we can now define environmental quality as the level and composition of the stream of all of the environmental services, except the waste receptor services. In economic terms, the ultimate measure of environmental quality is the value that people place on these non-waste-receptor services, that is, their willingness to pay for these services (3). This willingness to pay constitutes the demand for, or benefits of, environmental quality even though many of the services comprising environmental quality do not pass through markets and, hence, do not have prices attached to them. As a measure of the non-monetary income accruing to individuals because of the presence of environmental services, this non-monetary income is as much a part of their real income or welfare as their willingness to pay for marketable goods and services.

Again referring to the set of environmental services, we can also define the nature of damage induced by pollution. In economic terms, this damage is equal to the reduction in the value of environmental quality caused by the disposal of residuals. Hence, whenever residual disposal impairs life, reduces the value of property, or constrains the quality of natural recreation sites, the quality and quantity of non-residual-absorptive environmental services is reduced and environmental damages exist. These damages are measured by the value of the non-waste-receptor environmental services forgone because of the disposal or residuals. As such, environmental damage conforms to the classical economic notion of opportunity costs.

Given our definitions, environmental quality is maximised when no environmental damage is generated by residuals released into the environment. However, just as use of the waste-receptor services of the environment entails opportunity costs, increases in environmental quality from any given level also have opportunity costs. These costs represent the forgone waste receptor services of the environment and are manifested in the higher costs imposed on consumers and producers for disposing of the residuals flows from the economy other than direct disposal to the environment. Because of this, the fundamental economic issue is that of balancing at the margin environmental damage - in the form of reduction in life-sustenance services, amenity services, and material input flows — with the additional waste disposal costs which must be incurred in order to increase environmental quality.

One final and fundamental characteristic of the environment should be mentioned. As Professor Garrett Hardin has so clearly agued, the environment is the modern equivalent of "the commons". It is a commonly-held resource — an asset which cannot be reduced to private ownership. As a consequence, the services of the asset are available at zero price and as a result, there is overuse, abuse and quality degradation. The existence of environmental damage stems directly from this common property character of environmental assets. Because the services of these assets cannot enter into market exchange and be priced like other real economic inputs, they are progressively degraded. The use of the residual absorptive services of the environment appears costless to the industries, municipalities and individuals employing these services. This is so even though important values from other services of the asset are degraded or destroyed. The estimation of environmental damage for any economy, then, requires the estimation of the reduction in the non-residual-absorptive services of the environment due to the excessive use of environmental assets for residual-absorptive purposes.

II.   THE CONCEPT OF "ENVIRONMENTAL DAMAGE"

As the previous section has suggested, there are two types of costs or damage associated with the use of the waste-absorptive services of the environment. For example, if the discharge of residuals into the environment is <u>increased</u>, the value of the non-residual absorptive services of the environment would be decreased. The willingness of people to avoid this decrease can be interpreted as the environmental damages induced by the increased residuals flow. On the other hand, if the waste-absorptive services of the environment were to be <u>decreased</u>, society would be required to divert resources now being devoted to other production and consumption activities into the management of residuals flows. This diversion of resources is also a cost which is associated with the nature of and changes in the use of the environment.

Viewing the problem in this way, it can be stated that the attainment of the optimum level of environmental quality requires the minimization of the sum of these two costs. This proposition can be seen in the following simple model. Assume that prices can be attached to all flows of goods and services, which prices are satisfactory indicators of real economic values. Ignoring distributional questions, the two components of the aggregate output of goods and services are private consumption, government, and investment (N), and the stream of environmental services net of any environmental damages (E). Having defined pollution as the impairment of the flow of non-residual absorptive environmental services by residuals discharged, let E* represent the value of the flow of these environmental services in the absence of any residuals discharged. The difference, E* - E, is the reduction in the non-residual absorptive services of the environment due to residuals discharges, or D. Similarly, in the absence of any pollution control, the economy could produce N* worth of goods and services. Measures to reduce the residuals released to the environment absorb scarce resources (T), reducing the flow of non-environmental goods and services to N. This can be summarized as follows:

Economic welfare = W = N + E;

$$W = (N^* - T) + (E^* - D)$$
$$W = (N^* + E^*) - (T + D).$$

Only the levels of D and T are affected by the way in which residuals are disposed. Their sum $(T + D)$ is the total cost of residuals disposal and represents a reduction in economic welfare. Hence, the optimal level of the use of the environment for residuals absorption is that level of use which minimizes the sum of these two costs or damage.

From the above equations it can be seen that changes in economic welfare associated with altering the level of residuals absorption services are given by $\Delta W = - \Delta D - \Delta T$ where $- \Delta D$ is a reduction in pollution damage. An increase in welfare requires a decrease in damage $(- \Delta D)$ holding treatment costs constant, a decrease in treatment costs $(- \Delta T)$ holding pollution damage constant, or an increase in treatment costs which is more than offset by lower pollution damage. Steps taken to reduce residual absorption services should be undertaken as long as the reduction in pollution damage $(- \Delta D)$ exceeds the cost of achieving them (ΔT).

This simple framework can be made more concrete by referring to Figure 2. There the two cost functions are related to the concentration of residuals in the environment. The function labelled D indicates that the losses in non-residual absorptive environmental services rise at an increasing rate as the concentration of residuals in the environment rises. The cost function labelled T indicates that the value of resources required to reduce or otherwise handle residuals decreases as the concentration of residuals increases — or conversely, increases at an increasing rate as the concentration of residuals decreases. As indicated above, the total cost of residuals disposal is the sum of these two costs which, in the figure, is shown by the heavy line. As shown there, the total cost function attains its minimum at concentration level Q_2. Therefore, Q_2 is the optimum level of environmental quality. This

Figure 2

THE OPTIMUM ENVIRONMENTAL QUALITY

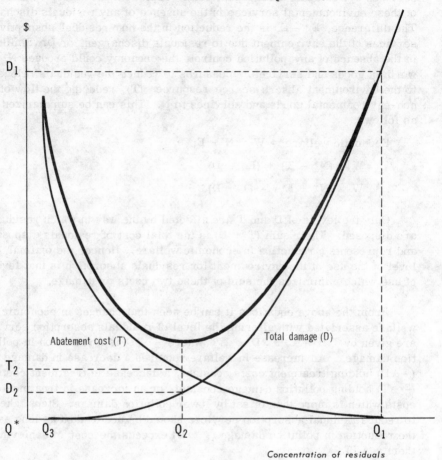

Concentration of residuals

indicates that costs equal to T_2 dollars should be incurred in order to reduce residuals concentrations and costs of D_2 dollars worth of reductions in non-residual absorptive services should be incurred.

The economic problem, then, is one of finding the optimal degree of residuals concentration, a task which can only be accomplished with empirical estimates of the two cost or damage functions — more specifically empirical estimates of the two marginal cost or damage functions.

This optimum level of the use of the waste-absorptive services of the environment has been described in terms of the levels of residuals

110

concentration. It is also possible to restate the problem in terms of the rates of discharge of the residual material. However, in order to do this, information is required on the relationships between rates of discharge of residuals and the resulting concentrations of materials in the environment. In reality these relationships are highly complex, depending on a host of environmental parameters, many of which are stochastic (e.g., temperature, wind, stream flow), as well as the rate and pattern of discharges of the residuals. Only if these relationships or transformation functions are known can we ascertain the optimal rate of residuals discharge consistent with the optimum level of environmental quality.

Having established that optimal environmental policy requires the empirical estimate of two marginal cost or damage functions, we would do well to explore some of the implications of this result. The first point concerns the cost function associated with the reduction in the residual absorptive services of the environment. This function indicates the lowest possible cost for attaining any given level of residuals concentration. As such it reflects the choice of the least-cost mix of technological options for reducing the discharge of residuals to the environment. From the viewpoint of the entire nation or of a single region within the nation, attaining the optimum necessitates choosing a mix of technological options within and among waste discharge activity such that the marginal cost of using each of the options is equal. Stated alternatively, to achieve any level of residuals concentration efficiently, each discharger must equate the marginal costs of all his residuals reduction options and, moreover, each discharger's marginal cost must be equal to the marginal costs of all other dischargers. If this condition is not met, the actual cost of any level of residuals concentration would be above that shown by the function.

A second point concerns the function displaying damages due to the reduced non-residual absorption services of the environment. Implicitly the function displayed assumes the existence of only one polluting substance. The existence of two or more residuals flows complicates the model substantially. First, as the Materials Balance Model showed, there are interdependencies among residuals in their generation and discharge. For example, a reduction in particulate emissions by a firm may be automatically accompanied by an increase in the discharge of solid matter into the water course. To take this into account, the estimated "treatment" cost curve for one residual (e.g., smoke) must include the environmental damages caused by the increased discharge of another residual (e.g., solids). Models must be constructed which account for these many interdependencies and solved simultaneously for the optimum degree of residuals discharge. A second way that the presence of two or more residuals can make the estimation of damage functions difficult is through interdependencies

111

in the effects of residuals on the environment. When there are synergistic relationships among pollutants, estimating and analysing this
damage function is difficult in concept and perhaps impossible in practice.
Information about the nature of these relationships is difficult to obtain
experimentally. Moreover, the economic analysis is complicated by
the fact that the damaging effect of one polluting substance depends not
only on the level of that pollutant in the environment but also on the level
of its synergistic partner.

Although data on both of these damage functions is essential for the
economic management of the environment, the choice of economically
efficient public investments for environmental control, and the administrative establishment of optimal prices and charges to be imposed on
uses of the environment imposing real social costs, the reliable
estimation of these functions has, heretofore, not been notably successful. The most formidable obstacle to the estimation of these functions
is the securing of the basic data and information implicit in them.
Essentially three kinds of data are required for determining these
relationships. First, the analyst must estimate the relationship
between residuals discharge reduction and the cost of securing that
reduction. Then, a model must be developed of the assimilation and
dispersion capacity of the environmental system in order to determine
the relationship between discharges and the environmental quality.
With these two pieces of information, treatment cost as a function of
environmental quality can be ascertained. Finally, and perhaps most
difficult of all, is the estimation of the relationship between concentration of residuals or levels of discharge and the dollar damages due to
such concentrations (in the form of reductions in non-residual absorptive
environment services).

Each of these three steps involves enormous difficulties in data
gathering and analysis. Consider first the treatment cost function.
In a river or airshed with a large number of dischargers all of whom
have a wide range of technological options for controlling residuals,
there are typically too many possible combinations for the analyst to
be able to estimate to a high degree of accuracy the least cost way of
achieving any given reduction of residuals discharge. Moreover, the
technology and cost factors are continuously changing due to innovation
and economic growth. Perhaps more importantly, the relationships
between discharges and concentrations in the environment are known
for only a few forms of residuals — for example, BOD and dissolved
oxygen in water, or sulfur dioxide in the atmosphere — and even these
are crude models which in several cases have not been adequately
tested for their accuracy. Finally, the presence of non-point residuals
sources makes both the estimation of control costs and the prediction
of concentrations in the environment more difficult.

112

Estimating the function describing the damage from reduced non-residual absorptive services poses the most formidable difficulties of all since it involves estimating the money values of environmental services which do not have recorded prices.

One major limitation to using these cost or damage functions in environmental planning stems from the randomness of nature and the lack of knowledge about the future. The natural phenomena that are represented in the function relating discharges to physical damage have elements of randomness to them. Hence, planning treatment facilities to prevent fish kills from occurring in a year with the lowest recorded streamflow is no guarantee that the treatment provided is sufficient.

Environmental management involves committing resources today to cope with expected future problems. It is inherent in the nature of things that the future may turn out to be different from our expectation. The use of damage functions based on past effects provides little assistance in perceiving that risk or estimating its distribution.

A second limitation has to do with possible cumulative and irreversible effects associated with some residuals discharges. The residual carbon dioxide being discharged to the atmosphere this year is not itself causing any environmental damage that we know of. But there is the possibility that it, in combination with the cumulative discharges of past and future years, could trigger major and essentially irreversible changes such as polar ice cap melting and flooding. Once those changes start, it is too late to begin controlling carbon dioxide emissions. For problems such as this, a model which focuses on present rates of discharge and present observable damage is of limited value.

A third limitation stems from the sequential dynamic nature of the real world. The use of empirically estimated damage functions assumes an unchanging static world in which the functions do not shift. However, in reality, the functions are in constant movement, and the process of change and sequence of policy steps may be more important than striving to attain the "optimum" at any point in time. For example, we presently have the choice of committing substantial resources to install the optimal air pollution control systems on automobiles. But we may be better off fifteen years from now if we devote those resources, instead, to research and development of alternative transportation systems.

This discussion is not meant to imply that the use of empirically estimated cost functions is of little value. Rather it is meant to emphasize the difficulty of estimating such functions and to suggest that their use applies only to a subset of all possible environmental problems.

113

III. SOME NATIONAL COST AND DAMAGE ESTIMATES

As the previous section emphasized, real economic costs are associated with both the existing level of residuals concentrations in the environment — commonly referred to as environmental damage — and with any policy effort designed to reduce residuals concentrations — called pollution control costs. Estimates of how these environment damages and pollution control costs vary with the level of residuals concentration or rates of residuals discharge require estimates of the functions referred to above. Heretofore, however, efforts to estimate the full functions have not been undertaken. Rather, point estimates have been made of the levels of the functions at some posited level of residuals concentration or discharge. Thus total environmental damage is often estimated at the existing level of concentration or discharge rate. Similarly, the "pollution control" costs are estimated to be the total cost required if concentration levels or discharge rates are to be reduced to the levels indicated by established environment quality standards (4). In this section several of the estimates of both environmental damage and pollution control costs appearing in official government documents will be reported.

Government Estimates of Environmental Damage

The most extensive description of the very skimpy evidence on the environmental damage imposed by existing levels of residuals concentration is contained in the Second Annual Report of the President's Council on Environmental Quality (5). As much to convey the rudimentary state of empirical estimates of the economic costs attribuable to pollution as to report those point estimates found in governmental documents, several statements from that Report will be quoted here.

The section in the Council's report dealing with "damages from pollution" begins with the following statement:

"Present levels of pollution and environmental degradation result in costs to society in the form of increased health services, lost productivity, and direct damage to crops, materials, and other property. The loss of scenic values and recreational areas, destruction of valuable ecological systems, and the loss of pleasant surroundings do not enter the traditional economic calculus directly, but they are no less economic costs... The evidence [of direct damage attributable to pollution] is not always clear-cut, and research on many environmental effects is only now beginning ... Even if the relevant data were available, it would be difficult to place a dollar value on these impacts"(6).

114

The estimate in the Report concerning the economic damage attributable to air pollutants was the most complete presented. The Report stated:

"The costs of damages attributable to the major air pollutants — surfur oxides, particulates, photo-chemical oxidants, carbon monoxide, and nitrogen oxides — have been estimated... [These estimates] are admittedly crude and at this stage, can only approximate the real costs of air pollution. In general, only direct monetary costs associated with air pollution damages to human health, materials, and vegetation and to property devaluation have been estimated. Even these studies rely heavily on judgment. Not yet available are data on aesthetic costs, visibility, odor, soiled clothing, dirty homes and the like. Yet these costs stir much of the public resentment to air pollution. "(7)

In referring to the effects of air pollution on human health, the Report states that "a 50% reduction in air pollution existing in major urban areas [in 1963] would lower the cost of damage to health by $ 2.08 billion in a single year"(8). Of this $ 2.08 billion of damages, the Council attributed 59% to respiratory disease, 19% to cancer, and 22% to cardiovascular disease. The Report goes on to state that the estimated health costs for medical care and work loss attributable to all air pollution was approximately $ 6 billion annually. With respect to the damage imposed by air pollution on vegetation and materials, the Council estimated the direct costs at $ 4.9 billion annually. In addition to health costs and damage to vegetation and materials, the Council referred to a study of the Environmental Protection Agency which suggested that property values are sensitive to pollution levels. It was estimated that air pollution lowered nationwide values of property by $ 5.2 billion annually (9).

In summing up these estimates of the damage from air pollution, the Council stated:

"The annual total cost of air pollution on health, vegetation, materials, and property values has been estimated... at more than $ 16 billion — over $ 80 for each person in the United States. In all probability, the estimates of cost will be even higher when the impact on aesthetic and other values are calculated, when the cost of discomfort from illness is considered, and when damage can be more precisely traced to pollutants. "(10)

While the Council's estimates of the costs of air pollution were skimpy, and perhaps double-counted some damage, their estimates of the damage from water pollution were even less well documented. Losses of ocean and coastal fisheries and shellfish production were cited as well as the effects of increased salinity due to the increasing use of water for irrigation, although no national estimates of the costs of these effects were provided. With respect to perhaps the primary cost of water pollution — namely, outdoor recreation — the Council suggested that "water pollution may cause recreational losses extending into many billions of dollars nationwide"(11).

Referring to the environmental damage other than air and water pollution damage, the Council said: "Costs of many other forms of pollution have not even been approximated." These additional effects which were mentioned in the Report included "aesthetic losses", "litter in parks and along roads and rivers", "transmission lines that traverse the countryside", land that has been surface mined, "noise pollution", "urban congestion", and "lack of open space"(12).

Governmental Estimates of Pollution Control Costs

Although the Report of the Council on Environmental Quality emphasizes the rudimentary nature of cost estimates for pollution abatement, substantially more evidence is presented on pollution control costs than on environmental damage. As noted above, however, such point estimates of pollution control costs must refer to some stipulated level of residuals concentration or rates of discharge which are below existing levels or rates. In the case of the cost estimates presented in the Council's Report, this reference level of pollution reduction is taken to be the air and water quality standards which have been established in response to federal legislation. Presumably these standards are to be interpreted as a community judgment on the acceptable levels of air and water residuals concentrations.

Table 2 summarizes the estimated costs for attaining existing legislated standards in 1970 and 1975 and the cumulative requirements over that six-year period. These estimates include measures for total capital investment, annual operation and maintenance costs, and the annualised equivalent of these costs. As the data indicates, the bulk of the water pollution control costs are attributable primarily to municipal and industrial waste treatment. The bulk of air pollution control costs are required to reduce particulates and automobile pollutants. Unlike the costs for water pollution control, air pollution control expenditures by state and local governments are primarily for planning and enforcement rather than treatment facilities. Also, because the major source of air pollution is the automobile, the major share of air pollution control costs will be borne by the private sector (13).

Finally, Table 2 also includes estimates of the cost for solid waste disposal. These costs are so large because of the inclusion of the costs

116

Table 2.   POLLUTION ABATEMENT
COST SUMMARY [1]

(in billions of dollars)

POLLUTANT/ MEDIUM	1970			1975			CUMULATIVE REQUIREMENTS 1970-1975		
	CAPITAL INVESTMENT		ANNUAL-ISED COSTS	CAPITAL INVESTMENT		ANNUAL-ISED COSTS	CAPITAL INVEST-MENT	TOTAL OPER-ATING COSTS	TOTAL EXPENDI-TURES
	CUMU-LATIVE[2]	ANNUAL		CUMU-LATIVE[3]	ANNUAL				
Air pollution									
Public[4]	$ 0.2	$ 0.1	$ 0.2	$ 0.5	$ 0.1	$ 0.2	$ 0.4	$ 1.2	$ 1.6
Private									
Mobile	0.1	0.1	-0.2	4.3	2.9	1.5	5.4	0.6	6.0
Stationary ...	1.0	0.7	0.5	7.7	1.8	3.0	8.0	8.1	16.1
Total	1.3	0.9	0.5	12.5	4.8	4.7	13.8	9.9	23.7
Water pollution									
Public									
Federal[5]	NA	NA	0.2	0.3	0.1	0.3	0.3	1.3	1.6
State and local									
Treatment systems ..	13.7	1.2	1.6	24.2	1.5	3.3	13.6	9.3	22.9
Collecting sewers[6] ...	(12.0)	NA	NA	(12.0)	NA	NA	(3.6)	NA	(3.6)
Combined sewers[7] ...	NA	NA	NA	NA	NA	NA	(15.0-48.0)	NA	(15.0-48.0)
Private									
Manufacturing	3.9	0.8	1.1	7.1	0.6	1.9	4.8	7.2	12.0
Other	0.9	0.3	0.2	1.1	0.1	0.3	0.5	1.0	1.5
Total	16.5	2.3	3.1	32.7	2.3	5.8	19.2	18.8	38.0
Solid Waste[8]									
Municipal									
Public	NA	0.1	2.1						
Private	NA	NA	2.3	NA	0.3	7.8	1.5	42.0	43.5
Industrial	NA	NA	1.3						
Total	NA	0.1	5.7	NA	0.3	7.8	1.5	42.0	43.5
Grand Total ...	NA	3.3	9.3	NA	7.4	18.3	34.5	70.7	105.2

NA = Non-available.
1.   For major air, water, and solid waste pollution control expenditures.
2.   Total capital in place as of the end of 1970.
3.   Total capital in place as of the end of 1975 is net of depreciation for the period.
4.   For construction and operation of Federal facilities only.
5.   For construction and operation of Federal facilities only. Does not include the Federal construction grant funds, which are included under State and local.
6.   Collecting sewers are shown as a non-add item due to lack of data.
7.   Combined sewers shown as a non-add item because of lack of data.
8.   Annualised costs exclude depreciation and interest because of lack of data.
SOURCE: Based on Environmental Protection Agency data.

117

of collection as well as disposal of residential, commercial and industrial solid residuals.

In referring to the data in Table 2, the Council Report stated:

"If standards are met on schedule, total annualised costs of pollution control in 1975 will increase approximately 97% over 1970. Annual investment will more than double. These cost increases from 1970 to 1975 vary greatly by type of medium. Air pollution annualised costs will increase 840%, water pollution control, 87%, and solid waste management, 37%. Total spending required for the major sources of environmental pollution between 1970 and 1975 is estimated at about $ 105 billion — 23% for air pollution control, 36% for water pollution control, and 41% for solid waste management."

As the Council Report makes clear, one additional pollution control cost should be mentioned. If sewage treatment plants are to successfully treat sewage during periods of heavy rainfall and heavy runoff, cities must separate existing unitary sewers that carry both sanitary and storm waste. It is estimated that between $ 15 billion and $ 48 billion is necessary to correct the combined sewers problem. These figures do not include the costs of increased urban congestion due to the disruption of US city streets required to accomplish sewer separation (15).

Although official estimates of the cost of pollution control are significantly more complete and detailed than estimates of environmental damage, the Council emphasized the tenuous nature of these estimates. It was noted that the interdependence of control costs was not included in the cost estimates and that while the cost estimates were based on standards existing in 1970, "upgraded standards, new pollutants covered by standards, and other factors will doubtless raise the total cost of attaining higher levels of environmental quality. On balance, the costs of environmental control — including just the controls over air and water pollution and solid wastes — are understated, probably significantly. "(16)

IV.   RECENT RESEARCH ON ESTIMATING
ENVIRONMENTAL DAMAGE

Given the fundamental weakness in the available evidence on the extent of environmental damage or the economic costs of improving environmental quality, this final section will describe the methodology and results of a number of the more important basic research efforts designed to measure environmental damage functions. Although full estimation of damage functions often requires research on both the

physical effects of alternative levels of residuals concentrations and
the economic costs related to these effects, we will largely neglect the
many studies of physical effects concentrating instead on the procedures
used to estimate economic costs (17). Because estimation of these
economic costs typically entails the evaluation of external or spillover
effects which have no market price attached to them, much of this
research involves the development of methodologies for estimating the
willingness-to-pay to avoid environmental damages. Studies of damage
functions attributable to waterborne residuals, airborne residuals,
and pesticide use will be discussed.

Damage Associated With Waterborne Residuals

The primary adverse effect of water pollution is the reduction in
natural outdoor recreation services yielded by the environment (18).
Two economic studies have directly addressed the estimation of the
economic value of this damage.

The earliest study is that undertaken by a group of researchers at
Oregon State University and reported in a paper by Joe B. Stevens (19).
In this study, a methodology was developed for estimating direct recreational benefits from improved water quality. Such benefit estimates
can be transformed into estimates of the costs of water quality deterioration. Stevens concentrates on that form of water-based outdoor recreation referred to as sports fishing. His problem is to estimate the
value which recreationists place on fishing at a given recreation site
as a function of water quality at that site.

As a first step, Stevens develops the concept of a biological production function for fishing which relates angler input to yield of fish
taken in a sports fishery. The level of the function is positively related
to the quality of the water in the fishery. He then incorporates this
function into a standard demand model in which the demanded "commodity"
is "units of sports fishing". Through multiple regression analysis, the
coefficients on all of the determinants of quantity demanded were estimated. From these regressions, the relationship of quantity to price
was estimated by incrementally altering price, holding all of the other
variables constant. Then, by altering the biological production function
because of water pollution effects, a second demand function can be
similarly estimated. The difference in the "consumers" surplus implied
in these functions represents the welfare loss — or damage — due to
increased water pollution.

Stevens illustrates this methodology by estimating demand equations
and success-effort functions for three estuarial sports fisheries on the
Yaquina Bay in the state of Oregon, and assuming a pollution-induced

119

reduction in the success-effort relationship. It is estimated that the annual loss from sports fishing in the Yaquina Bay would be $ 63, 000 if waste disposal resulted in a total loss of fishing. The present value of this loss in about $ 1 million if discounted at 6% (20).

Although this exploratory effort fails to include many of the quality related characteristics of an outdoor recreation experience, it does provide a consistent economic framework for estimating at least a portion of the real welfare losses associated with variations in residuals concentrations. As Stevens points out, however, a primary missing link in the analysis is the empirical estimation of variations in angler success attributable to various levels and compositions of residuals concentrations.

The second important study focused on the changes in the economic value of the recreational use which would be made of the Delaware estuary if the quality of the estuary were to be improved (21). While this study was done in a benefit-cost framework designed to guide decisions on the optimal level of water quality for the estuary, it yielded estimates of the extent of economic losses now and in future years attributable to the low water quality of the estuary. As the authors state, "upstream users have reduced the quality of the water in the Delaware River from Trenton to the sea to such a degree that it has been made almost unusable for water recreation"(22).

Adopting dissolved oxygen as the indicator of water quality, the authors statistically developed an estimate of the total number of swimming, boating, and fishing activity days which would be associated with various quality levels for the dates 1960, 1975, and 1990. In developing these activity day functions, data from a survey of 1350 households were used to isolate through multiple regression analysis those variables which influence participation in fishing, swimming, and boating and, for participants, the extent of participation. The independent variables included socio-economic characteristics, loca- tional variables, and, most significantly, an index of the quality of recreational facilities available. Using the most appropriate regression equations for fishing, swimming, and boating, the values of the relevant exogenous (independent) variables for residents of the Delaware estuary area were introduced to estimate the probability of participation and the number of participants by socio-economic group, given the current low quality of the estuary in 1960. Then, projections of the values of the exogenous variables were made for the 30 subsequent years and the same procedure followed to estimate the participation which would be anticipated in future periods, again with existing quality levels. As a last step, the quality of the Delaware estuary was artificially increased in the regressions and an estimate of the usage to be expected under these improved conditions was calculated. "The estimates indicate a large increase in activity resulting from an improved river. Combining the sports, the figures run close to 600,000 days for any year"(23). This figure is an estimate of the damage, in terms of recreation activity days forgone, attributable to the high levels of residuals concentration in the Delware.

As a last step, the researchers calculated the present value of the activity days forgone at various assumed levels of river improvement, and, using a series of arbitrary values for user days forgone, calculated a function describing the economic benefits from improving the quality of the river by various amounts. By combining these various marginal benefit estimates with the marginal costs of achieving various levels of improvement, guidance for decisions on the extent of river quality were provided. These results indicated that achieving a quality level of 3 ppm of dissolved oxygen could be justified if a value of $2.50 or more per day were assigned to boating (24).

While both of these studies have dealt with the damage in the form of recreation forgone from decreased water quality, other studies have explored other forms of damage from water pollution. These include the damage imposed on water using industries and municipalities which require water of some quality level. In general these studies have shown that both industrial and municipal costs for treating intake water are relatively insensitive to the quality of intake water (25).

Damage Associated With Airborne Residuals

While the damage associated with water pollution was primarily recreational opportunities forgone, that associated with air pollution is more diverse. It includes the costs associated with damage to human health, the costs of pollution-related cleaning and maintenance activities, the costs of inhibited growth and destruction of plant life, and the reductions in property values associated with air pollution. In this section, studies which have tried to estimate the economic value of the first and last of these effects will be discussed (26). In Appendix A, a tentative catalogue of the range of air pollution costs is presented.

Health-Related Air Pollution Damage

One of the earliest studies of the health related costs of air pollution was sponsored by the US Public Health Service and undertaken by researchers at Washington University (27). As a first step in this study, the total economic costs associated with a variety of respiratory illnesses potentially affected by airborne residuals concentrations were estimated. The components of these costs were defined as lost earnings due to premature death, premature burial costs, costs of absenteeism, and the treatment cost of illnesses.

It should be noted that other potential health related costs attributable to air pollution - moving costs for pollution stimulated migration, the value of non-priced labour services (e.g., housewife services) and the willingness to pay in excess of market costs to avoid sickness or accelerated death - were not analysed nor were the costs of diseases other than respiratory diseases.

The second step was to attempt to explain mortality and absentee rates by air pollution levels, after controlling for other factors which could affect mortality and absenteeism. After numerous efforts to develop such estimates, the researchers were unable to discern significant coefficients on the air pollution variables or coefficients with the right sign. The final step in this study was to estimate the maximum effect of air pollution on health - related costs by comparing urban and rural mortality rate differences after correcting for a limited number of socio-economic characteristics. Of the $ 2 billion of total health related costs for 1959 calculated in the first step, the researchers conclude that about 20%, or about $ 400 million, is accounted for by the urban-rural distinction and, hence, attributable to air pollution (28).

A more successful effort to measure the health-related costs of airborne residuals concentrations was made by Lester Lave and his associates (29). After analysing the extreme difficulties in measuring health - related damages from air pollution - lack of understanding of the physiological mechanism, lack of data on morbidity rates, absentee rates, and health expenditures, the "urban factor" in mortality, the potential interactions between smoking and air pollution, the statistical effects of errors of observation, and non-linear relationships between air pollution and health - Lave estimated the relationship between mortality rates and various measures of the dimensions of air pollution levels, controlling for a wide range of population size and socio-economic variables. The data used was for 117 SMSA's (Standard Metropolitan Statistical Areas) for the US. Both linear and non-linear relationships were estimated with least-squares regression techniques. Lave concluded that all of the alternative forms fit the data about equally well and that all indicate the significance of air pollution levels in determining mortality rates. All of the models suggested that minimum pollution readings were more important than maximum levels. Finally, Lave applied the linear model to explain age - specific mortality rates by various pollutants and measures of pollution. He concluded that pollution is a significant explanatory variable for death rates in all age categories although the effects vary by age category and the measure of pollution used. As to total air pollution damages in terms of mortality rates, Lave concludes:

"Abating pollution by 50% throughout the nation would add three to five years to the life expectancy of a child born in 1970 ... A 50% abatement would lower the economic cost of all ill health by just under 5% ... Abating pollution by 50% would be worth about $2 billion per year in terms of the economic benefits of (a) increased days work, and (b) decreased health expenditures."(30)

In a recent paper appraising the methodology of his study, Lave raises numerous conceptual and empirical difficulties which require careful appraisal and which raise serious questions concerning the meaning of his own results (31). These difficulties can be summarized as follows:

1. The lack of a theoretical model specifying the way air pollution affects health (p. 215);

2. Data on morbidity rates, absence rates, and health expenditure are not available on any extensive basis (p. 216);

3. The virtual impossibility of accounting for all possible factors that might be the real causes of ill health (p. 217);

4. Errors of observation in the data, which lead to potentially biased estimates (p. 218);

5. Health effects of air pollution which depend on past levels of pollution, while only recent indices are available (p. 219);

6. The unavailability of a single pollution index to appropriately characterize a region (p. 219);

7. The lack of knowledge concerning the shape of the function which describes the relationship between air pollution and health (p. 219);

8. The lack of a single appropriate measure of pollution although measures of only suspended particulates and sulphur compounds are available in acceptable form (p. 224);

9. The episodic nature of air pollution which makes estimates of its effects particularly difficult (p. 227);

10. The lack of age-specific mortality and morbidity data required for accurate estimates (p. 228);

11. The bias in consumer responses regarding the willingness to to pay for pollution abatement are likely to be biased because of a lack of information regarding the effects of pollution, the incentive to misrepresent preferences when being asked

regarding them (because of the public goods nature of pollution), the failure of adult responses fails to consider effects on children, the myopic nature of consumer evaluation of this sort, and, as Schelling has noted, the difficulty in appraising the value of marginal changes in very low probability events (p. 233).

The Effects of Air Pollution on Property Values

Substantial work in estimating the adverse economic effects of air pollution has been undertaken by relating air pollution levels to property values. The rationale for this estimation procedure is the belief that the rents for property capture the bulk of adverse effects from air pollution, including the health effect. According to economic theory, the price of a piece of real property equals the sum of the discounted present value of the stream of benefits and costs derivable from it. The effect of air pollution is to decrease the stream of benefits and increase the stream of costs. Because air pollution is site specific, the price of fixed real property will reflect these effects.

Regressing mean property values by census tract in the St. Louis metropolitan area on a number of explanatory variables, including air pollution control measures, Ridker and his associates found that air pollution levels - especially sulfation - were significant explanatory variables (32). In addition to air pollution measures, Ridker employed some of the following characteristics as variables expected on a priori grounds to affect property values: size, density, and quality of housing, locational advantages and disadvantages, neighbourhood characteristics such as school quality and crime rates, taxes and public services, racial characteristics, and median family income.

Because the objective of the study was to estimate damages from air pollution, the researchers were required to estimate the regression coefficients on the air pollution variables. As a consequence, problems of multicollinearity had to be dealt with as well as potential bias to due misspecification of the model. Several econometric techniques were used to deal with these problems and a number of regression equations were presented. The results from the best estimate are described as follows:

"This information can be interpreted as meaning that if the sulfation levels to which any single family dwelling unit is exposed were to drop by 0.25 mg/100 cm2/day, the value of that property could be expected to rise by at least $ 83 and more likely $ 245. Using the latter figure and assuming the sulfation levels are reduced by 0.25 mg but in no case below 0.49 mg (taken as the background level),the total increase in property values for the St. Louis ... area could be as much as $ 82,790,000."(33)

"To indicate the annual cost that is incurred because pollution is not at these lower levels, these figures must be multiplied by a rate of interest that reflects what could have been earned from investing these amounts. For example, using a figure of 6% ... we obtain an annual loss estimate for the whole St. Louis area of almost 5 million."(34)

While Ridker's analysis of the effects of air pollution on land values was the first of its type to appear, it has been followed by a number of others. Anderson and Crocker have studied the St. Louis, Kansas City, and Washington, D.C. SMSA's while Zerbe has studied the Toronto area (35). All of these studies have employed census tracts as the fundamental unit of observation.

More recently, Crocker has studied the relationship between air pollution and property values for the city of Chicago, employing data on each of 1288 individual single family - residential property trans- actions from 1964-1967 (36). The results of this study indicate that the marginal capitalized damages for an additional annual average of 10 mg per cubic meter per day of suspended particulates plus an additional annual average of one part per billion per day of sulphur dioxide ranged from about $ 350 to $ 600. Not only was the air pollution coefficient of the right sign but it was also significant, even after alter- ations in the specification because of multicollinearity. In addition to this finding, Crocker tested and accepted the hypothesis that marginal damages are inversely related to pollution levels, i.e., that the marginal damage function is declining and that land values are more sensitive to pollution levels than are improvement values. Finally, Crocker found that the skewness of the distribution of air pollution variables was positively related to decreases in property values.

While Crocker claims his results to be consistent with other property value studies, it should be noted that his methodology is sufficiently un- specified to enable the verification of this result. The choice of inde- pendent variables among those available appears judgmental and omission of some variables which would appear to be both important in explaining variation in the dependent variable and correlated with the pollution variables is troublesome.

These studies relating property values to air pollution levels have not been immune to criticism. In particular, it has been asserted that these regression results have been "over-interpreted". While the air pollution coefficient can be used to predict the differences in property values between two properties under ceteris paribus conditions, "these

conditions must include no change in air quality over all other land in
the system. But the regression equation cannot be used to predict the
general pattern of property values ... when the pattern of air quality
over the whole urban area has changed" (37). The point is that both
supply and demand factors must be consistently related in a general
equilibrium model if the true effect of air pollution on land values is
to discerned (38). In addition, Lave has emphasized the sensitivity of
the air pollution coefficient in these studies to other variables included
in the analysis (especially where there exists no theoretical way to
specify the model), the serious measurement problems associated with
the stochastic nature of the pollution phenomenon, the notorious difficulties of obtaining meaningful estimates of the value of land and property,
the difficulties of using aggregates such as census tracts, and the
problems of interpreting results when many of the effects of air pollution occur away from home (39).

Damage Associated With Pesticide Use

In the United States, the use of chemical materials to control pests
is widespread, especially in agriculture. In 1964, for example, farmers
used over 450 million pounds of active chemicals for pest control. Some
of these chemicals are very persistent, with residues remaining for
months and sometimes years. Because of this persistence, pesticide
traces have been found in human, animal, and fowl tissues. There is
some evidence that high dosages may induce carcinogenic or mutagenic
effects.

As with air and water pollution, existing levels of pesticide use
may entail real economic costs. Conversely, enforced reductions of
pesticide use will also generate costs, largely in the form of reductions
in agricultural output. Estimates of these latter costs have been made
by J. C. Headley, using 1964 data from a random sample of 393 counties (40). Estimating national and regional production functions,
Headley evaluated the contribution of pesticide use to agricultural
output. This contribution will be the cost which society will have to
bear if pesticide use is curtailed. For insecticides, Headley estimates
that the value of marginal product is about $ 1.50 per ounce of insec-
ticide, compared to a price of insecticides of about 10c to 15c per ounce.
Among the regions of the country, this estimated marginal product
varied from about 1c per ounce to over $ 10.00 per ounce. It is this
marginal product which will have to be sacrificed if pesticide use is
curtailed in the absence of substitute pest control.

To ascertain if the external, non-market damage from pesticide
use is sufficiently large to warrant enforced curtailment of pesticides,

researchers at the University of Florida attempted to measure these damages for a region in Florida and to incorporate them into a measure of social welfare (41). Two types of pesticides were evaluated and compared in an analysis of alternative policies for pesticide use. The two types of pesticides evaluated were acutely toxic (to humans) but non-persistent organic phosphates, and non-toxic, but highly persistent chlorinated hydrocarbons.

In their effort to measure the extent of external environmental damages, the researchers "aimed at relating a dollar measure of the social costs of externalities to the amount of a pesticide being used. (42) They stated:

> "This effort had some rather severe limitations. First, only those externalities which could be observed were measured. By and large these were acute external diseconomies which created controversy. Second, in many cases, the measurement of an externality was uncomfortably subjective in that it lacked a market determination. Finally, an estimation of this type overlooks moral and/or aesthetic considerations ... "(43)

Because the researchers had no access to time series or cross-sectional data, they were able to estimate only one point on a damage function. In estimating the total use of the two types of pesticides in the 1966-1967 crop year, records of individual farmers and pesticide firms were used. To estimate the damages from pesticide use, information was obtained from growers, insurance claims, veterinarians, biologists, conservationists, and public health personnel.

For the toxic organic phosphates, the researchers estimated damages of about $ 4, 600 per year for Dade County, Florida. This was associated with about 136, 000 pounds of pesticide use or damages equal to about $.035 per pound. These damages consisted of medical damage to humans (estimated by compensation payments and medical care expenses) and damage to domestic animals.

SOME CONCLUSIONS AND RECOMMENDATIONS

After this survey of the methodology and results of recent research, what can be concluded? In the following points, the primary conclusions regarding the meaning of this research will be described and an evaluation of the importance and potential of further research on damage functions will be offered:

1. No estimates of either full or partial environmental damage functions have yet been made in the US. Most of the estimates have been point estimates. Where changes in damages due to abatement

have been suggested, the estimates are based on the derivatives of arbitrary functional forms (Lave, Anderson and Crocker, Ridker) or assumed linearity in damage functions (Langham, Headley and Edwards).

2. Where studies with similar methodologies have been applied to various data sources, the estimates of changes in damage due to abatement or increased pollution loads have varied substantially. In the case of the property value studies (where the most replication has occurred), the highest estimate is about 3 times that of the lowest.

3. The theoretical basis for estimates of the health effects of residuals concentrations is very weak. For most of the important relationships, the relevant epidemiological data is unavailable. In addition, as Lave has noted, there are numerous unanswered questions of a conceptual, empirical and statistical sort. Most fundamental is the difficulty of separating the health effects of pollution from health phenomena which are influenced by a large number of other, non-pollution related and pollution interrelated variables. Analogous problems afflict estimates of soiling and materials damage effects from air pollution.

4. In the absence of specified general equilibrium models, the effect of air pollution levels on property values cannot be known. The meaning of the "willingness to bid" functions which have been estimated is not clear. They appear to have been overinterpreted, given the absence of such general equilibrium models.

5. The studies on soiling, materials damage, and vegetation effects of air pollution have been weak in the specification of the concept of damages and its relationships to the standard welfare economics framework. This, in addition to the lack of data and the absence of knowledge of physical effects, makes these studies of little use.

6. The social costs from water pollution stem primarily from forgone water-based recreation opportunities. The real cost of these opportunities depends on the sacrifices in consumers' surplus which in turn depends upon the availability of substitute recreation alternatives. The estimation of these marginal rates of substitution is most difficult, especially when outdoor recreation services are unpriced.

7. Studies which seek to estimate damages by asking people what they would pay to avoid various levels of residuals concentration or noise are likely to be of little use. Two problems appear fatal. First, there is substantial reason to believe that respondents' perception of damage and increased risks is sorely inadequate. Second, because of the public goods nature of the pollution problem, interviewees have incentive to understate their willingness to pay if it is anticipated that the costs of damage reduction will be related to their statements.

8. While most of the air pollution damage studies have yielded estimates of national damages, most of the important public decisions

must be local or regional decisions. They include the setting of emissions standards for various kinds of pollutants and sources, the setting of relevant emissions charges, the establishment of zoning regulations, or the undertaking of abatement investments. Such national estimates are of little help for these decisions. While such estimates could possibly be of help for, say, national decisions on research investments in transport systems as alternatives to automobiles, they are too unreliable to offer much assistance.

9. While the water pollution damage studies have been more limited in number, they have concentrated on regional problems (especially the Davidson, Adams and Seneca study) and have effectively used sensitivity analysis to shed light on relevant policy decisions. In this way, even if information and relationships are unknown, policy-makers can test out the results of alternative specifications (46). On the basis of these considerations, the following conclusions seem justified:

- For many of the categories of adverse effects of pollution, the economic concept of damage is not yet clearly specified. As a consequence, the appropriate empirical research methodology is not defined. Much basic research work is yet required.

- For other categories of adverse effects of pollution an economic concept of damage has been specified and research methodologies based upon the concept have been undertaken (especially the health and property value effects of air pollution, and the recreation losses from water pollution). However, the economic concepts of damage which have been employed have been subject to criticism on the basis of intergenerational effects, consumers' surplus effects (often called psychic effects), option value effects, and general equilibrium and dynamic adjustment consequences. Moreover, the data available for such studies is very limited. Again, basic research and data collection is of the first priority.

- Estimates of the national effects of residuals discharge are of substantially less importance than more limited local or regional studies which are directly related to imminent public regulatory, investment or pricing decisions. Even though the data limitations of such studies are substantial, as are estimates of the relevant physical relationships, sensitivity tests in the context of a benefit-cost framework can provide important information for decision-makers.

AIR POLLUTION

Health Effects

- Productivity losses from accelerated mortality.

- Incremental health care costs, including social overhead capital costs not included in many estimates of health care expenses.

- Productivity losses from morbidity.

- Reduced productivity not regarded as morbidity, e.g. increased lethargy.

- Moving costs for migration induced by desire to avoid health effects.

- Willingness to pay to avoid migration over and above moving and income loss costs.

- Income losses from migration induced by desire to avoid health effects.

- Willingness to pay to avoid induced morbidity, lethargy, or accelerated mortality in self beyond that indicated in productivity and health care costs.

- Willingness to pay to avoid induced morbidity, lethargy, or accelerated mortality in others (relatives, friends) beyond that indicated in productivity or health care costs.

Soiling Effects

- Incremental cleaning costs for clothing, person, buildings, autos, etc.

- Willingness to pay for elimination of soiling beyond that indicated by incremental cleaning costs.

- Moving costs for migration induced by desire to avoid soiling effects.

- Income losses from migration induced by desire to avoid soiling effects.

- Willingness to pay to avoid migration over and above moving and income loss costs.

Materials Damage Effects

- Incremental costs from accelerated replacement of metals, rubber, etc.

- Incremental costs from damages to historical monuments and other irreplaceable objects (involves estimation of option value).

Property Value Effects

- Reduction in property values due to pollution levels after general equilibrium adjustments over and above damages indicated in previously mentioned catagories. (The dangers of double counting are most serious in that property values will capture many of the above listed health and soiling effects.) The theoretical conditions which must exist for property values to capture air pollution effects are very rigorous ones. See Robert Strotz, "The Use of Land Charges to Measure the Welfare Benefits of Land Improvements", Resources for the Future, July 1966 (mimeo).

Damage to Vegetation

- Incremental costs of plantings required to compensate for growth retardation induced by air pollution. (If growth retardation results in higher prices, it is the loss in consumers' surplus which must be measured.)

- Incremental costs from damages to unique forests and landscapes (involves estimation of option value).

NOTES

1. This section and the next draws on material to be contained in
    A. Myrick Freeman, Robert H. Haveman, and Allen V. Kneese,
    The Economics of Environmental Policy (New York: John Wiley
    and Sons).

2. This model and principle are most fully developed in Allen V.
    Kneese, Robert U. Ayres, and Ralph C. d'Arge, Economics and
    the Environment: A Materials Balance Approach (Washington:
    Johns Hopkins Press for Resources for the Future, Inc., 1970).

3. For a more complete discussion of the willingness to pay concept
    and its tie to welfare economics, see J. M. Currie, J.A. Murphy,
    and A. Schmitz, "The Concept of Economic Surplus and its Use
    in Economic Analysis", Economic Journal, LXXXI, Dec., 1971,
    pp. 741-799.

4. It should again be emphasized that such point estimates of total
    cost or total damages are not relevant to decisions on the optimal
    level of environmental quality. It is the marginal cost and mar-
    ginal damage estimates which are needed for such environmental
    management decisions.

5. President's Council on Environmental Quality, Environmental
    Quality, the Second Annual Report of the Council on Environmental
    Quality, August, 1971.

6. Ibid., p. 104.

7. Ibid., pp. 104-105.

8. Ibid., p. 106.

9. Ibid., pp. 106-107. The study referred to is Larry B. Barrett
    and Thomas H. Waddell, "The Cost of Air Pollution Damages:
    A Status Report", Environmental Protection Agency, 1971,
    mimeo. The Barrett and Waddell study surveyed most of the

studies available which purport to estimate the damages from pollution. Their numerical estimates are based on linear extrapolations of the results of a few of these studies.

10. Ibid., p. 107.

11. Ibid., p. 108.

12. Ibid., p. 108.

13. The data shown in Table 2 are based on detailed estimates in US. Environmental Protection Agency, Cost of Clean Water, (Washington: Government Printing Office, 1971) and US Environmental Protection Agency, Cost of Clean Air (Washington: Government Printing Office, 1971).

14. President's Council on Environmental Quality, op. cit., p. 110.

15. Ibid., p. 114.

16. Ibid., pp. 116-117.

17. For a bibliography including many of the studies of the physical effects of air pollution see Paul H. Gerhardt, "Air Pollution Control: Benefits, Costs, Inducements," in Selma Mushkin, ed., Public Prices for Public Products (Washington, The Urban Institute, 1972), pp. 153-171. This paper also contains estimates of the pollution abatement costs required to meet the Clean Air Act. See also Lester B. Lave, "Air Pollution Damage: Some Difficulties in Estimating the Value of Abatement," in Allen V. Kneese and Blair T. Bower, eds., Environmental Quality Analysis (Baltimore: Johns Hopkins Press for Resources for the Future, 1972), pp. 213-242. For references on the physical effects of water pollution, see Clifford S. Russell and Walter O. Spofford, Jr., "A Quantitative Framework for Residuals Management Decisions," in Kneese and Bower, op. cit., pp. 115-180 and Allen V. Kneese and Blair T. Bower, Managing Water Quality (Baltimore: Johns Hopkins Press for Resources for the Future, Inc., 1968).

18. For a discussion of the relative importance of other damages from water pollution, see Kneese and Bower (1968), pp. 125-126.

19. Joe B. Stevens, "Recreation Benefits from Water Pollution Control," Water Resources Research, Vol. 2 (Second Quarter, 1966), pp. 167-182.

20. See Kneese and Bower (1968), pp. 128-129.

21. Paul Davidson, F. Gerard Adams, and Joseph Seneca, "The Social Value of Water Recreational Facilities Resulting from an Improvement in Water Quality: The Delaware Estuary," in Allen V. Kneese and Stephen C. Smith, eds., Water Research

(Baltimore: Johns Hopkins Press for Resources for the Future, Inc., 1966), pp. 175-211.

22. Ibid., p. 179.

23. Ibid., p. 206.

24. Ibid., p. 209.

25. See Kneese and Bower (1968), pp. 125-126.

26. The available studies of materials damage and soiling effects are partial, sketchy, and judged to be of limited reliability. See Barrett and Waddell, op. cit.

27. Ronald G. Ridker, Economic Costs of Air Pollution (New York: Praeger Publishers, 1967), Chapter 3, pp. 30-56.

28. Ibid., p. 56.

29. Lester B. Lave, op. cit., and Lester B. Lave and Eugene Seskin, "Air Pollution and Human Health," Science, 169 (1970), pp. 723-733.

30. Lave, op. cit., p. 240.

31. See Lester Lave, in Kneese and Bower (1972), op. cit.

32. Ibid., Chapter 6, pp. 115-140 and Ronald G. Ridker and John A. Henning, "The Determinants of Residential Property Values with Special Reference to Air Pollution," Review of Economics and Statistics, 49, May, 1967, pp. 246-257.

33. Ridker and Henning, op. cit., p. 254.

34. Ridker, op. cit., p. 137.

35. Robert J. Anderson Jr. and Thomas D. Crocker, "Air Pollution and Residential Property Values," Urban Studies, forthcoming; and R.O. Zerbe, Jr., The Economics of Air Pollution: A Cost-Benefit Approach (Toronto: Ontario Department of Public Health, 1969).

36. Thomas D. Crocker, "Urban Air Pollution Damage Functions," presented at the Econometric Society Meetings, New Orleans, December, 1971.

37. A. Myrick Freeman III, "Air Pollution and Property Values: A Methodological Comment," Review of Economics and Statistics, 53, November, 1971, p. 415.

38. Anderson and Crocker, it should be noted, dispute the Freeman criticism. While agreeing that the derivatives of the estimated functions are not market equilibrium price gradients. they claim that the function derivatives do indicate "a change in [bidding price] contingent on bidder income and other characteristics,"

and that there does exist a general equilibrium model that can
make use of the equations to generate equilibrium property
values predicated as alternative configurations of the environment. See "Air Pollution and Property Values: A Reply to
Professor Freeman's comment," Working Paper 14, Department
of Economics, University of California, Riverside, (October 1971).

39. Lave, in Kneese and Bower, op. cit., pp. 235-236.

40. W. F. Edwards, Max R. Langham, and J.C. Headley, "Pesticide
    Residues and Environmental Economics," Natural Resources
    Journal, 10, No 4, pp. 719-741; and Max R. Langham, Joseph
    C. Headley, and W. Frank Edwards, "Agricultural Pesticides:
    Productivity and Externalities," in Kneese and Bower (1972),
    pp. 181-212.

41. Ibid.

42. Langham, Headley, and Edwards, op. cit., pp. 195-196.

43. Edwards, Langham, and Headley, op. cit., pp. 732-733.

44. Ibid., p. 733.

45. Langham, Headley, and Edwards, op. cit., p. 209.

46. A similar approach has been followed in another environmental
    study not reported on in this paper - that by Krutilla and Cicchetti
    on the Hell's Canyon development proposal. (John V. Krutilla,
    Charles J. Cicchetti, A. Myrick Freeman III, and Clifford S.
    Russell, "Observations on the Economics of Irreplaceable Assets,"
    in Kneese and Bower, op. cit.). This study was an evaluation of
    the comparative benefits of using the Hell's Canyon for hydro-
    power as opposed to preserving it for recreation and scientific
    use. Again, much information on technological progress in
    energy production and consumer tastes for recreation was not
    available, and sensitivity analysis was artfully used with impor-
    tant results. It is the (i) policy relatedness, (ii) regional (or
    problem-area) focus, and (iii) use of sensitivity analysis in such
    benefit-cost type studies which has important lessons.

ESTIMATE OF THE ECONOMIC DAMAGE
CAUSED BY POLLUTION:
THE ITALIAN EXPERIENCE

Comments on the ENI-ISVET Research - 1969-70

by

Gilberto Muraro
Professor, Università Degli Studi di Padova
Facoltà di Scienze Statische
Padova, Italy

0.   INTRODUCTION

In 1969 the Italian national oil company ENI conducted a wide study
on the environmental problem in Italy, through the research centre
ISVET (1).   The outcome of the research has been published in ten
ISVET documents, each one devoted to a monographic study.   A summary report has been drawn up by G. Scaiola and the English version
of it was presented at the Stockholm Conference under the title "Economic Costs and Benefits of an Antipollution project in Italy" (2).
Chapter 3. 2 of that report contains a synthesis of the estimate of pollution damage and it is attached as an appendix.

The following notes take as known that synthesis and try to give
some additional illustrations about the approach utilized and about some
methodological tools that seem worthy of further application.

1.   THE MEANING OF THE ENI RESEARCH
IN THE ITALIAN FRAMEWORK

1.1.   The ENI research considered, on a national basis, the main
forms of air and water pollution due to the following sources: automobile emissions, industrial air discharges, domestic heating, civil and
industrial water discharges and the transport by sea of oil products.

In evaluating the abatement costs, the purification efficiencies
were fixed on the basis of the standards existing in Italy (domestic
heating), action taken in foreign countries (automobiles and industries),

the practice commonly followed in Italy for approving treatment plants (domestic waste water), and the limits fixed in other countries (oil products traffic). As for the pollution damage, it was classified, for operative purposes, into six categories that looked remarkably homogeneous as regards the nature of the assets and activities involved, i.e. :

- human health

- cultural assets

- agriculture and zootechnics

- tourism and free time

- drinking and industrial water supply

- ecological assets.

A seventh group covered all the main types of damage not considered in the previous sectors (for example: corrosion of some infrastructures, such as railways and bridges; additional domestic cleaning required, increased electric light consumption, fuel losses due to badly working plants).

For each category of damage, calculations of its amount for a base year (generally 1968) and of its growth up to 1985 (under the hypothesis of a neutral trend) were made. Then, the present value of the damage avoided, thanks to the anti-pollution policy proposed, for which a certain timepath was assumed (3) gave the benefits of the project. The time limit present in the benefit calculations was adopted because it was considered long enough to justify intervention on economic grounds and because the provisional estimates became increasingly imprecise as they went beyond 1985. There is no doubt, however, that the limit leads to an underevaluation of the benefits of the project.

1.2.   It is convenient to say once and for all that the estimates of the damage and of the abatement costs are very preliminary ones, due to the scarcity of significant precedents, to the impossibility of making too widespread enquiries and to the constraint of the national framework into which the estimate must fit.

In judging the research as a whole, one must strictly consider its objective which consisted of ascertaining the convenience of a wide public intervention against pollution; and since, in Italy, such an intervention could be started only by the central authorities on the basis of formal laws, it was necessary to act on a national basis, renouncing the higher accuracy in estimates that could have been reached on a smaller territorial basis (4). Notwithstanding the rough estimates, one must

consider that the objective has been reached, given the relevant superiority of the benefits over the costs related to the elimination of the
main sources of air and water pollution (5).

That does not mean that the research solved the optimization problem in pollution control. Note carefully that the research refers only
to two situations: the existing one and the one forecasted after the implementation of the significant purification efficiencies already mentioned.

Figure 1

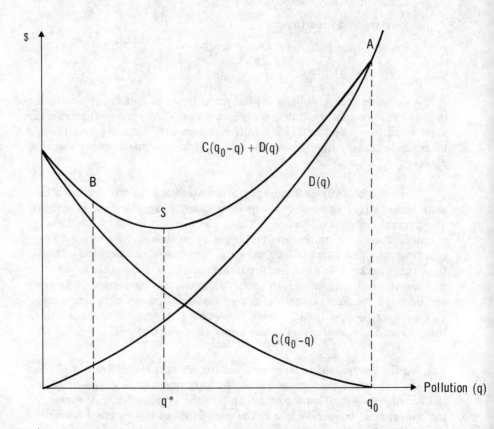

With reference to figure 1, the familiar graphs of environmental
economics are drawn: $C(q_0 - q)$ indicates the total cost of pollution
prevention; $D_{(q)}$ indicates the total damage of residual pollution; $C + D$
indicates the total pollution cost, i. e. the prevention cost plus the
damage cost. One can make a comparison of point A, corresponding
to the existing pollution q_0, with a point like B, finding that the total
pollution cost of B is less than at A. But no estimate was made of the

curves, thus no conclusion can be drawn about the position of B with respect to the optimal point S (where the total pollution cost is at a minimum) (6). This obvious limitation of the research must not be judged too severely when due account is taken of the difficulties of making a marginal analysis. It is worthwhile to recall that authorative students have suggested laying down environmental standards more or less in an arbitrary way - just being sure that in the new position the social welfare has improved but with no ambition to maximize it - and solving an optimization problem only as far as the way to reach those standards is concerned (7). Thus, the ENI-ISVET research may be seen as a first step in environmental policy, directed to demonstrate that it pays off to implement certain reasonable standards.

It must be added that some optimization problems concerning the timing, the territorial differences and the financial procedures of public intervention, have been the content of a successive research performed by ENI-ISVET under the sponsorship of the Planning Office (ISPE) of the Ministry of the Budget and Economic Planning (publication forthcoming).

2.   METHODOLOGICAL STEPS IN ESTIMATING THE POLLUTION DAMAGE

Let us now consider some methodological aspects of the ENI research. We will limit ourselves to commenting on the evaluation of damage in the basic year which presents more interesting questions in methodology: as for the extrapolation of damage up to 1985, the synthesis contained in the Summary Report may be considered sufficient.

2.1   As a foreword it must be said that a complete evaluation of the damage calls for an identification of the following relations :

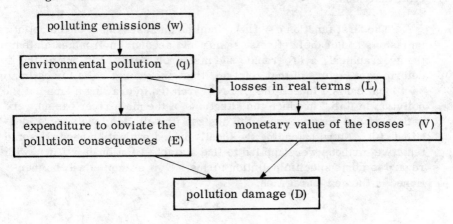

139

When in addition, one wants to find the optimal regulation of waste emissions, then the damage must be calculated in terms of w and compared with the cost of pollution prevention $C_{(w)}$.

Let us imagine that there is no way to obviate the consequences of pollution: one can only bear the pollution damage, that in this instance is represented by V. Then, figure 2 gives a complete picture of the relations involved in the evaluation of an optimal environmental policy: the optimal quantity of residual pollution is q^*, corresponding to w^* (8). Generally, however, there is some way of obviating the consequences of pollution: to build a swimming pool instead of giving up swimming, to restore a monument rather than accepting its deterioration and so on. Defining $E_{(q)}$ to be the expenditure of that nature, the damage function must be seen as the result of an optimizing behaviour on the side of the polluter, who, for each level of pollution, chooses the best combination between $E_{(q)}$ and $V_{(q)}$. That is shown in figure 3, where the marginal value of $D_{(q)}$ is determined through a continuous equalization of the marginal values of V and E (9). Plotting the pollution prevention costs (this time related to q instead of to w) in the same figure, the optimal quantity of pollution in the environment is given by q^* ($q^* = q_1 + q_2$): at that quantity the victims react, eliminating the consequences of a level of pollution equal to q_1 and bearing the welfare loss related to the quantity q_2.

2.2. With respect to the ideal representation of the problem illustrated in figures 2 and 3, the analysis performed by ENI is limited, as already mentioned above, in that it is concerned only with the existing level of pollution, so that only one final level of damage is assessed and is compared with the cost of pollution prevention. However, the different local situations examined give some aspect of a cross-sectional study to the research which in turn allows some understanding of the underlying functions.

The first function $q = f(w)$, implies an assessment of the polluting emissions and of their effects, taking into account environmental features: the geographical, hydrographic and meteorological conditions as the determinant factors of that relation, this, therefore, calls for estimates on a local basis. Indeed the ENI research led to drawing a "map of the pollution in Italy" in which the situations of the main river basins were estimated and the zones with the highest air pollution levels were identified (10). Notwithstanding the locally-based evaluation needed, some tentative methods were applied to find a stable relation $q = f(w)$, with regard to some specific pollution forms. Two examples will be mentioned in the next paragraph.

Figure 2

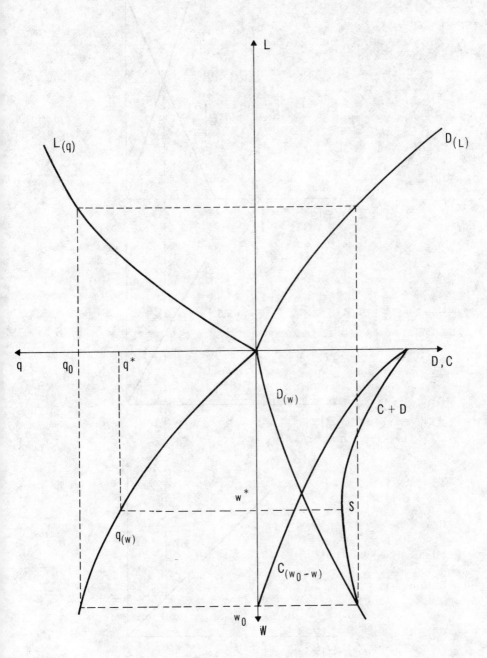

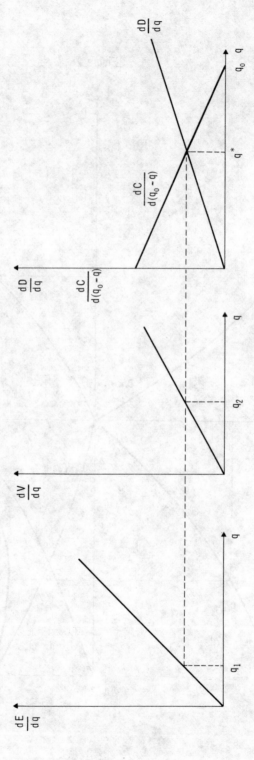

Figure 3

The second function, L = g(q), implies an assessment of the real losses due to pollution: disease, corrosion, soiling, decrease in productivity and so on. This relationship is troublesome to define, both for the scarcity of empirical data and for the difficulty of elaborating the data strictly respecting the ceteris paribus condition: synergism among various forms of pollution as well as among pollution and other natural and social factors, generally complicates the analysis. At the same time, there is a wider possibility of generalization than with other relations; thus, on this item an international effort in methodology promises to be highly productive. In paragraph 4 an example of the estimates made by ENI will be illustrated, namely concerning the effects of pollution on health.

As for the final estimate of economic damage, recourse was made in the ENI research, depending on the items considered, both to the monetary evaluation of the unavoidable welfare losses due to pollution and to the monetary estimate of the less costly means to avoid the consequences of pollution.

Examples of the first criterion are:

i)   the damage to the fishing industry due to sea pollution was calculated on the basis of the decrease in catch;

ii)   the damage to sport fishermen due to pollution of internal waters was calculated on the basis of their "willingness-to-pay" for fishing in non-polluted waters (willingness, ascertained through a wide enquiry).

In the majority of cases, however, the criterion utilized was that of the "best alternative means"; for instance:

i)   for cultural assets, the damage was measured as a percentage of the cost for restoring monuments in open spaces and for air conditioning in closed environments;

ii)   among the ecological assets, the damage suffered by the town parks was calculated as replacement costs;

iii)   for drinking water supply, the pollution damage was calculated as the additional costs (for treatment, for repair of plants, for modification of the supply) necessary to maintain demanded quantitative and qualitative standards.

It is easy to see that recourse to the criterion of the "best alternative mean" narrowed the field of the truly "intangible" effects that are the well known crux of the cost-benefit analysis. Note in addition, that the estimates made with that criterion may be valid also in other countries, since it is legitimate to assume that the techniques to avoid the consequences of pollution are available almost everywhere at roughly similar costs; while as far as the willingness-to-pay to avoid pollution is concerned, the values estimated are heavily influenced both by the level and by the distribution of national income.

3. ESTIMATING THE IMPACT OF POLLUTION EMISSIONS ON THE ENVIRONMENT: TWO EXAMPLES

As already said, the knowledge of the relationship between the environmental pollution and its causes is not strictly required in a simple estimate of pollution damage, but must be known when the target consists of an efficient regulation of the pollution. Now, the most straightforward way to find that relation is through field enquiries; and such a way is necessary when rigorous results must be achieved, given the relevance of the local, geographical, and meteorological conditions. However, it may be convenient to try to find approximate measures of that relation, starting from indirect and already available statistical data: that in order to reduce the cost of the research or to make forecasts in a territorial planning framework. The ENI research offers two interesting examples of such tentative methods.

3. 1. <u>Indirect method of estimating the coastal pollution from domestic and industrial discharges</u>.

For each coastal "Comune" (the smallest local unit in Italy) the following were calculated: the number of residents; the number of workers in each industrial sector; the equivalent population of industrial activity (on the basis of the sectoral coefficients that give the "equivalent population" for one worker), the density of the total population (resident plus equivalent), considering that the sea zone affected by the discharges reached 200 m from the coast. Such a limited zone was taken since the final target consisted of estimating the damage to marine tourism, whose activities take place mainly in that restricted zone. All the data necessary for calculating the density were available from official statistics. The levels of population density thus obtained were correlated to level of marine pollution and these were correlated with the damage through some "synthetic judgements". The damage was calculated in terms of tourism losses, namely as a depreciation of the economic value of the tourist flow for each "Comune" expressed in number of "activity days". Table 1 indicates these "subjective" correlations (11).

Table 1

LEVELS OF POLLUTION	POPULATION DENSITY POPULATION FOR km^2 OF SEA	DEGREES OF DEPRECIATION IN THE VALUE OF THE "ACTIVITY DAYS"
Absent	100	–
Very low	100 - 200	3
Low	200 - 300	5
Medium	300 - 500	8
Medium-high	500 - 1,000	12
High	1,000 - 3,000	16
Very high	3,000 - 5,000	20
Serious	5,000 - 10,000	25
Very serious	10,000	30

3.2. Indirect method of estimating the river basin pollution

A similar method was applied to estimate the pollution of the main Italian river basins expressed in terms of BOD_5. The elementary unit for the evaluation consisted of the river sub-basin, that is a section of the basin fairly homogeneous from the point of view of the hydrological features. For instance, the main Italian river basin, Po, with a size of 67,138.16 km., was divided into 22 sub-basins. For each sub-basin the resident population (except people living in dispersed houses), the industrial equivalent population, and the total population P_t as a sum of the two preceding ones were calculated. P_t was then divided by 54 g (which represents the average daily demand of BOD_5 per person), and the result thus obtained was divided by the m^3 of water that flows, in a day, through the section considered: the last result gave the BOD_5 for that section. The BOD_5 was calculated for four different flows: the average one and the flows related to a time-length of 91, 182, 274 days. Additional corrections were made in order to take into account the length of the river in the stretch considered and the corresponding self-depuration of the water from the points of discharge to the section of the river

to which the calculus of the BOD_5 was referred.   The measures thus obtained
were found to be approximate enough to the real values of pollution
determined in a sample of cases through direct control; so that the
theoretical measures were used to extrapolate the trend of water pollution, under hypothesis of no intervention (12).

4.   ESTIMATING THE REAL EFFECTS OF POLLUTION: AN EXAMPLE

As an example of the intermediary step necessary for estimating
the economic pollution damages and consisting of evaluating the effects
of pollution in real terms, it seems of some interest to state the case
of human health. Before putting a monetary value on the losses due to
premature death, to absence from work and so on, it is necessary :
i) to identify the diseases that are influenced by pollution; ii) to
estimate the incidence of those diseases due to pollution.   In the ENI
research, as for point i), recourse was made to the experts' judgement;
as for point ii), two sources were utilized: again the experts' judgement
and (only for the diseases attributable to air pollution) a statistical calculation (13).   This statistical calculation was made as follows:

(a)   National insurance data (INAM) for diseases of the respiratory
      system attributable to air pollution were recalculated by occu-
      pational categories, i.e. , they were disaggregated by the
      economic sectors;

(b)   For each category the percentage of the cases of disease
      attributable to air pollution over the total respiratory diseases
      for the same category was calculated: the rank of the per-
      centages resulting was strictly associated with the rank of
      air pollution levels for the various types of work;

(c)   For each disease attributable to air pollution, three groups of
      working categories were formed - respectively with high,
      average and low frequency (a, b, c) of the disease considered -
      calculating the frequency as the ratio between the number of
      cases of illness and the number of workers in the group;

(d)   For each disease attributable to air pollution, the ratios between
      the high and the low frequency and between the average and low
      frequency (a/c, b/c) were taken as an estimate of the higher
      risk due to pollution;

(e)   In extending the results thus obtained for the working groups to
      the whole population, the smaller ratio b/c was taken, as other

Table 2.   DISEASES ASSOCIATED WITH POLLUTION
AND PERCENTAGES ATTRIBUTED TO IT

DISEASES	% (EXPERTS)	% (STATISTICS)
Diseases associated with air pollution:		
Tumours of the respiratory system	10	10
Cancer of the larynx		
Cancer of the trachea, bronchi, lungs (not specified as secondary)		
Other malignant tumours		
Asthma (non allergic)	10	5
Congestive cardiac insufficiency	10	3
Acute infections of the upper respiratory passages (except acute tonsillitis)	10	Not considered
Acute broncho-pneumonias	15	12

Influenza with pneumonia or
    broncho-pneumonia
    lobar pneumonia		

broncho-pneumonia		

atypical primary pneumonia and
    other or non-specified types of
    pneumonia
    acute or sub-acute bronchitis and
    non-classified bronchitis		

Chronic bronchitis	20	19
Abscess of the lung	10	32
Congestion and hypostasis of the lung ..	5	7
Other diseases of the respiratory system	10	31
Diseases associated with water pollution:		
Typhoid fever	75	
Paratyphoid fevers and other salmonellae- induced diseases	75	Not considered
Amoebiasis	5	
Infectious hepatitis	25	
Gastroenteritis and colitis (from 29th day of life onwards)	20	

unfavourable factors may act together with pollution in the closed environment of a factory. The percentages imputed to pollution are indicated in Table 2. They were calculated for each disease as stated above: $(b/c - 1) \cdot 100$ (14).

Considering the two evaluations, the statistical one just described and the one due to the experts' judgement, some considerable difference exists for some specific diseases. However, on the whole the average imputed percentages - weighting the single percentages by the number of days absent for an illness - were quite close: 14.6% estimated by the experts and 17.4% estimated from the statistical calculation.

An intermediate percentage of 16% was adopted for estimating the economic damage.

1. The ISVET section for environmental studies is presently incorporated in TECNECO, a new research centre belonging to the ENI group.

2. This publication will be quoted in the following pages as Summary Report.

3. The time-sequence of investments was defined under a hypothesis of early approval of the anti-pollution laws, but allowing for some delay in building purification plants because of the technical time requirement for planning and building equipment, the necessity of implementing a programme of public works and infrastructures to include the installation of pollution control equipment, etc. The assumed length of time necessary for adapting pollution sources differed for the various sectors, with a minimum of one year for domestic heating and marine oil traffic to a maximum of ten years for domestic waste water. (See Summary Report, pp. 198-205).

4. Note also that the nation-wide effort for the analysis of environmental problems had the additional advantage of acting as a "catalyst" in regard to the still scarce resources devoted to environmental studies in Italy: students of various disciplines and of various regions were brought together, with the result that both specialized and inter-disciplinary researchers were highly stimulated.

5. For the period 1970-1985 and adopting a discount rate of 4%, the present values of the costs and of the benefits resulted in the following estimates (under minimum-maximum hypotheses: values in 1968 lire): 7,850-9,000 billion, for the costs; and 8,000-12,000 billion for the benefits. The benefit-cost ratio between the average values is 1.20; and it remains positive (1.12) at a discount

rate of 8%. Given the systematic under-evaluation of the benefits
- because of the limited period considered and of the lack of some
benefit evaluation in the various sectors - and the full estimation
of the costs, the economic expedience of the project seems well-
based. (See Summary Report, page 3).

6. This is true for the research as a whole; but in some instances
the cross-sectional nature of the study, dealing with different
local situations, allows an approximate estimate damage function.

7. See W. J. Baumol and W. E. Oates, "The Use of Standards and
Prices for the Protection of the Environment", The Swedish
Journal of Economics, 73(1), March 1971; A. D. Scott, "The
Economics of the International Transmission of Pollution",
OECD-AEU/ENV/71.8.

8. The functions plotted in the S-E quadrant of figure 2 are similar
to those in figure 1, but referred to w instead of to q.

9. $E_{(q)}$ must also be seen as the result of the optimal combinations
of the possible means to cope with pollution.

10. See Summary Report, pages 93-95 and 101-102. See amplius
in ISVET, Document No. 27 (L'inquinamento atmosferico in
Italia) and No. 27 bis (Inquinamento e risorse idriche)

11. See ISVET, Document No. 31 (Inquinamento, turismo e tempo
libero), pp. 83-93.

12. See ISVET, Document No. 32, op. cit., pp. 24-28.

13. See ISVET, Document No. 28 (Inquinamento e salute umana),
pp. 47-63.

14. Another example of the relationship between pollution and real
losses may be found in the Summary Report with regard to cultural
assets (pp. 112-114). On the basis of experts' judgement, "Pollution imputed percentages of the total damage to cultural assets,
according to the component materials" were calculated.

Appendix

Abstract from the summary report of ENI

ECONOMIC COSTS AND BENEFITS
OF AN ANTIPOLLUTION PROJECT IN ITALY

Stockholm Conference, June 1972

3.2. THE POLLUTED SECTORS: ESTIMATE
OF THE ECONOMIC DAMAGES DONE BY POLLUTION

We estimated the economic damages done by pollution with reference to the seven specific survey sectors, into which we divided the possible damages indicated by previous literature, research on the subject and by empirical experience, as possibly connected with the forms of pollution considered (see para. 2.2. and para. 1.4.).

This classification, made for operative purposes, gave six sectors that are remarkably homogeneous as regards the nature of the assets and activities involved (i.e. human health, cultural assets, agriculture and zootechnics, tourism and free time, the drinking and industrial water supply, and ecological assets); the seventh covered all the main types of damage not considered in the previous sectors.

ISVET set up seven working groups and asked each of them to estimate economic damages in one of these sectors. The groups were formed by external collaborators, usually technicians and experts specialized in the specific survey field, and ISVET research workers, generally economists and statisticians; the composition of the groups was therefore of an interdisciplinary type.

A central ISVET research group coordinated the sectorial surveys, particularly the unitary approach of the monographs drawn up, and discussed the conclusions with external experts to check their reliability.

151

Given the diversity of the problems to be examined, the methodologies and survey instruments used by the sectorial groups to evaluate the economic damages done by pollution varied greatly from case to case, although obviously all the criteria used conformed to the technical rules of cost-benefit analysis (120). Among other things, the groups adopted methodologies suggested in similar sample surveys made abroad; direct fact-finding through inspections and interviews by the research workers; demoscopic enquiries; investigations among operators or local governments through postal questionnaires; cross checking of the estimates and opinions of privileged witnesses; comparisons with data from foreign research adapted to Italian situations, and so forth. As a background to the sectorial estimates we drew an "air polluting effluents map", and a "map of the equivalent population density in the principal Italian water basins" (121), using the results to make forecasts up to 1985.

Given the number and complexity of the problems to be analyzed none of the benefits estimates in the different sectors served to establish the whole extent of the damage presumably caused by pollution. Although to a different degree for each sector, in practice these estimates are a minimum evaluation of the real damage, not only because of the cautious criteria adopted, but above all because the quantification usually included only the chief forms - and sometimes not even all of those - taken by the damage in the different sectors surveyed (122).

On the whole, the size of the economic benefits that would result from the elimination of the air and water pollution forms in the sectors examined should be as follows (figures in billion lire 1968):

	1970	1975	1980	1985
Minimum hypothesis	400	569	790	1 120
Maximum hypothesis	578	847	1 182	1 615

The significance of these values must be interpreted in the light of the previous considerations: they are minimum levels, which further evaluations and quantifications intended to come nearer the real scale of the damage might raise considerably. Above all, our figures indicate only the "direct" or primary benefits of depollution (122).

3.2.1. <u>Human Health</u> (123)

In cost-benefit analysis human health benefits are a classic example of "intangibles" not subject to economic evaluation. The problem of estimating economic damage is further complicated by our still insufficient knowledge of the relations existing between the spread of illnesses associable with pollution, and the presence and intensity of the latter; and as regards Italy the lack of data and statistics on the subject.

The working group therefore adopted a theoretical and methodological approach suggested by one of the very few existing researches on the subject, done by Ridker for the USA, and utilized official data as best it could.

3.2.1.1. <u>Defining the Field of Enquiry.</u> According to research made so far on the argument, the main economic damages due to the harmful effects of air and water pollution on human health may be classified as follows:

a. employees' wage losses and less domestic work in the home by housewives, due to premature death caused by illnesses correlated to pollution;

b. employees' lost income, due to absence from work on account of illnesses correlated to pollution;

c. loss of domestic work by housewives, due to illnesses correlatable to pollution;

d. increased expenditure for medical, ambulatorial, and pharmaceutical treatment and hospitalization caused by illnesses correlated to pollution;

e. prevention expenses;

f. less efficiency at work due to indisposition, ailments and nervous conditions not amounting to real illnesses, or due to the prodromic symptoms and after-effects of illnesses correlated to pollution.

For the present estimate we considered the first four damage categories, but omitted e. and f. as not expressible in economic terms. In practice we narrowed the field of enquiry to the unhealthy effects identifiable with real, acute or chronic diseases, although (according to the W.H.O. definition) the concept of human health signifies not only the absence of diseases or infirmity but "a state of complete physical, mental and social well-being". We had to set this limit, of course,

153

because of the necessity of basing the enquiry on available epidemiological data.

Our omission of pre-clinical or sub-clinical conditions means that the total damage shown by the survey is considerably underestimated (124).

3.2.1.2. <u>Disease Associated with Pollution.</u> Some pollutants in the air (ash, fuel residues, mineral dust, sulphur compounds, nitrogen oxides, carbon monoxides, hydrocarbons, aldehydes, lead compounds, etc.) and in water (toxic or infective pollutants such as chromium, fluorine and arsenic compounds) are certainly harmful to human health in the short or long run.

The nature and extent of their harmful effects, in particular the long-term ones, have not yet been sufficiently defined on the technical and epidemiological plane by adequate studies and surveys. However, there are a number of diseases for which a cause-effect relation with air and water pollution is fairly well certified, and which can therefore be defined as diseases "associable" or correlatable to it.

a.   The diseases associable with air pollution are :

    a. 1   cancer of the larynx;

    a. 2   cancer of the trachea, bronchi, and lungs, not specified as secondary;

    a. 3   other malignant tumours of the respiratory apparatus;

    a. 4   asthma (non allergic);

    a. 5   congestive cardiac insufficiency;

    a. 6   acute infections of the upper respiratory passages (except acute tonsillitis);

    a. 7   influenza with pneumonia or bronco-pneumonia;

    a. 8   lobar pneumonia;

    a. 9   bronco-pneumonia;

    a. 10 atypical primary pneumonia and other or non-specified types of pneumonia;

    a. 11 acute or sub-acute bronchitis and non-classified bronchitis;

    a. 12 chronic bronchitis;

    a. 13 abscess of the lung;

    a. 14 congestion and hypostasis of the lung;

    a. 15 other diseases of the respiratory system.

b.   The diseases associable with water pollution are:

    b. 1   typhoid fever;

    b. 2   paratyphoid fevers and other salmonellae-induced diseases;

    b. 3   amoebiasis;

    b. 4   infectious hepatitis

    b. 5   gastroenteritis and colitis (from the 29th day of life onwards);

    b. 6   nutritional illnesses of babies in their first year.

It is strongly suspected that air pollution causes some diseases not included in the previous list (such as cancer of the stomach, some forms of anaemia, some modifications of bodily growth, etc.). We did not include these in the study, however, because there is not enough scientific and epidemiological evidence that they are associated with pollution.

Some cases of acute or chronic intoxication are undoubtedly caused by chemical substances of industrial or agricultural origin, such as chromium, arsenic, DDT, anti-parasites and hydrocarbons in drinking water. Nor did we consider the increasingly frequent symptoms of intoxication in the survey, as they are not definite diseases and are often difficult to diagnose, especially if they are chronic.

These omissions undoubtedly lowered our overall economic damage estimate.

3. 2. 1. 3.   The Methodology adopted.   Following, with suitable modifications, the procedures suggested in a survey by R. Ridker (125), we estimated the economic damages by calculating the costs connected with the first four economic damage categories listed in para. 3. 2. 1. 1.

We calculated the cost due to premature deaths by capitalizing the present value of the presumable future incomes of workers who died from diseases associable with pollution and considering their survival probability at the age of death.

We followed a similar procedure for calculating the cost of the premature deaths of housewives, substituting an estimated value of services rendered for wages.

To calculate the cost of sick leave, we started by evaluating the days off for illnesses associated with pollution for the whole working population, a well as housewives' days in bed (for the same diseases). To the total days lost we applied wage estimates varying according to the economic activity sectors and value estimates of the domestic services performed, varying according to age and sex.

155

We estimated the cost of treatment connected with the diseases considered by extrapolating for all the resident population, INAM data on its total health expenditure on general and specialized medical treatment, casualties' and outpatients' treatment and medicines, as well as hospitalization expenses per patient.

To evaluate the quota of economic damage imputable to pollution, we applied an incidence percentage to each of these cost categories. Two different estimates, on different lines, were made of the imputability share: the first evaluation of individual associable diseases, made by a group of health experts, was based on current scientific and epidemiological knowledge and the results of some Italian and foreign surveys; and the second evaluation (of air pollution effects only) was based on a statistical procedure applied to INAM data on illness frequencies for particular nosological categories.

In spite of considerable differences for some of the diseases considered, the two evaluations tallied on the whole: the average imputability percentages (for <u>all</u> associable diseases) were quite close (14.6% and 17.4%), and we adopted the intermediate percentage of 16%.

3.2.1.4.   The Results of the 1966 Estimate.   Using this methodology, we evaluated the economic damages imputable to the effects of pollution on human health in 1966 at 84.2 billion lire.

In particular the economic costs calculated for each damage category were as follows (data in million lire):

	LIT.
Costs for workers' premature deaths	19,258
Costs for housewives' premature deaths	2,980
Loss of wages through illness	20,100
Loss of housewives' working time through illness	8,330
Treatment expenses	33,563
Total cost	84,231

The estimated damage (84.2 billion lire), though impressive, must certainly be considered lower than the real damage, because (as we have said) we had to leave out the damages resulting from physical and psychical distress, diseases not definitely linked with pollution, and ailments not constituting real diseases, as well as prevention and treatment expenses paid by private persons, etc., owing to the difficulty of putting a reasonable monetary value on them.

It is interesting to note the similarity of our estimates with those made by Ridker for the United States in 1958, with reference to air pollution only. In fact, the pro capite damage for the United States was equal to 1,350 lire, and for Italy (1966) 1,364 lire.

3.2.1.5. <u>Damage forecasts for 1985</u>. Finally, we tried to forecast the possible future damage trend, assuming the non-elimination and unchecked growth of pollution. Such a forecast is fraught with difficulties, especially as it is impossible to foresee the consequences of the progressive accumulation in human organisms of the effects of long periods of exposure to pollution.

We also had to formulate a series of hypotheses, often considerably simplified, on numerous parameters influencing future damage, such as population increase, the number of deaths, average <u>pro capite</u> income, the probability of the damaged persons belonging to the labour force, the average value of housewives' services, the rise in health expenses per patient and so on. We also assumed that the portion to impute to pollution would rise gradually from 16 to 20% (the value estimated by Ridker for the USA in 1958) until 1985 (126).

The entirely approximate extent of the damage, according to these forecasts, is 102 billion lire in 1968, 130 in 1970, 200 in 1975, 309 in 1980 and 490 in 1985.

3.2.2. <u>Cultural Assets</u> (127)

The estimate of the economic damage done by pollution to cultural assets in Italy proved particularly arduous, due both to the lack of any previous study on the subject in Italy or abroad, and the difficulty of treating cultural assets in economic terms.

It was impossible to assess the value of the assets damaged by pollution and consequently to quantify the relative economic damage. We thought that an indirect measurement of the benefits that would result in this sector from pollution elimination might be given (at least as a minimum level) by the difference between the expenditure theoretically necessary for the restoration and preventive conservation of cultural assets in the present pollution situation, and the (smaller) expenditure necessary in a hypothetical situation of non-pollution.

We therefore used a criterion similar to the "best alternative mean" suggested in cost-benefit analysis as a technique for the (indirect) monetary evaluation of intangible benefits. We were able to apply it, in practice thanks to the estimates made in the past by the Parliamentary Commission of Enquiry for the protection and improvement of cultural assets (the "Franceschini Commission" of 1964).

3.2.2.1. Delimiting the Field of Enquiry. To define the cultural heritage, we adopted the Franceschini Commission's suggested definition, according to which it includes all assets concerning "sociology, history, art, environment and landscape, records and books, and any other material evidence of civilization".

We left environmental and landscape assets out of our estimate, as they have been dealt with in other monographic studies (on tourism, free time and ecological assets).

We divided the cultural assets analyzed into four big categories: archaeological assets, medieval and modern works of art, monuments, books and records.

3.2.2.2. The Effects of Pollution on Cultural Assets. The damage pollution does to cultural assets varies with the intensity and nature of the pollutants, and the type of material affected.

As regards pollution intensity, we took the present average national situation as a reference basis. The pollutants that are obviously the most important in this framework are both "natural" air pollutants (sulphydric acid, carbon dioxide and natural aerosols) and "artificial" air pollutants (carbon monoxide, nitrogen oxides, artificial aerosols and ammonia, sulphurous anhydrides and ozone). We did not consider the effects of water pollutants.

The principal materials constituting cultural assets subject to the action of these pollutants are stone, stuccoes, mosaics, plasters, mortars, wall stones, cellulose materials, leather, parchment, painted canvases, painted tableaux and metals.

Existing information on the effects of the various pollutants (128) enabled a panel of experts to suggest an estimated pollution imputability percentage for the damage to (or total deterioration of) the different materials constituting cultural assets, as a result of natural and artificial pollutants (see table 3.2.2.2.a.).

3.2.2.3. The Methodology Adopted. To overcome the difficulties involved in directly defining the economic value of cultural assets, we assumed that the restoration and preventive conservation expenses necessary to keep the deterioration of the cultural heritage within reasonable limits (roughly corresponding to those of inevitable natural aging) are at least equal to the damage that might be done in the absence of this expenditure, and which it is therefore intended to avoid.

Table 3.2.2.2.a. POLLUTION IMPUTABILITY PERCENTAGES OF THE TOTAL DAMAGE TO CULTURAL ASSETS, ACCORDING TO THE COMPONENT MATERIALS

MATERIALS	ENVIRONMENT	
	INTERNAL	EXTERNAL
Stone	15%	50%
Wall painting	40%	
Canvas painting	40%	
Wood painting	5%	
Metals	20%	80%
Leather	50%	
Parchment	–	
Paper	20%	
Fabrics	40%	
Stuccoes, plasters, building materials	40%	60%
Mosaics	10%	20%

On the basis of this assumption we proceeded, with the help of experts (starting with the Franceschini Commission's suggestions for the protection and improvement of cultural assets), to estimate an expense budget theoretically needed by the Public Administration to implement an adequate programme for the restoration and preventive conservation of archaeological remains, medieval and modern works of art, monuments, records and books.

This estimate concerning the country's present situation (1968) and therefore the present degree of air pollution, is considerably higher than the actual expenditure (about 93 billion as against 30), and therefore highlights the present lack of public action in this section, and the consequently considerable damage to cultural assets each year.

Subsequently, the Antiques and Fine Arts Council surveyed a sample of various types of restoration by the Superintendencies of Antiques and Fine Arts. An analysis of the technical reports illustrating the cost evaluation of the restoration projects enables us to estimate separately for archaeological remains, monuments and medieval and modern works of art the composition of the total restoration expenditure per type of material used.

We used this structure to re-elaborate the expenditure budget theoretically necessary for an adequate protection of Italy's cultural assets (on the basis of the Franceschini Commission's data per expenditure heading), according to the different types of material. Finally we applied the different pollution incidence percentages for the various types of material to this volume of theoretical expenses.

To this amount we added the additional expense - due to pollution - necessary to preserve books and records, for which conditioning measures are planned, estimating their pollution imputability percentages in this case too.

Finally, we indirectly estimated the smaller expenditure needed for adequately protecting cultural assets in a hypothetical situation of non-pollution in Italy, compared with that theoretically necessary in the present situation.

3.2.2.4.   The Results of the Present (1968) Damage Estimate.   Using this methodology we obtained a minimum estimate of the economic damage done by pollution in 1968 of at least 36 billion lire, including 27 related to archaeological remains, monuments and medieval and modern works of art and 9 to museums, art galleries, libraries, archives and churches. We certainly underestimated the damage, in all probability to a considerable extent.

The basic assumption that the economic damage caused by pollution may be expressed through the cost of prevention and conservation aimed at avoiding it is quite insufficient, as the real damage would certainly be much higher (actually, with the definitive deterioration of the asset, the damage often becomes inestimable).

Secondly, the volume of theoretically necessary expenses proposed by the Franceschini Commission, (on which we based our evaluation of the expense budget necessary for an adequate conservation of Italy's cultural assets), must be considered as a minimum, as it was commensurate with the contingent possibilities of the State budget.

3. 2. 2. 5.   Attempted Estimate of the Possible Damage Increase in
1985.   Finally, we tried to forecast the possible increase in pollution-
induced economic damage to cultural assets until 1985, assuming that
pollution grows unchecked, i. e. that no action is taken to eliminate it.

We attempted this forecast using the methodology adopted for
estimating the damage in 1968. We also had to introduce some evaluations regarding not only the possible increase rate of air pollution in
the absence of any depuration, but the quantitative and qualitative increase of cultural assets, the growing social awareness of the cultural
value of artistic and historical assets, the passage to a policy of
prevention, and the increase of public expenditure in the field of social
action.

In short, the research group decided it could suggest a forecast of
possible future damage to cultural assets, in the theoretical hypothesis
mentioned, of 42-43 billion lire in 1970, 62-67 in 1975, 91-103 in 1980
and 134-158 in 1985 (still in 1968 lire).

3. 2. 3.   Agriculture and Zootechnics (129)

On the theoretical and conceptual plane, the evaluation of the
economic damage done by pollution in the sector of agriculture and
zootechnics presents relatively less complex problems than the other
sectors examined in the present survey.

Although the state of scientific knowledge and studies on the action
mechanisms of various pollutants on land, crops and livestock is still
limited and insufficient, it is possible to draw quite a clear distinction
between emerging damage, that would occur in all cases in which the
relation between pollutants and crops and/or livestock were translated
into immediate and intangible negative effects on their productive capacity; and potential damage, which would occur if these effects did not
appear immediately, but gradually, with the extension and accumulation
of the alterations produced by the action of pollutants on soil characteristics and agronomic processes, and consequently on the physiological functions of plants and animals .

Emerging damage may take three different forms, according to
whether the action of the pollutants has not brought about changes in
the crop arrangements and technical procedures previously used (cul-
tivation methods, the use of fertilizers, anti-parasite treatments, land
settlements, drainage, etc.); or whether this change has become necessary; or, finally, when the pollution of the irrigation waters reaches
such a point as to make farming impossible.

161

a. In the first case, the damage consists in the reduction of income due to the quantitative drop and/or qualitative deterioration of the product; or in the bigger current expenses and amortisation quotas of the capital necessary to keep the quality and quantity of the production up to the desired standards;

b. in the second case, when the harmful effects of pollution entail an alteration of crop arrangements and considerable changes in production organization - from the use of technical means, to crop practices and so on - the assessment of the emerging economic damage may be made by considering both the adaptation and re-conversion costs, and the profitability of the farm before and after pollution occurred;

c. in the third case, when the harmful effects of pollution become so serious as to prevent any form of farming, the damage is represented by the total loss of agricultural income and the disinvestment costs of the capital employed.

In any case market prices may be taken as a good yardstick for measuring the different types of damage. Usually the farm can realize these prices by selling the produce concerned; sometimes, in the case of crops to be used for internal farm transformation, it seemed more correct to apply the purchase price to the produce differences obtained.

3.2.3.1. Defining the Field of Enquiry. As the sources of water pollution abound mainly in the plains, we limited the survey to the irrigation areas in the plains. The territory considered, where the richest crops are concentrated and the highest unitary values of gross sellable produce are attained, represents about 12% of the total agrarian area (2,620,000 hectares) and 50% of gross national sellable produce (2,850 billion lire).

Further restrictions of the analysis were that we treated the effects of water pollution only, leaving out air pollution (due to the shortage of time and enquiry methods, and our assumption that the damage in this sector is small, at least in Italy), and assessed only the emerging damages, in the impossibility of proposing reasonable estimates for the potential ones.

In the agricultural and zootechnical sector too, therefore, our suggested economic damage estimate must certainly be considered as an approximate figure lower than the real amount.

3.2.3.2. Methodology Adopted. Although we limited the research field to 2,620,000 hectares of farmland, it was too large for us to be

162

able to make a detailed, direct survey of the damage all over the territory concerned with the time and means available.

We therefore made the survey at two complementary levels:

a. through some detailed analyses in sample zones which we found particularly significant, both on account of the presence and signs of water pollution, and the characteristics of the local agricultural structure. We made these field studies in seven zones (two in the Piedmontese irrigated plain, two in the Lombard irrigated plain, two in the Tuscan plain and one in the Agro Pontino), which we considered representative of wider territories. Our aim was to discover the relations between pollution levels and the emerging damage to crops and livestock. On the basis of the results, we drew up a scale of unitary values of the damage (in terms of net product) suffered by the main crops (130) and by livestock, in relation to pollution intensity;

b. by means of a subsequent general reconnaissance of the irrigated plain area, made in collaboration with the National Land Improvement Association and the CNR Water Research Section. We collected data through special questionnaires sent to the different Land-reclamation Syndicates, on the sources, nature and intensity of pollution, agricultural techniques, crops and organization, and the entity of any crop and livestock damages in the different localities. The picture that emerged from this general fact-finding survey, combined with specific indications given by the above-mentioned sample investigations, enabled us to formulate an estimate of the economic damages for the whole area considered.

3.2.3.3. The Results of the 1968 Estimate. The above-mentioned investigations enabled us to put forward an emerging economic damage estimate of 12/13 billion lire per year in terms of net product (1968). This figure represents about 19% of the value of the net produce from the area, which was appreciably affected by pollution (about 185,000 hectares, or 7% of the total considered), and corresponds to average values per polluted hectare of about 68,000 lire.

Nearly all the territory affected by pollution is in Northern Italy (95% of the territorial area), especially in the North-West (62%); this is understandable, considering the incidence of industrialization and urbanization phenomena localized there. In Central Italy there is a fair amount of pollution in about 4,000 hectares (forage, maize, vegetables), or 3% of the total irrigated plain area.

Of the damaged area, little less than half seemed to be subject to "medium" pollution, about 30% to "low" pollution and 23/24% to "high" pollution, distributed with considerable variation among the different crops.

In assessing the size of the proposed estimate (12/13 billion per year), it is useful to remember that this evaluation represents only a part, and presumably not the biggest part, of the total economic damage in agriculture. This is because of the omission of air pollution, the restriction of the territory surveyed, and the exclusion of potential damage, not to mention the cautious criteria followed in quantification.

3. 2. 3. 4.   Hypotheses on the Growth of Damage by 1985.   If we try to forecast, even very roughly, the possible future growth of the economic damage resulting from water pollution in agriculture (assuming the absence of any depuration) we come up against understandable difficulties. These include the necessity to put forward hypotheses as to the development of crop policies, the contents of agrarian policies and the use of new technologies.

Perhaps the only possible forecast is the size of the irrigated plain areas, which by 1985 should be about 3. 4 million hectares, compared with 2. 62 hectares now, expanding mainly in Southern Italy and the islands, which will probably be hardly affected by pollution.

Therefore, we forecast the possible level of future damage, taking as our basic hypothesis (a very restrictive and cautious one) conditions substantially the same as the present ones as regards crop uses, the technological level and therefore agricultural productivity and the amount of income produced.

Assuming that the new irrigated areas will be mainly in Southern Italy, pollution will continue to affect areas in Northern Italy only, where it is mainly localized today. In the great Northern plain, the industrial and urban expansion forecasts (in terms of population equivalent and resident population per area unit), suggest that there will be a much greater use of water, and therefore much greater water-polluting discharges.

To simplify matters, we may propose two hypotheses :

a.   the concentration of industrial and urban development in the zones where it is already present.

In this case the area affected by pollution might go up to about 250,000 hectares by 1985, with a unitary average damage value (for crops and livestock) of about 150,000 lire per hectare. At the same time, the effects of today's potential damage will appear, so that we can make a cautions average estimate of not less than

50,000 lire per hectare for 45% of the area with "medium" pollution intensity, and 80/100,000 lire per hectare for 25% of the area with "high" intensity.

On the whole, we might reach a total damage estimate of about 45 billion lire (in 1968 prices), with an average incidence of about 185,000 lire per hectare. If the damage rose above this level, in many cases there would be no economic expedience in farming;

b. industrial and urban development in areas that are different from the present ones, but have the same settlement density levels.

In this case the area affected by pollution might go up to 400,000 hectares. Considering that for this area the pollution intensity would not rise above present levels, that the distribution of the area in the various intensity degrees would remain unchanged, and that the arrangements adopted in the new polluted area would not differ substantially from those in the zones polluted today, the damage value in 1985 should be about 35 billion lire, including the potential damages that would appear, with a unitary incidence of about 90,000 lire per hectare.

It is superfluous to mention the cautious estimation criteria adopted for formulating these 1968-1985 forecasts.

Forecasts for the intermediate years may be worked out, utilizing as the only parameter the forecasts on the growth of population equivalent and resident population per area unit, as shown in table 3.2.3.4a.

Table 3.2.3.4 a. SUGGESTED FORECAST OF THE
FUTURE ECONOMIC DAMAGES THAT MAY BE
CAUSED BY WATER POLLUTION TO FARMING

	HYPOTHESIS a.		HYPOTHESIS b.	
	AREA (000 ha.)	VALUE (1968 BILLION LIRE)	AREA (000 ha.)	VALUE (1968 BILLION LIRE)
1970	180	13.5	195	13.0
1975	182	18.0	245	17.0
1980	205	30.0	320	25.0
1985	250	46.0	400	35.0

3.2.4.   Tourism and Free Time (131)

The problem of tourism and free time is hard to deal with using the traditional patterns of economic analysis.

As regards both production and recreational services and their consumption (the demand for these services), remarkable difficulties in economic measurement arise, because the two aspects of the problem are strictly interdependent and conditioned by income distribution, consumer behaviour models and collective welfare value judgements.

As an objective reference framework, the survey therefore took present supply of tourist and free-time services, the demand for these services by their users, the prices deriving from them at the market level, and so on. When evaluating the incidence of pollution on tourist and recreational activities, we used subjective judgements to attribute an "account price" to the smaller enjoyment/welfare connected with the fruition of these activities in polluted surroundings, or lower quantitative fruition levels (132).

3.2.4.2.   The Methodology Adopted. The procedures for quantifying these economic damages varied considerably in the different sectors examined.

Seaside Tourism.   An examination of the studies and researches on the situation of the Italian coasts, supplemented by a sample survey ISVET made by sending postal questionnaires to the Provincial Tourist Boards, the Local Residence Corporations and bathing establishments, revealed very high pollution levels all along the coasts of Liguria, Veneto and Romagna, and in short coastal stretches in Tuscany (Leghorn, Piombino, Portoferraio, Massa Carrara and Viareggio), Latium (Fregene, Fiumicino and Ostia), Campania (the mouth of the Volturno, the Gulf of Naples and the coastal waters of Salerno) and the Marches (from Ancona to Pesaro).

In Southern Italy and the islands, on the other hand, conditions were good on the whole, except in some zones with quite serious pollution: in Reggio Calabria, on the Calabrian coast, at Taranto, Lecce, Otranto, Gallipoli and Brindisi on the Apulian coast; Messina, Catania and Syracuse in Sicily and Cagliari and in the Gulf of Asinara in Sardinia.

The examination of the various types of damage to seaside tourism resulting from this situation, apart from the damage to human health (especially through bacterial sewage pollution) showed:

a.   psychic costs caused mainly by naphta and the excessive growth of algae due to the eutrophization and consequent putrefaction of sewage;

b. cleaning costs borne by district councils, bathing establishments and hotels in the attempt to restore the environment as far as possible to its original state;

c. "substitution" costs, as tourist operators (hotels, bathing establishments, etc.) tend to compensate for the decline of the natural environment with artificial equipment;

d. costs due to the destruction of natural tourist resources, and therefore of tourist income, when pollution reaches or approaches the tolerance limit;

e. development losses for the most polluted coastal stretches, in relation to their decreased ability to attract tourists.

We tried to make partial evaluations of some of these costs, especially the expenses incurred in cleaning beaches to remove naphta and other refuse.

For the purposes of quantifying the economic damage, we had to adopt a suitable methodology for the systematic collection of pollution data and our assessment of the damages. In this connection we referred exclusively to costs (a.), for the smaller enjoyment derived from tourist activities in polluted resorts.

We then:

- found the pollution level of all the coastal municipalities in 1968 (with an attempted forecast up to 1985) by elaborating data on the resident population and equivalent industrial population density, the sea area used for bathing in the individual municipalities;

- evaluated the annual supply capacity of "activity days" (recreational bathing days) of these municipalities in 1968 and for all the successive years considered, on the basis of coastal bathing - strip utilization standards;

- translated this supply capacity into monetary terms, attributing to the activity days values obtained through suitable market price corrections (133).

- determined a ratio scale between pollution levels and the degree of depreciation in the economic value attributed to the usable (or used) activity day. This correlation, based partly on the findings of a special demoscopic sample survey, is intended to give a synthetic evaluation (perhaps on the low side) of the various categories of damages connected with pollution, through a "smaller enjoyment" index.

167

We formulated the pollution smaller enjoyment correlation scale in such a way as to keep the inevitable degree of arbitrariness connected with this estimate within strict limits. In fact, very low degrees of depreciation in the economic value of the activity days, from a minimum of 3% to a maximum of 30%, correspond to very big variations in the pollution levels - based on density data for population units from below 100 to over 10,000 per km2 of sea. This certainly gave a lower-than-real economic damage estimate (134).

Lakeside Tourism. An ISVET survey made near the five major lakes of Northern Italy revealed serious pollution in Lakes Garda, Maggiore, Como, Iseo and Orta.

Once again we made this survey by sending questionnaires to the Local Tourist Boards, hotels and camping sites, aimed at establishing not only the whereabouts of pollution phenomena and their growth in time, but the decreases they cause in the tourist flow. Suitable elaborations of the replies received enabled us to reconstruct the 1968 decrease expressed as fewer potential activity days for the whole area; and we attributed a suitable value to the lost activity days to estimate the economic damage to lakeside tourism in 1968. We extended this evaluation for successive years until 1985, taking, as a reference parameter, the rate of pollution growth in the water basins where these lakes are situated, according to the forecast (in terms of the resident or equivalent population growth rate) made in another part of the present survey (135).

Free Time. The working group examined the problems of urban free time in relation to air pollution, and also dealt with some methodological questions on the evaluation of damage to "open space" recreational activities, in terms of time and space losses, and of the willingness to pay a surplus to enjoy free time in surroundings with non-polluted air. The group also put forward, as a guide, an attempted damage quantification, but as the grounds for this were very slight we kept it at the illustrative level.

However, a sample analysis leading to an effective damage quantification was made for a particular type of recreation, sports fishing in interior waters, through an enquiry ISVET made in collaboration with an authoritative review specialized in this sector.

We made the demoscopic survey by publishing a questionnaire in the review "Pescare" (Fishing). We estimated the damage borne by sports fishermen on the basis of the replies received (about 700) on two different lines:

- first, by evaluating the reduction in fishermen's activity days as a result of water pollution and the higher cost of transport over longer distances to reach clean water;

- secondly (as a check) by measuring, in two different ways, the willingness to pay a surplus for fishing in non-polluted waters.

We projected the result for 1970 until 1985, by calculating the average weighted pollution increase rate ISVET had elaborated for the water basins of the Po, Arno, Piave, Adige, Volturno, Tiber and Tagliamento, that is using a method similar to the one we used for our attempted forecasts of damage to lakeside tourism.

3.2.4.3.   The Results of the 1968 and 1985 Estimates.   We followed the procedures described to forecast the economic damage to seaside tourism, with the following results (in 1968 billion lire):

1968	1970	1975	1980	1985
46.6	50.5	60.3	71.8	86.8

In our evaluation of the lakeside tourist damages, we kept to the criterion of tackling the problem from the angle of the recreational services supply, using, as we have said, the fall in the tourist flow as our basis. We obtained the following damage estimates (in 1968 billion lire):

1968	1970	1975	1980	1985
2.9	3.1	3.8	4.8	6.0

The estimates for sports fishing in inland waters worked out as follows (in 1968 billion lire):

1968	1970	1975	1980	1985
12.5	13.7	17.3	21.9	27.6

The total damage estimates for seaside and lakeside tourism and free time spent on sports fishing are as follows (in 1968 billion lire):

1968	1970	1975	1980	1985
61.9	67.3	81.4	98.4	120.3

3.2.4.4. The Incompleteness of our Estimates. As we have observed, the quantifications of economic damage to tourism and free time made in the present research cover only part of the vast range of activities in this sector.

For example, we did not make any quantitative damage evaluations for urban "open space" free time (which are also very large) or other recreational activities such as hunting, excursions, etc. Nor did we consider "intangible" damages, such as the negative (though perhaps still largely potential) influence on foreign tourism, the flow of which might in future be diverted from Italy, because of the deterioration of the natural resources that form the basis for this activity. Finally, we should emphasize that even for the quantification we did make, for seaside and lakeside tourism and sports fishing only, we followed cautious criteria.

In short, the scale of economic damage the working group managed to quantify is to be considered only a fraction of the actual amount; what is more, this sector, together with the ecological sector, is perhaps the comprehensive research sector in which the estimated damage represents the lowest percentage of the real damage.

3.2.5. Water Resources for the Drinking and Industrial Supply (136)

The economic damage due to drinking and industrial water pollution may be considered as follows:

a. For drinking water: a.1 the additional cost of treating (137) surface, ground or spring water involving greater input and/or processing costs to reach the standards in force, when the water contains higher quantities of substances to be removed than are typical of water in "normal" conditions of natural evolution; a.2 increased wear and early repair of plants and equipment, and therefore bigger maintenance and amortization costs; a.3 enlargements, additions or modifications in plant components and/or processing stages (involving even bigger maintenance and amortization costs); a.4 the abandonment of polluted

170

wells, involving the recourse to substitute supply sources, with consequently bigger amortization and running costs, and/or disinvestment
costs;

b. Water for industrial uses: b. 1 additional treatment costs
(due mainly to an increase in the consumption of reactives), involving
bigger input and/or processing costs; b. 2 increased wear and early
repair of plants and equipment, involving bigger maintenance and
amortization costs; b. 3 enlargements, modifications or additions
in plant components or processing stages, involving bigger amortization and maintenance costs; b. 4 qualitative and/or quantitative
production losses due to plant stoppages for special maintenance, or
to pollution of the product by water (138).

Expenses a. 1, a. 2, a. 3, b. 1, b. 2 and b. 3 are usually involved
in the "basic" pollution water courses; damages a. 4, b. 4 , on the other
hand, are usually connected with incidental pollution of a special character, determined by localized factors that may put the plant out of
action or reduce its productive capacity.

In order to calculate these conceptually outlined damages concretely, one should have detailed information on the "normal" cost of treating
water in natural conditions, the volume of water drawn for various uses,
etc. As this documentation does not exist, it is a complex and difficult
job to evaluate the benefits deriving from a possible elimination of
water pollution, and the repercussions on drinking and industrial supplies.

In the present survey we tried to quantify all the cost categories
listed, although the complexity of the practical estimates obliged us to
simplify matters sometimes. For example, we took items a. 2 and a. 3
together, expressing them as additional amortization and maintenance
costs; we monetized the damage in item a. 4, taking the economic
value of the annual production lost through plant stoppages as an indirect
estimate parameter and omitted item b. 3 when evaluating the present
damage, but took it with b. 2 when forecasting the possible future damage
in 1981, still in terms of additional amortization and maintenance costs.

Considering this, and the entirely cautious criteria adopted when
estimating (e. g. the volume of water now needed for industrial uses),
we may conclude that our estimates are lower than the real damage.

3. 2. 5. 1. Effects of Water Pollution. Among the inorganic pollutants
that make water unfit for drinking, we should mention heavy metals
(As, Cd) and, as anions, the cyanides and chromates.

For industrial uses hardness, pH variations and salinity are the
most dangerous.

Soluble organic pollutants include many natural substances, as well as synthetic products such as tensioactives, pesticides, and colourants; the insoluble ones include oils, fats and suspended substances. In addition there is always a biological component which needs no particular treatment only if kept within very low limits.

Small amounts of inorganic pollutants are generally most harmful for drinking purposes, as the tolerability limits are extremely low and removal is very complex and costly (139).

For industrial uses the drawbacks caused by salinity, hardness, alkalinity and pH are connected with the stability index of the water examined, which varies according to the above-mentioned parameters and temperature. Water with a stability index, according to Ryznar, far from 6 may prove corrosive or encrusting and, unless suitably treated, entail the substitution or descaling of the equipment through which the water is circulated.

Soluble organic pollutants, fairly low concentrations of which are generally found in water to be used for the drinking supply, require continual chlorine or chlorine bioxide dosing to eliminate them. When, as often happens in industry, the dosing is insufficient or even non-existent, various kinds of drawbacks may occur, such as the formation of deposits, usually in connection with excessive biological growth, the clogging of equipment (filters, exchangers, etc.) the poisoning of active carbon or ion exchanging resin filters, deposits in steam generators and so on.

Besides the damage to the population that may result from the presence of tensioactives and pesticides in drinking water, trouble may also occur in industry due to surfactants in surface waters. The formation of foam in the cooling circuits and steam generators generally requires the use of anti-foam agents, and causes fairly serious trouble of various kinds.

Considerable negative effects also result from the presence of dissolved and suspended organic substances in the coagulation and flocculation of water subjected to a clearing and partial softening treatment, requiring a higher dose of chemical flocculants. The same applies to oils and fats that may interfere with filtration and clearing treatments, involving additional treatments or greater consumption of reagents and more frequent maintenance.

3.2.5.2. Pollution in the Various Italian Water Compartments. As the amount of economic damage done to the water supply varies according to the intensity of pollution, we made a preliminary evaluation of the degrees of pollution in the main Italian water compartments.

172

In the practical impossibility of collecting data directly, we made this evaluation by calculating the resident and equivalent population gravitating on the different basins, applying conversion coefficients taken from specialized literature. By comparing the total population thus calculated with the area in square kilometres, we obtained a pollution density index for the different basins. Using a similar method we calculated the BOD 5 level, one of the fundamental parameters for expressing pollution for the five rivers considered (Po, Adige, Reno, Tiber, Volturno).

Despite our simplifying hypotheses and approximations, the results obtained by this calculation seemed satisfactorily close to some directly collected data. The comparison therefore convinced us (though on merely indicative grounds) of the soundness of our pollution degree estimates, and enabled us to attempt a classification of the surface water courses based on the BOD 5 values for the different sections.

3.2.5.3.   The Methodology and Results of the Drinking Supply Estimate.
We started our estimate of the economic damage done by pollution to drinking water by establishing Italy's present annual requirements (166.4 m3/sec.), using data provided by Aqueducts Plan drawn up in 1967 by the Ministry of Works. Forty-eight percent of the water comes from springs, 42.8% from ground-water and 9.1% from surface water.

Using data collected directly from some of Italy's main aqueduct firms, we estimated an average unitary cost of making water drinkable, and the additional cost due to the present state of pollution. For surface water, this additional cost equalled 1/3 of the chemical reagents cost and 15% of the amortization and maintenance expenses (i. e. 1.45 lire/ m3); for the ground and spring water, it equalled the chlorination cost (or 0.20 lire/m3). On the whole, the 1968 annual damage imputable to basic pollution may be assessed at about 1.2 billion lire; to this sum we must add the damage done by localized, special pollution (for which official data are entirely lacking), estimable at about 3.1 billion, calculated assuming that the total flow lost through the break-down of aqueducts may be fixed at 2%.

3.2.5.4.   Methodology and Results of the Industrial Supply Estimate.
We found that the evaluation of the damage due to the pollution of water for industrial uses was more complex. Using an unpublished survey made by the CNR in 1969 on the industrial use of water, we calculated (using three alternative methods) the quantity of water drawn in the various basins from rivers or similar bodies of water by the five main water-using industrial sectors, forming about 70% of the national total (the paper, iron and steel, oil, electrical and chemical industries).

We then evaluated the cost of "normal" water treatment in the different sectors, subdividing the volume drawn into two fractions:

a.   for uses not requiring particularly intense treatment, such as clarification, and/or filtration and possibly disinfection;

b.   for uses requiring intense treatment, such as composting, softening or complete demineralization.

We evaluated the cost increase due to pollution by elaborating data from the CNR sample survey of industrial firms (about 400), mentioned above, specialized literature and experts' experience.

We applied the sample results from these sources to the national territory affected by pollution, divided into 12 water compartments, classified according to their estimated pollution levels (see para. 3.2.5.2.).

We estimated the additional costs due to pollution with reference to:

 - treatment costs, for which we considered the additional expenses for the greater quantity of reagents used, according to the types of treatment, sectors and class of pollution. We left out the expenses for energy, manpower and plant amortization, as we thought that they would not be appreciably affected by the degree of pollution;

 - costs of the outsize plants needed, because of pollution, to obtain an equal qualiquantitative production of water. We expressed these costs (for which almost no information is available) as annual amortization quota increases;

 - damage resulting from non-production, or lower-quality production, due to the use of polluted water. We calculated the damage assuming a loss of 2 °/$_{oo}$ per annum, corresponding on an average to two eight-hour shifts, to be applied to the value added (at the factors cost and at current prices) of water-using industrial firms. This value added may be cautiously estimated at about 7,500 billion lire, but drops to about 5,000 if we consider the incidence of the surface water drawn on the total uses of fresh water in industry.

Therefore, for the three above-mentioned cost-categories, our 1968 damage estimates were 8.7, 1.4 and 10 billion lire respectively, making a grand total of about 20 billion lire.

3.2.5.5.   Attempted Estimate of Possible Damage in 1985.   To make
a preliminary, rough estimate of the future growth of economic damage
caused by the purifying of water for the drinking and industrial supply,
assuming that no depuration action is taken, we made forecasts on:

- the degree of pollution of the water in the various Italian basins
  and subbasins in 1981. We made this forecast by calculating the
  resident and equivalent population density at this date, utilizing
  the methodology adopted for 1968 (see above, para. 3.2.5.2.), as
  well as forecasts relating to demographic expansion (140) in the
  various areas, and the production growth of Italy's main industrial
  sectors (141). On the basis of the estimated data thus obtained
  we made a new classification of the water basins according to the
  five reference classes (see above, para. 3.2.5.2.);

- water drawn, for drinking and industrial uses in 1981. For the
  former, we based our estimate on the Aqueduct Plan's requirement forecasts, (suitably elaborated); while for the latter we
  extrapolated the available 1968 data, on the basis of the foreseeable production growth rate in the main user industries and the
  results of the above-mentioned CNR survey (142).

Adopting the methodology used to make the 1968 estimates, the
working group proposed the following degrees of possible economic
damage (at 1968 prices) in 1981:

- for the drinking water required, 5.6 billion lire for the damage
  caused by current or basic pollution of surface, ground or spring
  water; and 7.8 billion for pollution caused by special, localized
  pollutants;

- for water drawn for industrial uses, 29.5 billion lire for additional
  treatment costs, 6.7 billion lire for additional amortization costs,
  34.5/35.7 billion for production losses or quality drops.

These forecasts may certainly be considered cautious, as assuming
that no adequate measures are taken to protect water, pollution might
reach such levels as to make the use of water for drinking and industrial
uses impossible or anti-economic, or require the substitution of the
present plants and treatment processes.

3.2.6.   Italy's Ecological Assets (143)

        The evaluation of economic damage to ecological assets poses
serious methodological difficulties on the theoretical plane. They concern our present insufficient knowledge of the consequences of pollution

on the various ecosystems, and the attribution of an adequate monetary value to express the overall utility of natural assets that, unlike those produced by man, are invaluable resources for society as well as being irreplaceable and rarely reproduceable.

From the first point of view, to measure the damage done by pollution we should need a thorough knowledge of the flora-fauna and microbiological composition of the various ecosystems, in the static sense, i.e. in terms of biomass and the dynamic sense, i.e. regarding the productivity of biomass in time. This degree of scientific knowledge exists neither in Italy nor in other countries, except for some simple ecosystems, for which the research done concerns few environments and groups of organisms, generally the most macroscopic, or those directly concerning human activities (such as hunting and fishing), or the most interesting from the point of view of scientific research.

The second order of theoretical problems to be solved, if we wish to measure correctly the economic damage done by pollution, concerns the calculation of the economic value of natural assets and resources, which are much higher than any market price.

In general, natural products expressible in monetary terms (such as fish, game, wood) account for a tiny part of the total value of the ecosystems, understood as functional systems in dynamic equilibrium, composed of a natural habitat, and living animal and vegetable communities which it enables to settle and feed. By far the most important (though unquantifiable) part of the economic value of the ecosystems and their components is constituted by the multiple direct and indirect uses that the natural assets are able to offer society in the medium and long run. Only some of these uses are known, as in the case of the functions and services connected with water and geology, hygiene and depuration, weather and climate, plant and animal health, recreation and tourism, the landscape and science, etc.

The utilities ecological assets procure for society belong, according to current literature on cost-benefit analysis, to the category of intangibles, the value of which cannot be expressed through market prices.

The most correct way to express these utilities or benefits in economic terms is to make a "social" evaluation for them by adopting shadow-prices (or account prices), although the difficulty of using these is well-known (144).

It is hard to apply the principal criteria proposed in literature on cost-benefit analysis for calculating account prices, the best-known of which are willingness to pay and the most economical alternative mean. The former, which measures intangible benefits through the theoretical

cost the individual would be ready to bear to enjoy that particular asset
or service, is hardly suitable, in the case of ecology, to express the
total objective and social value of the benefits deriving from natural
assets. The latter, which measures these benefits through the known
value of other substitutional assets or services, encounters its limits
in the frequent impossibility of finding substitutes or alternatives capable of giving society the same utilities as natural assets.

From the theoretical point of view, therefore, it is impossible today to calculate satisfactorily the damage caused by the pollution of
the ecological systems, both on account of the little scientific information available, and the lack of a monetary parameter through which
to express the value of the ecological systems and their components.

It is in the light of these problems that we must interpret the attempts made in the present research to quantify economically the
damage done by pollution to Italian ecological assets.

3.2.6.1. Defining the Field of Enquiry. Our estimate of the economic
damage done by pollution to ecological assets was restricted to some
ecosystems into which, somewhat arbitrarily, natural assets may be
divided. In the impossibility of estimating the economic value of the
entire ecosystem, we evaluated the damage for one of its components
or specific aspects. For coastal waters we considered fishes; for inland (fresh) waters we considered fishes and their habitat in a broad
sense; for forests, the productivity of coppiced woods; for urban parks
(which in themselves do not constitute a natural ecosystem), the soil-
covering of trees; and finally, for land ecosystems in general, game.

In practice, we limited our attempted damage quantification to the
principal components or aspects of the ecosystems for which we managed
to suggest a market or non-market monetary parameter, albeit indirect.
This implies that the estimated damage must be considered not only
approximate and rough, but also much lower than the real amount.

3.2.6.2. Pollution Effects. Very little is known about the action,
modalities and typologies of the main forms of physical and chemical
pollution in natural land and water surroundings. The lack of scientific
knowledge on the subject fundamentally regards the dynamic effects of
different types of pollution on various ecosystems; some of the static
effects, on the other hand, are better known.

The chief pollutants of ecological assets are biocides, automobile
emissions in general, hydrocarbon transport in particular, air and
water industrial effluents, and urban waste. These sources act on
natural resources (soil, air, water, flora and fauna) and through them

177

on the ecological systems, in ways and with effects that vary greatly
according to the natural environment, its living populations and the
dynamic equilibrium existing between habitat and populations.

3.2.6.3.   The Methodology Adopted.   We chose our criteria and
methodologies for estimating damage in 1968, bearing in mind the
difficulties mentioned above for measuring the effects of pollution and
the monetary qualification of the value of natural assets. For these
reasons they vary according to the ecological sector considered, partly
as a result of the statistical data, information and researches available.

We estimated the damage to fishes in the coastal waters on the basis
of the catch fall suffered by coastal sectors due to pollution. We calculated this fall on the basis of Gini's dissimilarity index, measuring the
absolute average variation existing, in terms of the amount of fish, in
the polluted and non-polluted sectors. The catch not made in the polluted sectors, multiplied by the wholesale price of coastal fish, gives
a rough estimate of the pollution damage. Using suitable coefficients
evaluated by experts we then extended the damage calculated to all
coastal fish.

We estimated the damage to inland (fresh) water by measuring the
cost of replacing the fish presumably destroyed by pollution. We extended this replacement cost, assessable for the fish repopulation
component only, on the basis of experts' estimates, to obtain the total
cost of dealing with habitat damage caused by pollution. The latter
cost component, practically neglected today, represents the largest
quota of the damage done to inland waters by pollution.

We calculated the damage to forests for copses only, on the basis
of their annual "productivity" value per hectare. We expressed this
productivity in calories, attributing to them an average (weighted)
economic value through the market prices of the main wood and animal
products. We distinguished the polluted copses according to the various
levels of air pollution expressed in SO_2, through a cross analysis of
the ECONSULT forest map and the ISVET air pollution map.

For town parks, which do not form a natural ecosystem but are
seriously affected by town air pollution, we estimated the damage for
the tree-covered top-soil, attributing to it a value equal to the replacement cost to be paid by the public administration if a tree is destroyed.
ISVET assessed the polluted assets, at the various damage levels, by
sending special postal questionnaires to all the main provincial authorities. We estimated the damage for the presumable parkland in the
main provincial towns, calculated on the basis of the minimum standard
in force today (9 m^2 per inhabitant), to obtain a figure nearer the real
area of green urban spaces equipped as parks.

178

We calculated fauna damage only for permanent non-hoofed plain and hill fauna, on the basis of the what it would cost society to prevent the depopulation by pollution of the potential wildlife the present Italian habitats could support. We evaluated the potential wildlife on the basis of the average density in other European countries, suitably reduced to cover the fauna and hunting policy differences in Italy and other countries.

3.2.6.4.   The Results of the 1968 Estimate.   Using the calculation methodologies described, we estimated the economic damage done by pollution in 1968 (145) at about 47 billion lire, classified as follows:

	ABSOLUTE VALUE (in billion lire)	DISTRIBUTION (%)
Coastal waters	6.0	12.7
Inland waters	19.0	40.3
Copses	3.1	6.6
Town parks	4.1	8.7
Game	15.0	31.7
Total	47.2	100.0

Given the (very partial) estimate criteria adopted, this value must be considered purely indicative compared with the damage actually done by water and air pollution to Italy's ecological assets.

We must point out that the above figures are only for the specific pollution damages considered in our more general cost-benefit survey, although ecological pollution is mainly identified with general human action altering our natural surroundings (urbanization, agriculture, noise, hunting and fishing, deforestation, and so on).

3.2.6.5.   Hypotheses on the Growth of Damage by 1985.   Forecasting the economic damage air and water pollution might do to ecological assets by 1985, (assuming that no measures to reduce or limit pollution are taken in the meantime) is problematical, because of the great difficulty of estimating the present damage, and the many queries on its prospects of future growth.

From the latter point of view, to formulate reliable forecasts we should assume, among other things, the structural changes that will occur in the natural surroundings and their living populations, and the future uses of natural surroundings, as the amount of damage done by pollution will vary according to the uses these surroundings are put to in the meantime.

Finally, if pollution were really to continue, growing at its "spontaneous" rate, some natural surroundings still existing in Italy today might disappear forever by 1985, so that the damage done by pollution might become incalculable, as many natural assets are not reproduceable or replaceable.

Granting this, we still made a tentative forecast, of the damage in 1985, although it is very low mainly because it is based on the extrapolation of the damage estimates for 1968, and leaves out many cumulative factors, which might increase the future damage at exponential rates until in some cases the asset is completely destroyed.

In the absence of other parameters to judge by, we assumed, to simplify matters, that the damage considered might grow at the same rate as the pollution of the environments concerned.

Our suggested estimate (see table 3.2.6.5 a) is the result of extrapolating the 1968 damage estimates for coastal waters, inland waters and copses until 1985, according to the average pollution increase rates for coastal waters, inland waters and air respectively. For town parks, we first extended the 1968 damage estimate to the parkland theoretically existing in 1985 (calculating 9 sq. metres per inhabitant in the main provincial towns) and then raised it according to the air pollution increase rate. For game damage, we projected the 1968 estimate to 1985 on the basis of forecast increases in biocide and pesticide consumption.

Table 3.2.6.5 a. SUGGESTED 1985
ECOLOGICAL DAMAGE FORECASTS

	ABSOLUTE VALUE (in 1968 billion lire)	DISTRIBUTION %
Coastal waters	13.0	14.3
Inland waters	42.0	46.0
Copses	8.6	9.4
Town parks	6.7	7.3
Game	21.0	23.0
Total	91.3	100.0

3.2.7. Damage through Deterioration, Dirtying and Depreciation
of Real Estate and Personal Effects; Various Damages (146)

Besides the economic damage done by pollution in the sectors
considered in paras. 3.2.1 - 3.2.6, we cannot ignore a set of less
easily classifiable and fairly heterogeneous damages, involving a
considerable economic burden for society. Various authors and empirical experience have shown that these damages may be directly or
indirectly traced to pollution (particularly air pollution). For the
purposes of the present research, we may link them together as they
supplement the pollution damage categories given above (see para. 2.2).

It is well-known that pollution, especially air pollution, damages
and dirties real property (buildings, houses, factories, etc.), infrastructures (e.g. bridges, railways,etc.), and personal effects (clothes,
furniture, goods and so on). It has also been observed that various
drawbacks connected with decreased air transparency (lighting, traffic,
variations in weather and climate, etc.), may be traced to pollution.

Of course, the sum of these damages may weigh heavily on the
economy, as has been proved by the few sample surveys attempted in
this field. However, with very few exceptions, reliable Italian estimates
have not yet been formulated, although there is now a great deal of technical literature on the effects of air pollution on various materials (147).

Apart from the entirely unsatisfactory state of empirical researches,
on the methodological plane, too, the attempts at evaluating these damages (especially those made by Ridker, as part of a preliminary study
for the US Public Health Service) have been far from successful. For
this damage category, collecting the direct information necessary to
make a well-founded economic damage estimate is particularly difficult
on the operative plane, too, as has been shown by the poor results of
the surveys made so far.

In the present study we made an analogical evaluation of this damage category as lack of time and funds prevented us from making a
direct, analytical collection of basic data.

3.2.7.1. Defining the Field of Enquiry. The damage categories we
examined are as follows:

a. damages connected with the deterioration and dirtying of residential,
    commercial and industrial buildings and property in general;
b. damages through the deterioration (corrosion) of some infrastruc-
    tures (railways, bridges, etc.);

181

c.   damage through additional domestic cleaning and increased wear
     and tear on clothes, domestic furnishings, and goods in general;
d.   damage due to increased electric light consumption;
e.   damage through traffic (especially air and road traffic) due to
     decreased visibility;
f.   damage through fuel losses due to badly working plants;
g.   depreciation of building plots and real estate.

We cannot suggest a reliable quantification for e.; and we included
f. in our purification cost estimate (see below 3.3.3). For g. we made
a pilot study for a sample town, Genoa, the only one where we could
find the separate data, on pollution levels in the main urban zones,
indispensable for our estimate.

3.2.7.2.   The Methodology Adopted.   Estimating the damages listed
in para 3.2.7.1 is very difficult, due to the lack of adequate statistics
and approved methodologies.   It would really be necessary to make
direct sample surveys similar to those made abroad in some limited
cases, but these are costly and laborious.

For the purposes of the present research we attempted to quantify
the damage, as mentioned above, on the basis of crossed judgements
given by experts in the various sectors, and through analogical comparisons with similar estimates made abroad, adjusted to make them
comparable to the Italian situation (148).

To apply this methodology, we used the ISVET air pollution map
(149) to evaluate the population resident in the polluted zones in 1967
and formulate two hypotheses: a very restrictive one for the "black"
zones, corresponding to the epicentres of pollution sources; and a
wider one, considering all the communal territory in which the above-
mentioned areas are situated as polluted.   The first "low" hypothesis
corresponds to an area with a population of about 3.67 million residents,
rising in the "high" hypothesis to 13.95 million (150).

3.2.7.3.   The 1967 Damage Estimate.   The methodology adopted provided the values summarized in table 3.2.7.3 a.   The average pro
capite damage per annum for each category considered,according to
the experts' estimate and the comparison with similar estimates in
foreign studies, is given in the first column.

We assumed a 50% higher clothes-washing frequency for 150 days
per year in the polluted zones than in the non polluted ones, and a useful
life shorter by one twentieth, due to wear and tear.   For domestic cleaning we estimated 15 minutes' additional work per day, for 150 days a

year, for each family residing in the polluted zones (151); for lighting, a greater annual consumption of 6 Kwh. per person, and so on. The cautious hypotheses adopted for calculating these damages considerably lowered the values suggested by experts or foreign estimates.

The adoption of the two hypotheses concerning the number of residents in the polluted zones (the restrictive one for the "black" zones, and the wider one for all the communal areas in which these zones are situated), gave a damage variability band with the maximum about four times bigger than the minimum (about 167 billion and 46 billion respectively). This difference seemed justified by the relative reliability of the basic data utilized, so that the estimate was necessarily very rough. However, for some categories, we did not try to quantify the damage, mainly concerning road and air traffic trouble, due to decreased visibility.

3.2.7.4. 1985 Tentative Damage Forecasts. Extrapolating estimates with such a wide margin of indetermination to 1985 involves further possibilities of error. We had to forecast the size of the polluted areas at that date, the population resident there (taking urbanization into account), the pollution level, the size and composition of the assets concerned, and so on. At the present stage of information it seems practically impossible to make well-founded forecasts of this kind; at best we can suggest reasoned hypotheses purely as a guide.

On the basis of some 1985 pollution growth forecasts calculated (in terms of the quantity of effluents over the national territory) elsewhere in the present study (152), we estimated that a population of about 6.37 million (on a restrictive hypothesis) and about 26.7 million (on a wider hypothesis), might reside in the polluted zones. We then estimated a certain unitary value for the individual costs or damages (deterioration, cleaning, wear, lighting) for 1985 and obtained possible damage forecasts ranging from a minimum of 143 to a maximum of 602 billion lire (see table 3.2.7.4a.). This impressive value points to the desirability of making further estimates in this sector with more detailed direct procedures and more ample means. The amount is perfectly comparable to foreign estimates. In fact, for damages similar to those examined in this sector, some direct surveys made recently, especially in the USA, give pro capite values like $ 60 for Pittsburg (1959, Schmidt), $ 84 for Ohio (1960, Michelson and Tourin) and $ 200 for Washington (1968, Yokom).

3.2.7.5. Reduction in the Value of Building Plots. Some economists include the reduction in value of urban areas and consequently of the property built on them in economic damage due to the effects of air pollution. Cost-benefit analysis doctrine suggests that we should not

Table 3.2.7.3a.   ESTIMATE OF AIR POLLUTION DAMAGE TO REAL ESTATE,
SOME CONSUMER GOODS AND VARIOUS ACTIVITIES (1967)

TYPE OF DAMAGE	AVERAGE ANNUAL PER CAPITA DAMAGE IN POLLUTED AREAS (IN LIRE)	POPULATION RESIDING IN THE POLLUTED AREAS a. "BLACK" ZONES b. "POLLUTED" ZONES (IN THOUSANDS)	TOTAL DAMAGE a. MINIMUM b. MAXIMUM (IN 1968 BILLION LIRE)
Metal buildings and structures		a. 3,675 b. 13,950	a. 12.0 b. 45.4
Clothes: cleaning	3,125	as above	a. 11.5
Clothes: wear and tear	2,000	as above	a. 7.4 b. 27.9
Automobiles	800	Automobiles in circulation a. 710 b. 2,466	a. 0.6 b. 2.0
Home cleaning	(per family) 11,250 (300 per hour for 37 1/2 hours per year)	resident families a. 1,020 b. 3,870	a. 11.5 b. 43.5
Lighting	192	a. 3,675 b. 13,950	a. 0.7 b. 2.7
TOTAL			a. 43.7 b. 165.1

184

take this value into account, as it represents a redistribution benefit: with the disappearance of pollution the increase in property values in certain areas would probably be compensated by a corresponding decrease in other previously non-polluted zones. Although it does not seem quite unjustified to consider some indirect benefits connected with a more rational territorial organization that the elimination of pollution would make practicable, for the purposes of the present research we decided not to include the benefits from an increase in real estate value in our cost-benefit calculation (153).

Even so, we thought it would be useful to make an <u>ad hoc</u> survey of the city of Genoa, as a sample study to test a methodology proposed by Ridker. This study may be extended to other Italian towns, as and when the necessary statistics are available, particularly those results from a desirable increase in air pollution survey points.

The methodology adopted, borrowed from the research done by the working group directed by Ridker for the city of St. Louis in 1960 (154), utilizes multiple regression techniques to measure the specific incidence of pollution level variations on plot price variations, compared with a series of other variables. We chose 17 variables to justify the values of the plots in an urban zone, and divided them into three general categories: town planning variables (building density, accessibility to the centre, industry and the port, beaches and bathing establishments, and the motorway network; the adequacy of roads and parking places, free time and open space facilities, public transport, schools, and commercial structures); social and economic variables (housing density, upkeep and prestige of the area) and environmental variables (the orographic situation).

We chose the city of Genoa as statistics on the above-mentioned variables were available, and calculated their specific values for 67 urban zones. To measure the air pollution levels we used the results of recent surveys made by Genoa University Hygiene Institute, in 17 points of the city between Pegli and Nervi, for the minimum and maximum amounts of the 4 chief pollutants (sulphurous anhydride, benzopyrene, iron oxide and suspended dust).

After a laborious statistical elaboration, aimed mainly at eliminating the effects of multicollinearity, the survey produced very significant results tallying with Ridker's (155). It emerged in fact that variations in the value of the residential areas in the whole city of Genoa of 9.2, 27.6 and 46 billion lire would correspond in theory to 10%, 30% and 50% decreases in the level of pollution. Considering that the price of the areas is on an average equal to 1/3 of the value of the immovables, the influence of pollution on the value of real estate turns out to be quite high.

Table 3.2.7.4a. SUGGESTED FORECAST OF FUTURE ECONOMIC DAMAGE CAUSED BY AIR POLLUTION TO REAL ESTATE, SOME CONSUMER GOODS AND VARIOUS ACTIVITIES (1985)

TYPE OF DAMAGE	AVERAGE ANNUAL PER CAPITA DAMAGE IN THE POLLUTED AREAS (IN LIRE)	POPULATION RESIDENT IN THE POLLUTED AREAS a. "BLACK" ZONES b. "POLLUTED" ZONES (IN THOUSANDS)	TOTAL DAMAGE a. MINIMUM b. MAXIMUM (IN 1968 BILLION LIRE)
Building and metal structures		a. 6,370 b. 26,750	a. 33.1 b. 139.1
Clothes: cleaning	4,000	as above	a. 25.5 b. 107.0
Clothes: wear and tear	3,000	as above	a. 19.1 b. 80.3
Automobiles	1,500	automobiles in circulation a. 2,088 b. 8,776	a. 2.5 b. 10.5
Home cleaning	34,000 (850 per hour for 40 hours per year)	resident families a. 1,800 b. 7,600	a. 61.2 b. 258.4
Lighting	250	a. 6,370 b. 26,750	a. 1.6 b. 6.7
TOTAL			a. 143.0 b. 602.0

NOTES TO THE APPENDIX

120.   Even in the "modernized" version mentioned in para. 1.3.2.2.

121.   Cf. above, para. 3.1.1., and below, para. 3.2.5.

122.   See the considerations in paras. 4.1.2. and 4.1.3.

123.   The monographic study for this sector was made by a working
       group with the following members; Prof. L. Villa, Ing. G.
       Scaccia Scarafoni and Dr. S. De Fulvio of the Italian Health
       Institute; Prof. A. Serìo, of INAM, lecturer in Health Statis-
       tics; and Dr. P. Gardin and Dr. M.T. Marignetti for ISVET.
       The complete text of this monograph appears in ISVET Document
       no. 28 (Inquinamento e salute umana, Rome, 1970).

124.   Theoretically, we could indicate the probable economic extent
       of category e. damage, which we also left out of our quantifi-
       cation; think for example, of the cost of mountain sojourns,
       sea cures, etc. often necessary for the treatment or prevention
       of air pollution effects in urban zones.

125.   See R. Ridker, Economic costs of air pollution, op. cit. chap. 3.

126.   In situations of particularly serious air pollution, e.g. in certain
       zones in Tokyo, about 30% of the population is already suffering
       from some form of respiratory disease brought on by pollution
       (see The most polluted city, Newsweek Nov. 1969). The recent
       estimates by L. Lave and E. Seskin, of the Carnegie-Mellon
       University of Boston, on air pollution damage to human health
       in the USA, are also quite significant.

127.   The complete text of this monographic survey is carried in
       ISVET Document no. 29 (Inquinamento e patrimonio dei beni

culturali, Roma, 1970). The survey was made by a working group whose members were Dr. G. Torraca, of the International Centre for the Conservation of Cultural Assets; Prof. M. Leoni, of the Experimental Institute of Light Metals, Novara; Prof. M. Paribeni, of the Technical Physics Institute of Rome University; Dr. F. Capuano, of the Antiques and Fine Arts Council (Ministry of Education); the Central Restoration Institute, the State Records Office (Ministry of the Interior) and "Italia Nostra" experts.

128. For a thorough analysis of this information we refer readers to the complete text of the survey (see above, note 127).

129. The complete text of this monographic survey is given in ISVET Document no. 30 (Inquinamento e agricoltura, Rome, 1970). The survey was made by a working group coordinated by Dr. M. C. Cesaretti, with the help of Dr. G. De' Rossi and Dr. T. La Noce, and formed by agrarian economy experts Dr. A. Bartolo, Dr. M. Cellerini, Dr. G. P. Pallavicini, Dr. N. Pavan, and Dr. G. Stupazzoni, who supervised the local surveys in their respective zones of competence. Dr. La Noce of the CNR gave his help on the technical and chemical aspects, Dr. De' Rossi collaborated in the survey outline and in drawing up the text. ISVET was also given vital assistance by the National Land Improvement Association: thanks to the helpful attitude of its President, G. Medici (M. P.) and of its Director, Dr. E. Giuliani, we were able to make the general reconnaissance survey, in collaboration with the CNR. Several agricultural experts, including Dr. G. Andreoni (M. P.) contributed useful ideas and suggestions.

130. Grain, maize, rice, vegetables, sugar beet, peach trees, alternated and permanent fields, (water meadows), forage fields.

131. The complete text of the present monographic survey is carried in ISVET Document no. 31 (Inquinamento, turismo e tempo libero, Rome, 1970). The survey was made by a working group formed by Prof. I. Insolera, Dr. P. Kammerer, Dr. M. Mazzarino and Dr. M. A. Milani of ISVET. Dr. M. T. Marignetti (who also edited the statistical elaborations), the ISVET-LINEA Division and the specialized review "Pescare", and the Merchant Navy Ministry provided most useful data on the juridical regime of the Italian coasts.

132. In cost-benefit analysis the repercussions of a particular programme on free time, tourism and recreation in general, pose extremely complex problems of methodology and practical calculation.

Only in some cases can we evaluate the benefits, or at least the effects, in terms of market prices, in theory, comparing the situation of the area under review with or without the programme. In general, however, market prices are not available, and we have to use shadow prices estimated or obtained by comparing them with market prices for similar goods or services.

Actually, as is shown by a survey on the methodologies followed in a sample of 170 projects authorized by the US Congress to evaluate the effects on recreation (excluding fishing, hunting, excursions and ecology), "arbitrary prices are generally used to evaluate the relevant services ... the statistical bases of these prices are not illustrated in the reports" (cf. I. K. Fox, O. C. Herfindahl, Efficiency in the use of natural resources, in "American Economic Review", May 1964).

Even more often the effects are treated as intangibles, i. e. benefits inexpressible in significant monetary terms, and not included, except indirectly, in the comparison between the costs and benefits of a particular project.

On the methodologies proposed in the cost-benefit analysis for the tourism and free time sector, see for example A. Majocchi, Sulla valutazione de tempi non monetari della spesa pubblica, Fusi, Pavia, 1968; R. Mack and S. Myers, Outdoor Recreation, in R. Dorfmann, Measuring benefits of Government Investments, Brookings Institution, Washington, 1965; M. Clawson, J. L. Knetsch, Economics of Outdoor Recreation, Johns Hopkins Press, Baltimore, 1966, Chapters 5 and 11; P. H. Pearse, A New Approach to the Evaluation of Non-Priced Recreational Resources, in "Land Economics", February 1968, pages 87-99.

133.   To express the activity days in monetary terms we referred to ISTAT statistics on average daily tourist expenditure (at present about 10,000 lire per day). Only part of this sum may be attributed to specifically tourist activities, as it also includes board and lodging expenses, which would in any case have to be paid even in the tourists' own homes, so we made a correction to find out the quota attributable to specifically tourist activities.

134.   In cases where awareness of the pollution situation is high, the drop in activity days is certainly sharp: for example, in the 1970 season it was about 50% for the beaches along the Latium coast.

135.   See below, para. 3.2.5.

136.   The complete text of this monographic survey is carried in ISVET Document no. 32 (Inquinamento e risorse idriche, Rome, 1970).

The survey was made by a working group formed by Ing. M. A. Arista and Dr. F. Gallo of ISVET, Dr. C. Merli of CNR and Ing. G. Silvestro of the Ministry of Works, and supervised by Prof. R. Passino, Director of the CNR Water Research Institute. Thanks to the collaboration of the CNR Water Research Institute, the group was able to utilize some of the as yet unpublished preliminary results of an enquiry on the use of water in Italian industries (1969).

137.   Mainly through increased chlorination.

138.   We might also consider the hypothesis that water pollution will become so intense as to cause the utilizing companies to cease their activity or to move. This eventuality turned out to be quite abstract (the working group found no cases of the kind in Italy), so that we did not consider it when we estimated the economic damage.

139.   The upper limit established by the WHO for the most common toxic ions that may be found in surface and ground-water are: lead 0.05 mg/l; arsenic 0.05 mg/l; selenium 0.01 mg/l; (hexavalent) chromium 0.05; cadmium 0.01; barium 1.0 mg/l.

140.   Taken from M. Livi Bacci, F. Pilloton, Popolazione e forze di lavoro delle regioni italiane al 1981, Giuffrè, Rome, 1968.

141.   Taken, with suitable elaborations and adoptions, from F. Forte, L. Carcassi, B. Ferrara, l'Economia industriale italiana al 1980, CSPE, Rome, 1969

142.   These indications gave data about 15/20% higher than those calculated, as the methodology adopted does not sufficiently consider the increase of recycling, consumption reduction techniques and so on.

143.   The complete text of this monographic survey is carried in ISVET Document no. 33 (Inquinamento e patrimonio ecologico, Rome, 1970). The survey was made by a working group formed by Ing. P. Cannavò of ENCONSULT, Dr. S. Panella of the Central Hydrobiology Laboratory, Rome, Arch. F. Pratesi of EN-CONSULT and Dr. T. Tassi, Director of the Abruzzo National Park, with the coordination of Dr. L. Piazza of ISVET. The economic approach and statistical elaborations were made by Dr. G. Ricoveri and Dr. M. T. Marignetti of ISVET. The working group received valuable suggestions and advice from numerous experts, including: Dr. A. Alessandrini, Inspector-General of the Agriculture and Forestry Ministry; Dr. F. Baschieri

Salvadori, Vice-President of the Italian Association for the World Wildlife Fund; Prof. G. Bini, lecturer in Hydrobiology at Rome University; Prof. E. Bronzini, Director of the Rome Zoo; Dr. A. Carraro Moda, of the Rome City Council; Dr. A. Cederna of "Italia Nostra"; Dr. P. Chilanti, Director of the Game Producers' Association; Prof. C. Maldura, Professor of Oceanography, Rome University; Prof. F. Matta, of the Central Laboratory of Hydrobiology; Dr. F. Muzzarini, Secretary of the Game Producers' Association and Prof. P. Turli, Director of the Central Hydrobiology Laboratory.

144. The relation between man and nature is historically determined and varies according to the overall level reached by each society at a particular stage of its social and economic development. The value a society is ready to attribute to natural assets therefore changes according to the variation of the degree of overall development reached by that society.

145. We calculated the damage for the coastal waters, in relation to the available data, for the year 1967.

146. The complete text of this monographic survey is carried in Inquinamento e patrimonio immobiliare, ISVET Document, no. 34, Rome, 1970. The first part, on damage through the deterioration, soiling and wear of immovable and movable assets and various types of damage, was edited by Prof. L. Mammarella; the second, a pilot survey of the city of Genoa to evaluate the effects of pollution on the value of urban areas and therefore on real estate, was made by a working group composed of the architects M. Birindelli and A. Saraceno and Ing. G. Santese.

147. See, for example, John E. Yocum, Effects of air pollution on materials in "Air Pollution", Arthur Stern, New York, Academic Press, 1962.

148. The most important foreign studies on this are for the United States and Great Britain. As early as 1913 the Mellon Institute had estimated a damage of 20 dollars pro capite, due to losses through bad combustion, for the town of Pittsburg. Additional costs for laundering and cleaning clothes; maintenance and domestic lighting; maintenance, lighting and goods deterioration in shops; internal and external cleaning of public buildings, hospitals, etc. A subsequent estimate made in 1959 for the same town put this damage up to 60 dollars per inhabitant. Similar surveys were made later in other towns in the United States without satisfactory results. A survey made by Ridker in 1965 at Syracuse, following an episode of massive pollution,

gave a total estimate of about 38,500 dollars, with an average cost of 11-12 dollars per family, mainly attributable to cleaning costs. In 1960 Michelson and Tourin, examining two towns of similar size, urban density, average income, weather and climate, one situated in a highly polluted zone and the other in a relatively clean area, estimated for the former an additional cost of 84 dollars pro capite per annum for external and internal house maintenance, laundry and cleaning and personal (hair and face) care. In Great Britain the Beaver Commission estimated damages to real estate and personal assets in 1954 as part of a wide survey to evaluate the economic damages caused by air pollution. The Commission's total estimates for laundry expenses, the cost of cleaning, painting and maintaining buildings, and metal corrosion damages amounted in 1953 to 150 million pounds sterling (see above para. 2.1.1.).

149.   See above, para. 3.1.1.

150.   According to the Beaver Commission estimates, about 50% of the population of Great Britain in 1913 was considered as resident in the "black" zones; for the USA, Michelson and Tourin estimated in 1966 that 25% of the inhabitants resided in zones with serious pollution problems, and a further 34% in urban areas with moderate and minor problems.

151.   Miss Brand-Konheim has estimated that in the city of New York housewives' work is lengthened by at least half an hour per day to remove the dirt produced by air polluting emissions.

152.   See above, para. 3.1.1.5.

153.   See below, para. 4.1.2.5.

154.   Cf. R.G. Ridker, J.A. Henning, The Determinants of residential property values with special reference to air pollution; and R.G. Ridker, Economic costs of air pollution, op. cit. Chap. VII.

155.   Air pollution alone would explain in particular about 1% of the area value, as in the results of the St. Louis survey.

DAMAGE FUNCTIONS,
SOME THEORETICAL AND PRACTICAL PROBLEMS

by

Hans Opschoor
Instituut voor Milieuvraagstukken,
Vrije Universiteit, Amsterdam
Netherlands

INTRODUCTION

In this paper, the term "damage function" will be used to indicate the relationship between, on the one hand, the amount of exposure (of materials, plants, animals, men; generally: receptors) to a certain pollutant and, on the other hand, a quantitative expression of the effect of that exposure. One can think of an expression in monetary units, in which case one might speak of "monetary damage functions" (MD functions). On the other hand, one can stop one step short of MD functions and think of an expression in, what the economist often calls "physical" units (as opposed to monetary ones, physical units are entities that enter utility functions or production functions directly) in which case one might speak of "non-monetary damage functions" (ND functions). The relations between MD functions and ND functions will be dealt with later in this paper.

The concept of "damage function" (D function) is closely related to, e.g. those of "dose-effect relation" and "stimulus-response function". All three describe chains of reactions to predetermined "actions". Dose-effect relations and stimulus-response functions describe relations within their original terms of reference, i. e. , that of the toxicologist and the psychologist. D functions describe negative (external) effects of pollutants. As such, MD functions may be derived from dose-effect and stimulus-response functions and ND functions are often identical with them.

This paper will indicate some of the theoretical and practical problems associated with D functions. Some examples will be given, taken mainly from the fields of health effects of air pollution and noise. The main object is to arrive at some opinion as to the usefulness of damage functions as a tool in decision-making.

In what follows I shall confine myself mainly to effects on the human organism. Since in many instances dose effect relations and stimulus response functions are equal to the relevant ND functions, it might be expected that, in general, ND functions "behave" much like them. Thus one may expect the amount of a certain type of damage (ND_i) not only to depend on the amount of the pollutant under study (P_j) that the organism is exposed to, but also on the level of state variables characteristic of the organism (S_k), including the amount of P_j still left within the organism from previous exposures, and other input variables I_l (1).

For a given period, then,

$$(1) \qquad ND_i^h = f^h \left[P_j^h, \ S_k^h, \ I_l^h \right]$$

where superfix h indicates the organism we are studying. Thus, moving from one organism to another, a given exposure may easily lead to a different ND; moving with the same organism through time may reveal a time-dependent ND function; moving from one region to another may even reveal that <u>average</u> reactions over larger populations are not comparable. Note, that if (1) contains not only additive terms (between P, S and I), <u>marginal</u> damage too will be influenced by S and I.

Following Zielhuis, it may be useful to distinguish three types of "factors" (chemical elements and compounds, radiation, energy, etc.) that an (human) organism is exposed to:

   i) factors having a <u>first-order link with the organism</u>; stimuli necessary for remaining at equilibrium or moving towards it. These contain: food, light, heat, etc. In general we need something of all these factors, but not too much: there exists an <u>optimal</u> value;

   ii) factors that are <u>primarily alien to the organism</u>; these contain, e.g. the chemical additives to foods, certain chemicals in air and water, etc. The optimal value for these factors is at (or below) the threshold value in the dose-effect relation, i.e. that value where no (significant) effect has been recorded;

   iii) factors that have a <u>second-order link with the organism</u>. Some of the factors discussed in (ii) may, in themselves, be antagonistic towards a given individual, but from the point of view of the community they may be judged unavoidable; e.g. SO_2

pollution can be avoided by abandoning the products that entail that kind of pollution, but from a social point of view, this solution might be too high a price.

It follows that health damage occurs, when exposure to certain stimuli differs from that "optimal" value which, in some cases, may be zero, e.g. when the ND functions pass through the origin. Of course, in this context "optimal" refers to the health of the organisms only, although acceptance of arguments as discussed in (iii) will bring in economic arguments (among others) as well.

Let us now consider an example from the air pollution field; let us take the relatively well-documented case of SO_2 pollution. The pollutant under study has been identified, but <u>what</u> do we take as a measure of P_{SO_2} ? There may be long-term effects of exposure to low concentrations, and rather vehement effects of high short-term exposure. These have been combined in diagrams such as in figure 1. From such information, Joosting and Van Houten generalize that for practical purposes, one may take a given effect to be roughly dependent on

(2) $K \log C + \log T$

where K = some constant, C = concentration, T = exposure times.

Figure 1

TRADE-OFFS BETWEEN CONCENTRATION AND EXPOSURE TIME

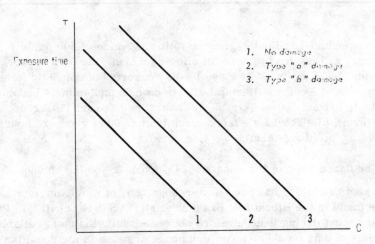

1. No damage
2. Type "a" damage
3. Type "b" damage

(Both axes have a logarithmic scale)

Source : Biersteker, Brasser et al.

A numerical illustration taken from Brasser et al. is given in Table 1.

Table 1.   EFFECTS OF SO_2 EXPOSURE,
EXPOSURE TIME, CONCENTRATION

| | EXPOSURE TIME | | | | |
	LONG PERIOD	7 DAYS	3 DAYS	1 DAY	2 HOURS
	AVERAGE 24 HR. CONCENTRATION (μg/m^3)				
Effects on Man:					
1. Harmful 3rd degree [2]		1,300	2,000		
2nd degree	250	650	800	1,400	
1st degree	180	400	480	680	
2. Transitional area	130	240	280	350	
3. No harm	100	150	170	200	
Effects on Plants:					
1. Harmful effect	400	580	680	850	1,400
2. Transitional area	350	500	560	700	950
3. No harm	300	430	480	580	700

(These data are reported to be on the low side for the Netherlands due to low soot-concentrations there).

Joosten and Ten Houten give the following values: 200 μg/m^3 (24 hours) will not lead to harmful effects on man; the long-term equivalent is 75 μg/m^3. At these levels "deserts" of epiphytic lichens and mosses will occur. Harmful effects on man and animals become detectable around 500-600 μg/m^3 (24 hours) and around 150 μg/m^3 (long-term). Deleterious effects occur from 2,000 μg/m^3 (24 hours) and 300 μg/m^3 (long-term).

The dependence of the effects of SO_2 exposure on the amount of suspended particles, has been well-recognized, of which ample evidence can be found in the literature (Brasser et al.; US dept. of HEW). Perhaps the most daring (but therefore not necessarily the most reliable) synthesis of data on short-term high concentrations in metropolitan areas such as London and New York has been given by Larsen (1970). He postulates the following relation between the number of excess deaths per period D and "pollutant" concentration p;

(3) $D = a \cdot p^b$

(a and b are constants).

More specifically, the following equation resulted from the London and New York data:

(3 a) $D = 0.6 \, P_{SO_2} \, P_{part.}$

when SO_2 and particulate concentrations were used; the value of b seems to have been estimated on a priori grounds. Unfortunately, no information about the equation was given, except R being .98. SO_2 concentrations were measured in ppm; suspended particulates were measured in $\mu g/m^3$.

The number of excess deaths, D, will for any combination of P_{SO_2} and P_{part}, depend on the density of population of a given area; apparently, such variables have similar values in both cities, according to Larsen. Of the possible interactions of chemicals: independence, additivity, antagonism or synergism, the latter would, according to (3a), be the case, since

$$\frac{\delta^2 D}{\delta_{P_{SO_2}} \, \delta_{P_{part}}} > 0.$$

Up till now, of the several variables that can be classified under S_k and I_k, only the concentration of one other pollutant has been discussed. As one of the relevant state variables, mainly in periods of very high concentrations, one must consider the amount of SO_2 within the organism, built up as a result of previous exposures.

Very important, especially under more "normal" conditions than those on which (3) is based, are input variables from other (socio-cultural and economic) aspects of the environment of the system. An early attempt to complete pollution damage functions in this respect has been reported by Gardner et al. Apart from some climatologic and meteorologic factors and factors related to the Ca content of water,

197

they used "domestic air pollution" (derived from energy sources bought for consumption on domestic fires) and a "social factor score" (a weighted combination of factors such as population density, education, income levels etc.) in a multiple regression analysis, to "explain" differences in death rates due to several causes, in several age and sex groups, between UK towns.

In a well-known article, Lave and Seskin have applied a more elaborate version of this approach to mortality rates due to various diseases of 117 standard metropolitan areas (year: 1960). In their model, the mortality rate depends on: age, sex, various genetic factors, nutrition, smoking habits, exercise habits, income, race, quality and frequency of medical care, occupation mix, climatological factors, air pollution for both pollutants, particulates and sulphates, measurements of 26 bi-weekly periods were used to derive three variables in the regression: minimum reading, maximum reading, annual arithmetic means, and, of course, an error-term. (However, not all variables were used in the regression analysis.)

Their main conclusion is that "air pollution has a marked effect on the mortality rate". Using different functional forms or adding additional explanatory variables does not change the basic implication.

Some figures: a 10% decrease in "air pollution" will, according to the outcome of the regression analysis, reduce the total death rate by 0.9%. A 50% decrease in air pollution will increase the life expectancy of a baby by 3 to 5 years.

The so-called "body burden" (the amount of a chemical present in an organism at a given moment; clearly a variable of the S type) has been briefly mentioned above, in connection with SO_2. In connection with pollution by toxic metals such as lead, however, they deserve more attention, due to the much longer half-life (10 years for lead, stored in the bones, where 90% of the lead goes and 3 years in the body as such, according to Zielhuis, 1971). Thus, exposure to low concentrations may eventually build up to a high body burden. In such cases effects have to be related to exposures during the relevant number of periods.

For air pollution, the following model might be appropriate. Let the body burden in period t be B_t; let A_t be the addition to B_t due to intake from exposure at t, and let E_t be the sum of expiration, excretion, etc. at moment t. Then:

(4) $\quad\begin{cases} B_t = B_{t-1} + A_t - E_t \\ \\ E_t = \alpha\, B_{t-1} \\ \\ A_t = \overline{A}_t \text{ and we get} \end{cases}$

As-
sume

(5)

(4 a) $\qquad B_t = (1-\alpha)^t\, B_o + A_t\, \dfrac{1-(1-\alpha)^t}{\alpha}$

For A_t we have in fact:

(6) $\qquad A_t = V(C_b - C_e).\ T$

where V = volume breathed in per unit of time

$\quad\ C_b$ = concentration of pollutant in air breathed in

$\quad\ C_e$ = concentration of pollutant in expired air

$\quad\ T$ = number of units of time per period,

so that the assumption made about A_t in (5) is justified, when (6) holds
and V, C_b and C_e are given.

The health of the organism exposed, is another one of the variables
relevant to the determination of the effect. For example, SO_2 is assumed
to influence the energy-transportation system within the body – a system
that is usually well-balanced and capable of returning to its steady state.
A loss of vital energy could be camouflaged by those feed-backs, if the
organism is healthy. But it might well appear to have negative effects,
if the organism is ill (Joosting and Van Houten).

Some authors warn against thinking in terms of specific effects.
Often, an observed health deterioration is the result of many factors,
including the pollutant studied, but also, one pollutant may cause various
specific effects in terms of specific diseases.

Non-monetary damage due to noise

So far, we have concentrated on effects of pollution on mortality
and morbidity. However, following WHO, in defining health as a state
of optimal physical, psychical and social well-being, annoyance due to
pollution may become a health effect as well. At this moment, damage
functions relating air pollution to the resulting annoyance are being

constructed in the Netherlands; in this paper we will take a closer look at annoyance due to noise, generated by road traffic and aircraft.

From the literature (3) one may deduce the following:

Aural effects due to traffic noise are likely to be very rare. Extra-aural physiological effects of noise have been reported, but the evidence does not, as yet, lead to very firm conclusions; there are physiological reactions that may be the result of a stimulation of the vegetative nervous system, some of them may be subject to adaptation, but not all. A very notable effect is that on sleep. Griffiths and Langdon found that approximately 30% of the people living in the north-west of London were awakened by a traffic noise of 70 TNI (4). Jansen, reporting on a laboratory experiment, mentions shortening of deep sleep to occur at noise bursts only 20 dB above ambient levels, whereas long lasting noises of 70 dB cause considerable shortening of deep sleep stages. An interesting result of experiments by Steinecke has been reported: subjects, asleep in their own bedrooms, were exposed to a noise, increasing with 3 dB every 3 minutes, starting from 30 dB; about 50% of the subjects were awakened at 45 dB. However, it is not clear to what extent these influences of the sleep pattern are being compensated at later hours, during the rest.

There is some - not yet entirely satisfactory - evidence supporting the assumption that noise may have an effect on mental health.

The most widely reported effect of noise is of a psychological kind: it may cause annoyance.

Some of the problems in formulating damage functions for annoyance are similar to those already discussed. First, how does one measure "noise"? A number of measures have been suggested, and they also differ when one is dealing with aircraft noise or with road-traffic noise. This aspect will not be dealt with here - suffice it to say that the question has not yet been settled. Second, how does one measure "annoyance". Two approaches have been followed, so far: (i) one can ask a person how annoyed he is, using some scale of annoyance, (ii) one can ask a person whether he is disturbed in the execution of several activities, such as reading, speaking, watching TV, sleeping, etc. , and whether he finds this disturbance annoying, and then use the number of the activities that are disturbed to an annoying extent, as a measure of annoyance. In using the first approach, one also wishes to substantiate the annoyance score given by asking questions about what disturbances are "behind" the annoyance reported.

Thus, annoyance may be regarded as a second order effect of noise, built up from several "causes" such as sleep disturbance, fear of aircraft falling on one's house, etc. In trying to measure annoyance, one in fact tries to measure some individual aggregation of noise effects on individual well-being. And, of course, there may be other second-order effects derived from the same disturbances: sleep disturbance may lead to a reduced productivity, noise may reduce the efficiency of communication at school and at work, thus leading to efficiency losses; noise may reduce the value of a recreational area, etc. We shall come back to this "joint-product" type aspect later.

Alexandre has reviewed research on noise annoyance around airports in France, the UK, and the Netherlands. In all cases, annoyance was measured according to method (ii) described above, but some harmonization as to the length of the scale was necessary. Noise was measured in different units, but these could be transformed into NNI, the British unit (5).

Median annoyance in a given noise climate, on the transformed scale, A_R was then plotted against the NNI value characterizing that noise climate, using the data of all three countries. The resulting equation (derived from a diagram by Alexandre) must have been close to:

(7) $\qquad A_R = 1.25 \ NNI - 10 \qquad$ (6)

The reported correlation coefficient is .916. The basic calculations in the individual countries' studies also produced correlation coefficients of that order.

However, if _individual_ scores had been used, the correlation coefficient would have been much less.

There have been some attempts to measure the annoyance due to road-traffic noise; the best-known are being made by Griffiths and Langdon. They measure annoyance according to method (i) mentioned above, using a dissatisfaction scale from 1 to 7 (7).

Some of our own work, when compared with Griffiths and Langdon's results leads to the conclusion that there are significant differences between median annoyance scores, as they report for a given noise situation, and the median score found at some Amsterdam sites with a similar noise in terms of TNI. Also, at similar noise situations we found different effects in terms of disturbance of sleep. These differences may have been the result of differing other conditions (type of house, etc.) and influences - the S and I of equation (1). Thus, again one has to take care in using "borrowed" dose-effect relations from others or in extrapolating with those relations.

Figure 2

RELATIONS BETWEEN VARIOUS EFFECTS OF NOISE AND EXPOSURE

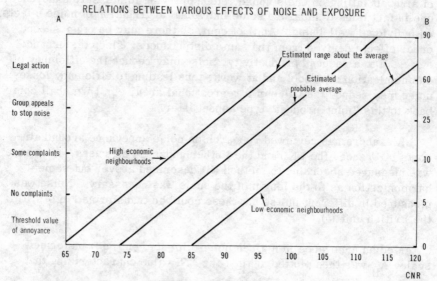

Notes : For practical purposes : CNR = $\overline{PN \, dB}$ + 10 log N - 12

where PNdB is average perceived noise level in decibels, N = number of aircraft

On axis A, some reactions to noise are plotted ;

On axis B, the average percentage of people rating the noise environment unacceptable is given.

To further substantiate these numbers :

at CNR = 90, indoor conversation is assumed to be inaudible for 1 minute/day
at CNR = 100, indoor conversation is assumed to be inaudible for 15 min/day and 5 per cent of the people
between 41 and 57 years are assumed to be awakened per flight (1 per cent in age class 5-8,
23 per cent in age class 69-75)
at CNR = 110, indoor conversation is inaudible for 1 hr/day, and the corresponding awakening percentages
are 21, 4, 33.

Source : Kryter

Figure 3

DISTRIBUTION OF NUISANCE-SCORES REPORTED
AS A FUNCTION OF MEAN NUISANCE AT PARTICULAR LOCATION

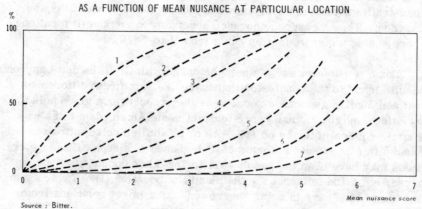

Source : Bitter.

A very interesting intervening variable is the satisfaction with general dwelling conditions in the area studied. This has been reported by Aubree et al. , and it is confirmed in our own field studies in Amsterdam. There is some trade-off at work, in that the subjective evaluation of high noise exposures can be compensated by the evaluation of other, more positive characteristics of the area.

Some quantitative and qualitative evidence and hypotheses are represented in figures 2, 3 and 4.

Figure 4

Regression of dissatisfaction on TNI with confidence
limits at t±2x standard errors of estimate

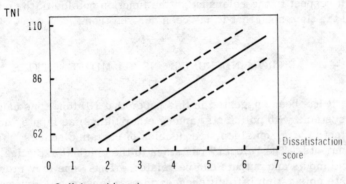

Source · Griffiths and Langdon

ND functions: some generalizations

The observations and results mentioned above can be summarized as follows. Non-monetary damage to health due to pollutants is not only a function of the concentration of that pollutant, but also of factors such as the general health condition of the individual or population studied, previous exposure, exposure to other pollutants, socio-economic variables, etc. Summing over individuals to get ND functions characteristic of a population may yield functions that can shift over time, because preferences change, adaptation (or the opposite) occurs, because some individuals "drop out", thus changing the composition of the population, and because state variables may change to levels where the predictive value of the original ND function is limited. It appears that, ceteris paribus, ND functions relating health damage to levels of pollution are not very well known. Some better-known examples have been discussed. In a large number of cases present knowledge is, mostly, of a qualitative kind, and only the top of the iceberg may be assumed to be known. Apart from these aspects, debates are still going on regarding the terms in which the "amounts" of pollutants are to be expressed, and as in the case of subjective evaluations such as annoyance due to noise etc. , regarding the scales invented to quantify the effects.

A pollutant may have several "specific effects", each of which one might wish to describe in a separate dose-effect relation, if that were possible. This procedure would tremendously enlarge the number of studies to be undertaken. One may wish to avoid this by aggregating to some "states of health"; so far, to my knowledge, attempts to define such states in a manner useful for analysis in an economic context have not been successful.

In those cases where some insight in the damage functions at work has been gained, it is not yet clear to what extent one may generalize with respect to the relevance of the function outside of the population and the time span that it has been derived from.

FROM ND FUNCTIONS TO MD FUNCTIONS

It has been suggested in this paper that ND functions can be seen as systems with pollutants (among other things) as inputs, and certain "effects" (e. g. on sleep, frequencies of certain diseases, mortality, etc.) as outputs. The "closer" one stays to the original exposure, the easier these inputs and outputs can be related. Thus, one may more easily relate noise stimuli to differences in skin tension or dilation of the pupils than, e.g. , to reductions in efficiency. And yet the latter information may be of more relevance on some level of decision-making than the former. That is, in trying to apply damage functions in decision processes, one has to attempt to translate the "direct" outputs of a system as discussed here, in terms of the variables of the objective function of the decision-maker, or find transformations that will ultimately connect the two sets of variables. Variables appearing in the objective function of the decision-maker may include consumption per capita, employment, public health, etc. In many cases the decision-maker will not be fully aware of the exact shape of his objective functions. It is obviously of great help, then, to reduce the number of dimensions of his decision problem - by attempting to transform all aspects into numbers of units of one dimension only, e. g. money. This aspect is linked with the delicate matter of the extent to which the values of the policy-maker reflect those of society, that is: to the degree of consumer sovereignty.

Some of these issues will be discussed in the following paragraphs.

Exposure to pollutants may result in some set of direct, or first-order consequences, which may lead to a set of second-order consequences, etc. Some of these patterns take little time, and may therefore be relatively easily perceived - both by experts and by the public. Others extend over a longer period of time, and the consequences are then usually less well known or perceived. A further distinction that can be applied is that between effects on human well-being and effects on non-human receptors that are not relevant to our well-being. The first category contains "technological" and pecuniary effects, that is, direct reductions of welfare levels or reductions of our means to welfare (consumer goods, factors of production). If these effects are associated with specific geographical locations, the value of these locations and the uses to which they have been applied (dwelling zones, recreational areas, natural reservations, etc.) may well decline. One must, in these circumstances take care not to count a given damage twice; declines in, e.g., amenity values (taking surpluses into account) would reflect at least some of direct physical damage (8).

I would argue then that one should distinguish between actual effects of pollution associated with our economic behaviour and the values we attach to these effects, thus making it quite clear that:

i)   the second category follows the first one logically, and not all information is necessarily used when we go from one level of effects to another;

ii)   it is our evaluations that are established (if this can be done at all), and not those of other generations possibly affected or non-human living organisms. MD functions could be taken to be the result of rather anthropocentric-egocentric evaluation procedures.

Problems of estimating monetary damage

We shall confine ourselves mainly to the aspects that have been dealt with earlier in this paper: effects on the health (in a wide sense) of human beings (9). Health damage may have several consequences that suggest a monetary evaluation:

a.   i)   It may lead to expenses, associated with visits to doctors, hospitals, and with the consumption of drugs, medicines, diets, etc., thus reducing the amount of resources available for consumption directly;

ii)   it may lead to reductions of productivity (or fraction of time worked), leading to reductions of income or profits, thus reducing the total amount of resources available for consumption indirectly;

b.   iii)   it may lead to a welfare-loss on the part of the receptors, quite apart from (i) and (ii).

Type (i) damage obviously leads to market behaviour (at least in those countries where medical care is not provided free of charge), and can be evaluated with market-signals as transformators.

Type (ii) damage will be more difficult to evaluate: often it will only show up partially or not at all. In some cases, however, evaluation seems possible at least to some extent.

As an example let us look at one aspect of pollution by suspended particulate sulphates and the associated incidence of respiratory diseases as reported by the US Department of HEW (pp. 135-136):

Figure 5

Frequency of absenteeism, due to pollution

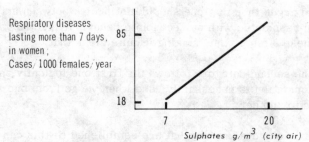

Source : U.S. Department, of Health, Education and Welfare ; approximate ranges are indicated.

Given some data such as average length of the disease and wages, one could use ND functions like this one to calculate corresponding MD functions.

Although it is true that anticipated or experienced welfare losses due to pollution may lead to changes in the behaviour on certain markets, with the purpose of reducing the effects of pollution, taking the value of those changes in market behaviour may yield very partial results, as the noise example in the next paragraph will show. There may still be welfare effects that have not appeared in behaviour as such, but yet are to be imputed to the pollution input. These are what have been called "type (iii) damage". It is with these types of damage that concepts such as "compensation", "willingness to pay", and the techniques to estimate them, have to be considered.

But, confining ourselves, momentarily, to changes in market behaviour, there are still some serious problems to tackle.

First, there is the obvious question whether the markets may be assumed to produce the "correct" prices to be used in building MD functions. Even apart from matters like market power, the influence of the income distribution on demand functions, increasing returns to scale, and other well known market imperfections there are some important considerations.

One may well question the individual's ability to be fully aware and/or fully informed of pollution and its consequences. That this may influence market behaviour so as to create divergences between actual behaviour based on anticipated relations between the relevant variables, and _ex post_ optimal behaviour, has been noted before (10). Of course, this bias may operate in two directions, depending on whether actual interdependencies are weaker or stronger than the anticipated ones.

A second difficulty can be introduced with the following example. Suppose, someone has bought a second house to spend the week-ends in, thus to evade exposure to very heavy road traffic noise. The individual or its family will be exposed during the other days of the week, but this leads to much lower annoyance levels. Is one to count expenditure on the second house as representing "total noise cost", 2/7 of "total noise cost", or should one not count the entire expenditure as related to noise cost, since having and using a second house may lead to increases in the individual's welfare quite apart from the noise matter?

More formally, a given action does not necessarily have but one "cause"; pollution may be one of the factors leading towards certain behaviour or effects. In addition, the resulting action may have joint products; it may have side benefits and/or disbenefits that lead to significant changes in welfare compared with the situation in which they are absent. Allocating costs in these circumstances can at least be called a very difficult job.

Next, is one to base evaluation upon observed actions and behaviour, or, rather, on more efficient ways to achieve the same ends? The latter seems preferable (but it implies that the evaluator will need much more information at his disposal, than if one can assume behaviour always to follow least cost paths).

There are several monetary values to be established, given the effect E_o of the initial exposure P_o, and the effect E_1, after the individual has taken some measure:

- the costs of methods of preventing (E_o - E_1) by sufficiently reducing pollution to, say, P_1;

- the costs of methods of "curing", that is, while leaving P_o as
  it is, somehow reduce E_o to E_1;

- the sum of money large enough to compensate receptors; that
  is, while leaving P_o and E_o as they are, the sum of money that
  will make receptors as well off as without the extra money, but
  at (P_1, E_1);

- money values associated with combinations of the activities
  underlying the previous valuations.

It may be the lowest one of the values defined above, that is wanted
for MD functions, or it may be that it is decided to take the value
corresponding with actual behaviour which, obviously, must be included
in the strategies distinguished above.

A final problem is the extent to which all three types of damage
will be considered relevant. Already, the relation between damage
and the policy-maker's objective function has been mentioned.

If the policy-maker is allowed to consider individuals as factors
of production solely, then damages of type (i) and (ii) are relevant,
and that of type (iii) only insofar as they may have long run consequences
for the productivity and "maintenance costs" of the individuals. If, on
the other hand, subjective individual valuations are to count, type (iii)
damage enters into the picture. As will be seen in the noise example
yet to be presented, this will not always be allowed to take the form
of an absolute conformity to individual evaluations.

The remaining category of damage to be discussed is that of
(parts of) damage not showing up in actual behaviour. It may be thought
of as changes in the "level of satisfaction", without leading to different
solutions, when utility functions are confronted with the relevant constraints. There may be some amount of money that will compensate for
the change in pollution levels (for some, there is not, as the next paragraph shows). This sum of money one usually tries to establish by
asking people, through enquiries and social surveys. There are many
points that can be made on this subject, but they fall outside the scope
of this paper (11). One main point in this context is that asking questions
about hypothetical compensations for hypothetical exposures to noise or
air pollution, etc. may indeed yield answers in terms of money values,
but it seems difficult to have enough confidence in them.

The cost of noise of airports and motorways

Damage functions with regard to noise exposure could be important
pieces of information in planning motorways, airports, etc. Non-monetary

consequences of noise have been discussed above; we assume here that we may concentrate on the annoyance aspect alone. The question then is, what money value can be attached to annoyance due to noise?

Prediction models for noise exposure have been developed and are being improved; relating annoyance to noise exposure is a difficult task. So far, in several countries one has relied upon statistically found relationships between the two. Recent work in the UK casts some doubt upon the predictive value of these models (12). Nevertheless, annoyance may be assumed to increase with noise exposure, appropriately measured.

Once an airport or a motorway has been constructed, the noise it emits will become one of the characteristics of the areas around it. As such it will influence the quality of those areas as dwelling zones, etc. Property prices may then be taken to decline. It is this decrease in value that has been used as a starting point of the evaluation of the cost of noise annoyance, especially in the case of the Third London Airport (13).

Several approaches have been put forward, that apparently try to fully measure the cost of noise annoyance, based on a model where individual households are assumed to decide whether to move out of the area or not, following the outcome of:

$$(8) \qquad N \gtreqless S + R + D \qquad (14)$$

where N = cost of enduring the noise,

D = depreciation of house value,

R = cost of moving,

S = surplus associated with living in present area.

The left-hand side is supposed to measure the cost of staying in the area; the right-hand side is supposed to measure the costs associated with moving. The direction of the inequality determines whether a household moves (with imputed costs $S + R + D$) or stays (with cost N).

Other models concentrate mainly on the D term: the depreciation of house values (15). The (absolute and relative) merits of several of these methods have been discussed and shown to be doubtful (16); nevertheless, so far no better method has been suggested, which leaves us with the choice of either using one or more of these methods, or abandoning trying to measure noise annoyance costs at all. Here, we shall confine ourselves to describing some of the results of applying these methods.

We may conclude that depreciation of house values may be a quantifiable effect of exposing an area to noise (17), but that it is not certain to what extent this may be taken to represent total noise costs.

In this paragraph, some of the evidence concerning the depreciation of house values is given as an example of a partial MD function; some results of attempts to build "complete" MD functions for the annoyance aspect in the London Airport case will be repeated as well.

The following data have been taken from the Roskill Commission Final Report (op. cit.). They relate to inquiries of house agents familiar with aircraft noise and its effects on house prices, in the Gatwick and Heathrow Airport areas.

Table 2.   AVERAGE PERCENTAGE DEPRECIATION
OF HOUSE PROPERTY VALUES
(RE HOUSES OUTSIDE 35 NNI)

PRICE RANGE (£)	NOISE EXPOSURE		
	35-45 NNI	45-55 NNI	> 55 NNI
A. Heathrow Area			
0 - 4,000	0	2.9	5.0
4,000 - 8,000	2.6	6.3	10.5
> 8,000	3.3	13.3	22.5
B. Gatwick Area			
0 - 4,000	4.5	10.3	
4,000 - 8,000	9.4	16.5	
> 8,000	16.4	29.0	

In another British study (concerning the costs and benefits of retrofitting aircraft), the following relation between noise exposure and and house price depreciation (based on estate agents' estimates in the Heathrow area) was used: (Table 3).

Table 3

NOISE EXPOSURE	% DEPRECIATION
< 35 NNI	0
35–40 NNI	3. 5
40–45 NNI	7. 5
45–50 NNI	10. 0
> 50 NNI	15. 0

In the Metra report mentioned above, one can find the result of a regression analysis based on a survey of estate agents around (outside) London:

(9) $\qquad X_1 = 1.73 + .00107 \, V$

$\qquad X_2 = 0.0295 + .00070 \, V$

where X_1 = % depreciation of houses assumed to be in the 45–50 NNI zone (compared < 35 NNI value),

$\qquad X_2$ = % depreciation of houses assumed to be in the 35–45 NNI zone,

$\qquad V$ = value of the house (£) when in < 35 NNI zone.

These data have been assembled in Figure 6.

It appears that important differences between depreciation data exist, even if price and noise exposure are controlled as far as possible. Several notes may be added:

- Gatwick houses suffer from a rapid growth in air traffic forecasts; it is at a greater distance from London, and it is more rural, thus having a lower background level (18). One can perhaps imagine other significant variables to differ at the two locations, thus leading to differences in house price depreciation.

- Price differentials have been established by consulting a sample of house agents. These agents will not all give the same answers. Exactly how much they vary can be shown for the Gatwick data; the outcome may surprise some and they certainly cast further doubts on the figures quoted:

211

Figure 6

HOUSE PRICE DEPRECIATION PERCENTAGES AS A FUNCTION OF NOISE EXPOSURE

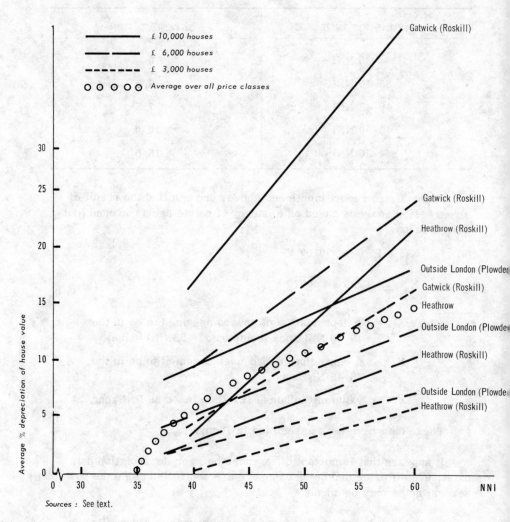

Sources : See text.

Table 4. RANGE OF DEPRECIATION ESTIMATED (PERCENTAGE) (NNI 35-45)

HOUSE PRICE RANGE	< 4,000	4,000-8,000	>8,000
Highest estimate	10	15	25
Average estimate	5	9	16
Lower estimate	0	3	5

In situations with noise due to road traffic, house price depreciation has also been reported. In our previously mentioned Amsterdam case study, we made some investigations, with the following result. Along the road studied there are several apartment buildings, some of which are owner occupied. They have been erected in 1961; the road was built later and was opened for traffic in 1967. The actual prices at which these apartments have been sold, in the period 1961-1972, are known, and they reveal the following picture:

From 1961-1967 prices rose, following a trend representative for similar houses in urban areas in the Netherlands. In 1967 and later, house prices oscillated roughly around the 1964 level reached previously. Using simple statistical techniques to extrapolate to a no noise 1971 value that could be compared with actual selling prices, yields depreciation values of - roughly - 25%. Some house agents have been asked to officially estimate the loss of value due to the road and the nuisance it generates (mainly noise) arrive at lower levels, but again the difference would be in the neighbourhood of 25%. The noise at the particular location may be taken to be of the order of magnitude of l_{eq} = 70 dB(A) or 95 TNI (19).

As has been stated, house value depreciation may be only partial approaches to the damage due to noise, even if one restricts oneself to effects of human noise annoyance. Other elements might be those appearing in equation (8). That particular model has been used by the Roskill Commission, and (adapted) by Plowden, although principally different methods were used to estimate N (20). The latter's calculations have yielded the following results: (Table 5).

The term "modified moving costs" merits some explanation. Many people (18%) stated that no sum of money would induce them to move out of the area they lived in, thus in fact placing an infinite surplus value upon this property and its surroundings. For these people (and also for those mentioning a compensation of more than 50% of their

213

Table 5

NOISE LEVEL	TYPE OF SOCIAL COST	% OF HOUSE-HOLDS FOR WHICH EACH TYPE IS SMALLEST	AVERAGE MINIMUM COST
50 NNI	Endurance costs	37	951
	Moving costs	35	2,599
	Modified moving costs	28	4,396
	Total	100	2,506
45–50 NNI	Endurance costs	42	689
	Moving costs	33	2,184
	Modified moving costs	25	4,128
	Total	100	2,028
35–45 NNI	Endurance costs	55	571
	Moving costs	23	1,791
	Modified moving costs	22	3,615
	Total	100	1,508

house value) a cut-off figure of 50% of their house value has been used, yielding the so-called "modified moving costs" in those cases where moving was the outcome.

The above figures were then applied to yield noise cost estimates for the four alternative possible airport locations. The Roskill report does not give its results in this damage function type form; rather it gives the outcome of the calculations for the four sites directly. For two locations, the Roskill cost figures have been compared with those that would have resulted using Plowden's damage function. The Roskill cost figures appear to be lower: approximately £ 96.6 million as opposed to £ 72.2 million for the Nuthampstead site, and £ 40.9 million as opposed to £ 15.6 million for the Thurleigh site. These gaps would have been greater if the cut-off procedure discussed above had not been followed.

It seems that these two approaches, although very similar in logic, cannot be taken to verify one another.

Some comments

The amount of faith invested in the individual's ability to produce reasonable figures, is enormous. The development of the noise over time, its effects in terms of annoyance and associated costs, etc. , are all taken to be known; furthermore, individuals are taken to be capable of discounting annual costs to one period; all this must lead to a money answer, produced, say, within ten minutes from the question being asked.

There are some arguments for assuming the depreciation to grow with time. In the first place, quiet housing is likely to become scarce in absolute terms, and more demanded, as income rises. The model discussed by Pearce (op. cit.) takes such factors into account. Our own case study supports this hypothesis: since the opening of the road, the price difference between the exposed houses and their hypothetical non-exposed equivalents increased every year, both in absolute and in relative terms.

Rising price differentials may also be a consequence of changing preferences due to, e. g. increased information.

CONCLUSIONS AND FINAL REMARKS

A distinction has been made between "non-monetary damage functions" and "monetary damage functions", whereby the latter are taken to be based upon the former. Within the category of non-monetary damage one can imagine several "levels" of effects, all being elements in some causal chain, that may be taken to have "monetary damage" as (one of) its ultimate element(s).

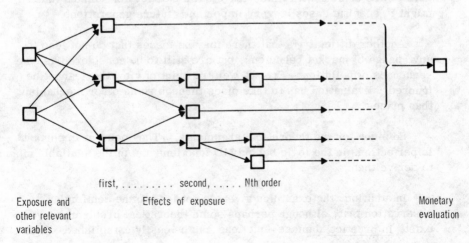

first, ... second, ... Nth order

Exposure and   Effects of exposure   Monetary
other relevant   evaluation
variables

215

Going from one level to another, one must take care not to lose information, by disregarding some effects. It is not at all certain, that monetary evaluation will take all effects into account; neither can one assume that it will take account of the effects adequately. A given set of effects at any level is not only determined by some exposure, but by several other variables, reflecting pollution by other pollutants, physical and mental health, socio-economic circumstances, etc. and theoretically the time-paths of these variables. It appears that it is going to be a job worthy of Hercules to attempt to find all, or even only the more important monetary damage functions. Perhaps one could be satisfied with a smaller amount of information: some points on the ND functions, or best informal guesses as to these points. In trying to attach money values to physical damages one meets with some additional difficulties.

Damage may lead to changes in market behaviour that can as such, be, in principle, observed and assessed. Other effects that seem relatively easy to evaluate are those on the human being as a factor of production - the human resource point of view. It must be mentioned that prices and market behaviour reflect present supply and demand conditions, including preferences, the income distribution, etc. , and that these preferences may change as the level of information changes. To put it differently, if the consequences of pollution are but poorly known, even to the experts, individual market behaviour can hardly be regarded as being optimal.

It must also be mentioned that it will not always be easy to identify a certain change in market behaviour as being a result of pollution; many factors may be responsible for a given action, one of them perhaps being pollution. In these "joint input" cases, it is hard to allocate costs over causes. Furthermore, it is present supply and demand conditions that we are dealing with which leave out a category of humans that might in specific cases be very important: future generations.

Another difficulty is that there may be losses that do not lead to any change of market behaviour, but are still to be considered as consequences of pollution. From a welfare point of view they cannot be ignored. Evaluation has to take place through some other mechanism than prices.

So much for the theoretical arguments. They point at important imperfections in the logic behind MD functions and in the available means to derive them.

In addition, the examples given do not lead to the comforting observation that, although perhaps some theoretical problems may exist, in practice damage functions can be easily established. This

216

may be due to the fact that although non-monetary damage functions may somehow be of a "general" nature, evaluations by people may differ from one region to another, as well as many other data that go into the damage-function concept. In other words, one may very well expect (sometimes large) regional differences in MD functions.

My conclusion is, that although conceptually damage functions are to be considered as extremely useful tools in decision-making with respect to pollution, the moment that they can be used as such on any relevant scale must still be far ahead. Monetary damage estimates can so far be used as "circumstantial evidence" only; and the ranges of values that one may obtain when using several methods of estimation simultaneously, may even make the word "evidence" doubtful. For problems that require solution in the shorter run, the policy-maker may expect more from informed guesses and sometimes estimations as to the non-monetary effects of alternative levels of pollution to be decided between, and set standards on the basis of that information mainly.

REFERENCES

The following list contains those items that have not been already referred to in the footnotes.

Alexandre A. : Prévision de la gêne due au bruit autour des aéroports et perspectives sur les moyens d'y remédier, Centre d'Etudes et de Recherches d'Anthropologie Appliquée, Paris 1970.

Aubrée D. , Auzou S. , and Rapin J. M. : Etude de la gêne due au trafic automobile urbain, Centre Scientifique et Technique du Bâtiment, Paris, 1971.

Biersteker K. : Kwaliteitsnormen Buitenlucht, Tÿdschift voor Sociale Geneeskunde, 1968.

Bitter C. : La gêne due au bruit des avions, Revue d'Acoustique n° 10, 1970.

Brasser L. J. : Joosting, P. E. , Van Zuilen D. : Sulphur Dioxide, To What Level is it Acceptable ? I. G. -T. N. O. , Delft, 1967.

De Bruin A. , Zielhuis R. L. : Toxicological Appraisal of Lead as a Public Health Hazard, Tÿdschift voor Sociale Geneeskunde no. 23, 1971.

Gardner M. J. , Crawford M. P. , Morris J. N. : Patterns of Mortality in Middle and Early Old Age in the County Boroughs of England and Wales, Brit. J. of Prev. Soc. Med. , 1969.

Griffiths I. D. , Langdon F. J. : Subjective Response to Road Traffic Noise.

Izmerov N. F. : Establishment of Air Quality Standards, Arch. of Environmental Health, Vol. 22, 1971.

Joosting P. E. , Ten Houten J. C. : Biological Effects of Air Pollution, Toekomstbeeld der Techniek, no. 7, the Hague, 1971.

Kryter K. D. : Non-Auditory Effects of Environmental Noise, Am. Journ. of Publ. Health, no. 3, 1972.

Larsen R. I. : Relating Air Pollutant Effects to Concentration and Control, Journ. of the Air Poll. Ass. , Vol. 20, no. 4, 1970.

Lave L. B. , Seskin E. P. : Health and Air Pollution, Swed. Journ. of Economics, 1971.

US Dept. , of HEW: Air Quality Criteria for Sulphur Oxides, Nat. Air Poll. Control Adm. publication no. AP. 50.

Zielhuis R. L. : Het Vaststellen van Aaanvaandbare Concentraties, Tÿdschift voor Sociale Geneeskunde, Vol. 47, no. 20, 1969.

NOTES

1. Joosting and Ten Houten list the following factors (relevant to health effects of air pollution): (a) physical and chemical properties of the pollutant, (b) its concentration, (c) duration of exposure, (d) environmental conditions, (e) susceptibility of the organism, (f) locus and mode of uptake, (g) metabolism and rate of elimination. The latter factor will determine what fraction of P_j^h will be stored as "body burden", and will therefore be important in studying the time-path of that body burden.

2. It is not fully clear what the authors mean with "1st, 2nd and 3rd degree effects": from the context, one can deduct that 1st degree effects include symptoms of illnesses, disease and death to occur approximately 1.5 to 2 times some set of reference values; when this rate increases to 2.5 to 3, one is dealing with the 2nd degree effects, etc.

3. This section is based on a number of reports, some of which only have been included in the list of references at the end of this paper.

4. TNI is a measure of exposure to road traffic noise, which is built up from peak level noise and back-ground levels, as follows:

$$TNI = 4(L_{10} - L_{90}) + L_{90} - 30$$

where L_{10} and L_{90} are the 10 and 90 percentile sound levels in dB(A).

5. $$\text{NNI} = 10 \log \frac{1}{N} \sum_{N} 10^{\frac{L}{10}} + 15 \log N - 80$$

where L = peak noise level (PNdB) and N = number of aircraft.

6. On several grounds, one must take care in using such equations to predict noise annoyance; some of these are: (i) individuals may, and will, move thus leaving a changed population; (ii) reactions towards noise may change over time; (iii) the "theory behind" this equation is weak insofar as it can be shown that the value of the correlation coefficient is quite insensitive to changes of the regression coefficients connected with N in the second term of the expression for NNI.

7. They have estimated $D = \beta \, \text{TNI} + \alpha$, and found $\alpha = .101$, $\beta = -3.87$, with $r = .89$, var $(\alpha) = 13.741$, and var $(\beta) = 0.002$. Thus, TNI seems to be a good "predictor" although the constant term is rather shaky. D is the mean disturbance score at a given location; the correlation coefficient drops to .29, when individual scores are regressed against TNI. A similar position has been reported by Aubree et al. , for the Paris situation, with $r = .97$ and $r = .37$ respectively. The relatively small range indicated in fig. 4 must be interpreted with this aspect in mind.

8. I know of no example where this has occurred as yet, but in the discussions on airport location and noise effects, the possibility of double-counting seems to have invaded at least one proposed (though not officially used) method of assessing the monetary value of noise annoyance. See E. J. Richards, "Noise and Society", Journal of the Royal Society of Arts, Sept. 1971, where annual noise costs are estimated by determining the annual lack of appreciation of house values in noisy areas, and where, in addition, a value is sought for sleep and conversation disturbance, etc. The author argues that "This is nothing to do with house value... ".

9. Other types of monetary damage can of course be easily imagined: reduced protective capacity of paint, corrosion, damage to crops and livestock, etc. It might be that damages of these kinds can be more easily assessed than those associated with health effects, because they may be taken to have no direct welfare loss over and above the reduction of income disposable for consumption, due to pollution.

10. See, e. g. : A. Coddington, J. B. Opschoor, D. W. Pearce: "Some Limitations of Benefit Cost Analysis in Respect of Programmes with Environmental Consequences", in Problems of Environmental

Economics, OECD 1972, and: J. B. Opschoor, "Opinie-enqetering en Informatie", Economisch Statistische Berichten, May 1971.

11. See, for some of these, Peter Bohm: "A Note on the Problem of Estimating Benefits from Pollution Control", in Problems of Environmental Economics, OECD, Paris 1972, and "An Approach to the Problem of Estimating Demand for Public Goods", Swed. Journal of Economics, 1972.

12. Second Survey of Aircraft Noise Annoyance around London (Heathrow) Airport, HMSO, 1971, pp. 186-188, and p. 9.

13. Other aspects, such as reduced recreational value of areas, etc. would still have to be assessed; this section ignores these valuation problems.

14. This model may be taken to be representing that of the Roskill - Commission advising the British government (Roskill Commission, "Final Report", HMSO 1970) and, with some alterations, that of the Metra Consulting Group (SPC Plowden, "The Cost of Noise", 1970).

15. D. W. Pearce: "The Economic Evaluation of Noise-Generating and Noise Abatement Projects", in "Problems of Environmental Economics", OECD, 1971; and Richards, op. cit.

16. M. E. Paul: "Can Aircraft Noise Nuisance be Measured in Money?" Oxford Economic Papers, 1971, and also Pearce, op. cit.

17. This is not to say that it will be easy to show differences in prices when actual market transactions are studied; to the contrary, in several cases this has appeared to be very difficult. For this, many arguments can be put forward which, however, will not be discussed here. We shall concentrate mainly on depreciation figures derived from surveys among house agents.

18. Richards, op. cit.

19. Of course, these figures cannot be used to derive a reliable damage function: we have data of only one sample area and, according to the experiences with aircraft noise, one may expect large differences in comparing values for other areas having the same noise exposure; also: we only have values for one noise level. However, perhaps the information may be used to formulate some expectations as to the order of magnitude of amenity loss due to noise in urban dwelling zones for this particular type of house. Assuming that noise below l_{eq} = 45 dB(A) will not lead

to any reductions in house values (which seems not unreasonable, in view of the ISO standards) and assuming that analogous to the effect of aircraft noise we may expect a linear relationship between noise exposure and its effect on house prices, we could hypothesize:

$$
\left.\begin{array}{ll}
d = -45 + 1_{eq}, & \text{for } L_{eq} \geqslant 45 \\[2ex]
d = 0, & \text{for } L_{eq} \leqslant 45
\end{array}\right\}
$$

where d = % depreciation with reference to "no-noise" value.

However, one might just as well assume some sort of step function to hold, where depreciation percentages will rise as the noise index will pass some new perception thresholds. Depreciation of 25% has been reported elsewhere in the Netherlands and other figures have not. However, in view of the hypothesis embodied in fig. 2, this could be due to the fact that only when certain exposure values are passed will people start to take some form of action.

20. Roskill assumed that median annoyance at a given noise level can be set equal to the depreciation in house values due to the noise, a procedure that has been thoroughly criticized by Paul (op. cit.). Plowden estimates N through a social survey; a procedure that again necessitates some drastic assumptions.

DAMAGE FUNCTIONS AND THEIR ESTIMATION:
A THEORETICAL SURVEY

by

Karl-Göran Mäler*
Department of Economics, University of Stockholm
Sweden

INTRODUCTION

This paper is an attempt to present, in a systematic way, the
theoretical difficulties which occur in defining and estimating monetary
damage functions. In doing this I have been drawing freely on existing
literature, without always giving the proper references. The paper is
mainly based on two chapters in a forthcoming book (5). For further
details and for more extensive references, the reader is referred to
this book.

On can regard this paper as a translation of familiar welfare theory
to the field of environmental pollution. It is divided into two parts. In
the first part, monetary damage functions are defined. The definition
depends, however, on the assumptions we make about the existence of
ethical norms in society. Different norms imply different damage
functions. But the definition is also closely related to the instruments
we have to redistribute income in society.

The basic value judgement underlying the whole paper is that it is
individual preferences which are important. This means that the damage
functions will be closely tied to the marginal willingness-to-pay concept.

The second part deals with theoretical problems connected with an
estimation of damage functions. A few approaches to such estimation
problems are discussed, but not one is found to be satisfactory. In
view of the difficulties present in defining damage functions and the
difficulties in estimating them, it may be better to use so-called
"physical" (or "non-monetary") damage functions as a means to represent information about the environment, except in those cases where
it is possible to define and to estimate monetary damage functions.

* Presently Professor at the Stockholm School of Economics, Stockholm.

Part I

THE DEFINITION OF SOCIAL DAMAGE FUNCTIONS

1. Environmental quality

We start from the assumption that there exist well-defined characteristics of the environment, it being possible to measure each characteristic in some way. Moreover, we assume that these characteristics
fully describe the quality of the environment. These assumptions imply
that it is possible to characterize environmental quality completely by
a vector

$$Y \in R^m$$

The first component of Y may stand for the ambient concentration of
SO_2 at some grid point, the second may be the concentration of SO_2 at
some other grid point. One component may be the population of trout in
some specific lake, another may be the level of noise along some main
street in a city, a third component may be a probability distribution of
getting a disease. It is obvious that the number m may be very large.
We assume, however, that it is finite.

Y is, in general, a function of human activities, such as discharges
of residuals, highway construction, artificial aeration of a water body,
destruction of old buildings and so on. Let the symbol z stand for these
activities. Then we can write:

(1) $Y = F(z).$

We will call the function F the environmental interaction function. It
could equally well be called a physical damage function, because it
gives the physical changes in environmental quality due to changes in
human activities.

From now on we will assume that the environmental interaction
function is known and that it is deterministic. Both these assumptions
are far from being realistic. One of the main problems in management
of residuals is that the effects of discharges of residuals are not known.
It is, however, not the job for an economist to discuss methods of
estimating this function, it is a job for ecologists, meteorologists and
other natural scientists and engineers. The second assumption is
equally dubious, and in some cases is directly misleading. We know
that temperature and rainfall determine the speed of the degradation
of organic matters in a stream and, therefore, also the dissolved

oxygen concentration. But weather must be regarded as a random variable and the environmental interaction function should be stochastic.

In spite of these remarks we will maintain the assumption that F is completely known and deterministic. The importance of studies that give us more information on the environmental interaction function must be stressed, however. It is probably the field which should be given the highest priority in connection with damage functions.

2.   Environmental quality as a public good

We will assume that the vector Y has the character of a public good in the sense of Professor Samuelson (11). This means that everyone is faced with the same environmental quality, and no one can change the quality only for himself, but the change will occur to all other individuals. This does not mean that an individual cannot try to avoid some deterioration of the environment. He can, for example, move to a neighbourhood with a better environment, but the quality of the environment is in our terminology still the same.

This is a very reasonable assumption, and almost any facet of the environment may be interpreted in this way. For some variables, this is self-evident: air pollution in a city is one example. But even such variables as air quality inside an air-conditioned building may be interpreted as a public good. However, in this case, presumably only those who live in the building have definite preferences for air quality.

3.   Consumer preferences

This section contains an elementary exposition of consumption theory that can be found in almost any textbook on the subject. I have included it in order to present the terminology that is going to be used. Needless to say, it is possible to generalize the discussion considerably without changing the conclusions. For such a generalization see chapter IV in (5).

In this paper we will use the classical idea that consumers have preferences that can be represented by a twice continuous differentiable utility function, defined on R^{n+m}:

(2) $u(c, Y)$

where c is an n-vector interpreted as the vector of net demands for private marketable goods and services. Positive components indicate consumption, while negative ones indicate a supply of goods and services.

The consumers do, therefore, have preferences both for their own private consumption and for environmental quality.

As usual, u is not uniquely defined by the preferences of the consumer, but only up to a strictly increasing transformation. As Y is a vector of public goods, the consumer cannot himself change Y, and so his budget constraint is

(3)
$$p^T c \leq I,$$

where I is his wealth or lump sum income; and $p^T c$ denotes the inner product of the price vectors p and c.

Utility maximization subject to the budget constraint yields the following necessary conditions

(4)
$$u_i - \alpha p_i = 0, \quad i = 1, \ldots, n,$$

where

$$u_i = \frac{\partial u}{\partial c_i}, \quad \text{and } \alpha \text{ a Lagrangean multiplier.}$$

These conditions determine the Marshallian demand functions

(5)
$$c = c(p, Y, I).$$

If we substitute these demand functions into the utility function, we obtain the indirect utility function v:

(6)
$$v(p, Y, I) = u(c(p, Y, I), Y).$$

Consider now the dual problem of minimizing the expenditures necessary to sustain a given utility level $\bar{u}$:

$$\text{minimize} \quad p^T c$$

$$\text{subject to} \quad u(c, Y) \geq \bar{u}.$$

The first order necessary conditions are

(7)
$$\beta u_i - p_i = 0, \quad i = 1, \ldots, n \quad (\beta \text{ is a Langrangean multiplier)}$$

and the solutions are the compensated demand functions

(8)
$$c = c^*(p, Y, \bar{u}).$$

The function

(9)
$$m(p, Y, \bar{u}) = p^T c^*(p, Y, \bar{u})$$

226

is called the expenditure function. The expenditure function gives the least income necessary to sustain the utility level $\bar{u}$ as a function of prices and environmental quality.

It is easy to derive the following properties of the expenditure function (for a derivation, see chapter IV in (5)).

i) $\dfrac{\partial m}{\partial p_i} = c_i^*$, $\quad i = 1, \ldots, n$

ii) $c(p, m(p, Y, \bar{u})) = c^*(p, Y, \bar{u})$

iii) $c(p, I, Y) = c^*(p, v(p, Y, I), Y)$

iv) m is a concave function in p

v) $\dfrac{\partial^2 m}{\partial p_j \partial p_i} - \dfrac{\partial c_i(p, Y, m)}{\partial I} \dfrac{\partial m}{\partial p_j} - \dfrac{\partial c_i(p, Y, m)}{\partial p_j} = O$

   (Slutsky equations)

vi) $\dfrac{\partial c_i^*}{\partial p_j} = \dfrac{\partial c_j^*}{\partial p_i}$

vii) if u is quasi concave in (p, Y), then m is convex in Y.

The Slutsky equations are a system of total differential equations. Property vi) which is equivalent to (because of i) and ii))

(10) $\qquad \dfrac{\partial c_i}{\partial p_j} + c_j \dfrac{\partial c_i}{\partial I} = \dfrac{\partial c_j}{\partial p_i} + c_i \dfrac{\partial c_j}{\partial I}$.

(10) is, however, a necessary and sufficient condition for complete integrability for the Slutsky equations. It is thus possible to solve the Slutsky equations in order to obtain m as a function of p, if the demand functions are known and satisfy (10). The demand functions are at least in principle observable relations, and if they, furthermore, are consistent with our consumption theory, then it is possible to compute the expenditure function as a function of prices. It is not possible to estimate m as a function of Y in this way, however.

4. Definition of damage functions for one individual

We are now in a position to define damage functions for one individual rigorously. The damage function, to be denoted by $CV(p, Y, \bar{u})$ is defined as the compensating variation or as

227

(11) $CV(p, Y, \bar{u}) = m(p, Y, \bar{u}) - I,$

where $\bar{u}$ is the utility level at some predetermined situation, in which the consumer's income is I.

The damage function is thus defined as the amount the individual must be compensated because of a deterioration of the environment.

In order to see how this definition works, let us consider two situations, characterized by Y' and Y'' respectively. In Y' the individual is healthy, but in Y'' he is sick. We have

$$CV = m(p, Y'', \bar{u}) - I =$$

$$\sum_{i=1}^{n} p_i (c_i^*(p, Y'', \bar{u}) - c_i(p, Y', I)).$$

Let there be only three goods, the first one is labour supply, the second medical care, and the third consumption in general. Assume that the sickness prevents the individual from working, so that

$$c_1^*(p, Y'', \bar{u}) = c_1(p, Y'', I) = 0$$

Assume also that when he is healthy, he does not spend any money on medical care. This means that

$$c_2(p, Y', I) = 0$$

Assume also that the income effect on the demand for medical care can be neglected so that

$$c_2^*(p, Y'', \bar{u}) = c_2(p, Y'', I).$$

The damage can now be written

$$CV = - p_1 c_1(p, Y', I) + p_2 c_2(p, Y'', I) +$$

$$p_3(c_3^*(p, Y'', \bar{u}) - c_3(p, Y', I)).$$

The first term is the loss in wage income (recall that c_1 is negative because it represents a supply of labour), the second term is the increase in expenditure for medical care. The third term can be interpreted as the psychic cost, because it gives the increase in expenditure on consumption in general that is necessary in order to compensate the individual for the sickness.

In most applications, only the first two terms are considered. Our derivation shows that such an approach may be greatly misleading. It is quite possible that the third term is the largest term.

The problem of estimating individual damage functions is thus the same as the problem of estimating the individual expenditure functions. As we have seen above, it is possible, from a knowledge of the individual demand functions to compute the expenditure function as a function of prices. It is, however, not possible to compute the expenditure function as a function of environmental qualities in that way without further assumptions.

Note that one important component in the usual concept of a damage function is not formally included in our definition, namely, the direct effects of pollution on materials owned by the individual. For completeness, let us therefore discuss briefly this component.

Let, as before, c be a vector of consumption goods and services. These goods and services have certain qualities, which we suppose can be represented by the vector $r \in R^k$. The consumers are assumed to have preferences not only for the amounts they consume of the different goods and services, but also for the qualities of these goods and services. We will, therefore, write the utility function $u(c, r, Y)$. Due to pollution some components in the quality vector r may fall. It is, however, possible to counteract this quality deterioration by maintenance. Let $x \in R^n$ be a vector of goods and services used as inputs for maintenance. r will then be a function of x and Y:

$$r = G(x, Y)$$

where G is a vector-valued function with components G^i. The control variables for the individual are the c-vector and the x-vector. We can therefore define a new utility function $\hat{u}$ by setting

$$\hat{c} = (c, x)$$

$$\hat{u}(\hat{c}, Y) = u(c, G(x, Y), Y).$$

The utility maximization problem and the expenditure minimization problem can equally well be formulated with this new utility function $\hat{u}$ as with the old one $u(c, r, Y)$, and the results will be the same. But the utility function $\hat{u}$ is exactly of the form we have previously been using. Therefore maintenance is included in our first formulation.

Note also, that our formulation includes the cases when pollution affects the production possibilities. If pollution decreases the daily catch a fisherman can obtain, this will decrease the profit of his small enterprise by say ΔI. The compensating variation is here equal to ΔI. In general, the income I consists partly of shares in different producer surpluses, and if pollution affects the production possibilities, this will be reflected in the producer surpluses, and accordingly in the damage functions for those who have such shares.

We have so far only considered a static situation (it is quite possible, however, to interpret the components of c as dated commodities). It is straight forward to generalize the analysis to include several time periods as long as we neglect uncertainty and risk. We will not do that because no new insights will thereby be gained. In applications such extensions must of course be done.

Finally, let us define for future reference, the demand price δ_j for environmental quality as

(12) $$\delta_j = - \frac{\partial m}{\partial Y_j} \qquad j = 1 \ldots, m.$$

5. Social damage functions

Let us consider an economy with H consumers. Each consumer will be denoted by a superscript h, $h = 1, \ldots, H$. Assume that we can ignore all second-best problems arising from market imperfections, external effects (besides those that are reflected in the vector Y), indirect taxes and so on. This means, in particular, that all markets are cleared and all prices reflect social costs minus environmental costs.

It is obvious that we cannot define a social damage function without a discussion of the ethical norms of the decision-maker who is going to use the damage function. The purpose with a damage function is to make it possible to judge whether a change in the human activity vector z is desirable or not. Suppose that the change in z yields a revenue equal to R and that the damage from this change is according to the damage function D. Then the change is desirable if $R - D > O$. The change will, in general, affect different persons differently, so the decision-maker must in some way evaluate and compare these different individual effects in order to be able to make a decision. It is thus clear that his subjective evaluation of different individuals' importance must be included in this cost benefit analysis. Of equal importance is his means to redistribute income and thereby change the situation for each individual.

In view of these remarks, it is convenient, in the following discussion, to separate between cases when lump sum transfers are feasible and when they are not, and between cases when the only criterion is the Pareto-criterion (namely, that a change is desirable if no one is made worse off by the change, and at least one is better off) and when the preferences of the decision-maker can be represented by a social welfare function.

230

The discussion is very much tied to the discussion of compensation criteria in welfare economics (see (3) and (4)).

5.1.   Pareto-criterion, lump sum transfers are feasible

In this case we can define the aggregate expenditure function $m(p, Y, \bar{u}^1, \ldots, \bar{u}^H)$ as the sum of the individual expenditure functions.

$$
(13) \qquad m(p, Y, \bar{u}^1, \ldots, \bar{u}^H) = \sum_{h=1}^{H} m^h(p, Y, \bar{u}^h).
$$

Let I be the total lump sum income or wealth, i.e.

$$
(14) \qquad I = \sum_{h=1}^{H} I^h.
$$

Then it is natural to define the social damage function as

$$
(15) \qquad CV = m(p, Y, \bar{u}^1, \ldots, \bar{u}^H) - I = \sum_{h=1}^{H} CV^h
$$

where CV^h is the compensating variation for individual h.

If the revenue from the change in z is R (for example the producer's surplus increases with R), and if $R > CV$, then it is clear that it is possible to transfer this revenue to the individuals in such a way that every one gets at least the amount necessary to compensate him, and some individuals will get more. The change will therefore satisfy the Pareto-criterion. The definition (15) of the damage function is thus a very reasonable one.

One should note one difficulty, however. The aggregate expenditure function will, in general, not satisfy the Slutsky equations, and so it is not possible to compute the m-function from a knowledge of the aggregate demand functions. This can most easily be seen from the conditions (10) for complete integrability. There is no reason why the aggregate demand functions should satisfy these conditions, even if the individual demand functions do it. One can show that only if all individuals have the same utility function, and if this utility function is homothetic (that is a strictly increasing transformation of a homogeneous function) will the aggregate demand functions satisfy the complete integrability conditions, (see chapter IV in (5)).

5.2. Pareto-criterion, lump sum transfers are not feasible

We can still define the damage function as in (5), but this definition loses much of its previous appeal. The reason is simply that even if $R > CV$, the change may no longer satisfy the Pareto-criterion. It seems that it is impossible to define a reasonable damage function without specifying the mechanism with which income is distributed. But even if such a mechanism is specified, the concept of a damage function may be without any greater interest, because probably very few changes will satisfy the Pareto-criterion.

5.3. Social welfare function, lump sum transfers are feasible

We will assume that the preferences of the decision-maker can be represented by a) the idea of consumer sovereignty, and b) by certain preferences on the distribution of real income and environmental quality. We assume that these preferences can be represented by an indirect social welfare function

$$(16) \qquad V(p, \ Y, \ I^1, \ldots, \ I^H).$$

We assume that welfare function is of the Pareto-type (see (3)) i.e.

$$\frac{\partial V}{\partial I^h} > 0, \ h = 1, \ldots, \ H.$$

It seems natural to assume that

$$(17) \qquad \frac{\partial V}{\partial p_i} = - \sum_{h=1}^{H} c_i^h \frac{\partial V}{\partial I^h} \quad i = 1, \ldots, n,$$

because this condition says that it is real income that matters for social welfare, not nominal income.

Let us also assume that the following conditions also hold for the social welfare function

$$(18) \qquad \frac{\partial V}{\partial Y_j} = \sum_{h=1}^{H} \delta_j^h \frac{\partial V}{\partial I^h}, \quad j = 1, \ldots, m.$$

This condition simply means that it is the individual preferences on the environment that are to be counted, and that the decision-maker has no preferences himself about the environment. This condition may be hard to accept, but it will simplify the following analysis. Furthermore, it is not critical to the analysis, but can be dropped without changing any results substantially.

232

One can show (see (5)) these conditions imply the existence of a function $W(x_1, \ldots, x_H)$ such that

$$(19) \qquad V(p, Y, I^1, \ldots, I^H) = W(v^1(p, Y, I^1), \ldots,$$
$$v^H(p, Y, I^H)),$$

where $v^h(p, Y, I^h)$ is the indirect utility function of individual h.

The reason why we started with the indirect social welfare function and derived the social welfare function W, instead of following the usual path that goes in the opposite direction, is that the indirect welfare function seems to be a much more operational concept than the direct welfare function.

We can now define a social expenditure function exactly as we defined the individual expenditure function. We are looking for the least expenditure necessary to sustain a given social welfare level $\bar{U}$.

$$\text{Minimize} \quad p^T \sum_{h=1}^{H} c^h$$

subject to $W(u^1(c^1, Y), \ldots, u^H(c^H, Y)) \geq \bar{U}$.

We will write the solution to this problem as

$$(20) \qquad c^h = c^{h*s}(p, Y, \bar{U}), \quad h = 1, \ldots, H$$

and these functions will be called the social compensated demand functions. The social expenditure function is then, of course, defined as

$$(21) \qquad M(p, Y, \bar{U}) = p^T c^{h*s}(p, Y, \bar{U}).$$

It now becomes a matter of importance to investigate the relation between the social expenditure function and the individual expenditure functions $m^h(p, Y, \bar{u}^h)$.

Assume that

$$(22) \qquad \bar{u}^h = u^h(c^{h*s}(p, Y, \bar{U}), Y), \quad h = 1, \ldots, H.$$

This can automatically be achieved by the use of lump sum transfers. It now turns out that the social expenditure function is equal to the sum of the individual expenditure functions, or

$$(23) \qquad M(p, Y, \bar{U}) = \sum_{h=1}^{H} m^h(p, Y, \bar{u}^h). \quad \text{(see (5))}.$$

If we had not made the assumption (18) we could still have been able to derive (23), but this should not any longer be an identity in Y.

The definition of the social damage function is now obvious:

(24) $CV = M(p, Y, \bar{U}) - I.$

One can show that the M-function will satisfy the Slutsky equations, and that the aggregate demand functions will satisfy the conditions for complete integrability.

One should note that our discussion in this section is equivalent with Samuelson's discussion of the existence of a social utility function in (10).

5.4. Social welfare function, lump sum transfers are not feasible

We maintain the assumption that the preferences of the decision-maker can be represented by the indirect social welfare function (16), and that the conditions (17) and (18) are satisfied.

Let us first consider the case when it does not matter for the decision-maker who receives the income, the important variable for him is the size of the total income. This means that

(25) $\dfrac{\partial V}{\partial I^h} = \dfrac{\partial V}{\partial I^{h'}}$ $h, h' = 1, \ldots, H$

This implies that

(26) $W_h = W_{h'},$

where $W_h = \dfrac{\partial W}{\partial u^h}$, for a proper choice of individual utility functions.

We can, without any loss in generality, assume that the partial derivatives W_h are constants and equal one. The social welfare function can then be written

$$W = v^1(p, Y, I^1) + \ldots + v^H(p, Y, I^H)$$

Note that as one representation of the indirect utility function of the individual we can take the negative of his compensating variation, i.e.

$$I^h - m^h(p, Y, \bar{u}^{-h}).$$

234

If we take this representation, the social welfare becomes

$$\sum_{h=1}^{H} (I^h - m^h(p, Y, u^h)),$$

and the damage function

$$CV = \sum_{h=1}^{H} (m^h(p, Y, \bar{u}^h) - I^h) = m(p, Y, \bar{u}^1, \ldots, \bar{u}^H) - I.$$

We have thus once more obtained (15) as a definition of the damage function. This definition is thus reasonable, either when lump sum transfers are feasible, or when it does not matter for the decision-maker how the income is distributed.

Let us now turn to the most interesting case, namely when lump sums are unfeasible and when income distribution matters.

Let us first define the equivalent variation EV^h for one individual as

$$(27) \qquad EV^h = m^h(\bar{p}, \bar{Y}, u^h) - I^h.$$

Symbols with a bar are referring to the initial situation, while symbols without a bar are referring to some other situation. The equivalent variation is thus the amount one has to compensate the individual with so that he will choose the initial situation in comparison to the other.

Let us now compare two situations. The welfare difference is

$$(28) \qquad \Delta W = W(u^1, \ldots, u^H) - W(\bar{u}^1, \ldots, \bar{u}^H).$$

We assume that W is continuously differentiable, so that the mean value theorem of calculus can be applied. This theorem yields.

$$(29) \qquad \Delta W = \sum_{h=1}^{H} \bar{W}_h \Delta u^h,$$

where $\bar{W}_h$ is the partial derivative W_h evaluated at some point between $(u^1, \ldots, u^H)$ and $(\bar{u}^1, \ldots, \bar{u}^H)$, and $\Delta u^h = u^h - \bar{u}^h$.

As $\bar{p}$ and $\bar{Y}$ are regarded as constant vectors, $m^h(\bar{p}, \bar{Y}, u^h)$ is a strictly increasing transformation of the utility function u^h; and is therefore one representation of the preferences of individual h. We can also imagine that W is defined on this representation of the preferences. The welfare difference can therefore be written

$$\Delta W = \sum_{h=1}^{H} \overline{W}_h \left\{ m^h(\bar{p}, \ \overline{Y}, \ u^h) - m^h(\bar{p}, \ \overline{Y}, \ \bar{u}^h) \right\} =$$

$$\sum_{h=1}^{H} \overline{W}_h \left\{ m^h(\bar{p}, \ \overline{Y}, \ u^h) - I^h \right\}, \quad \text{or}$$

$$(30) \qquad \Delta W = \sum_{h=1}^{H} \overline{W}_h \ EV^h$$

It is easy to show that

$$(31) \qquad \frac{\partial V}{\partial I^h} = \frac{\partial W}{\partial u^h}, \qquad h = 1, \ \ldots, \ H.$$

In order to apply (30) we must thus know how the decision-maker values the nominal income of each individual and we must also know the equivalent variation of each individual. This last requirement is equivalent to a knowledge of the individual expenditure functions.

Equation (30) does not give a monetary measure of the welfare change, and cannot therefore be used as a starting point for a definition of a damage function. In fact, we are faced with the same difficulties we encountered in 5.2., namely that it is impossible to define a damage function without specifying the mechanisms with which income can be redistributed.

One can, however, take (30) as a starting point for a new kind of cost-benefit analysis, in which one does not try to express all costs and benefits in monetary terms but in welfare terms. If we can find a suitable division of the individuals such that individuals in the same class can be regarded as homogeneous, then it seems probable that the conditions for complete integrability will be satisfied for the aggregate demand functions in each group, and that consequently, the aggregate expenditure functions for each group can be computed. It seems improbable that a decision-maker has preferences for the income of each individual, but he will certainly have preferences for the income distributions of different social groups. All this adds up to the conclusion that it should be possible to use (30) in an operational way. The purpose of this paper, is to discuss monetary damage functions, and so we will not pursue this interesting topic any further.

6. Summary of Part I

We have in this first part of the paper tried to define, in a rigorous way, the concept of a monetary damage function. Intuitively the damage function should give a monetary value for the deterioration of environment which is connected with certain human activities. The definition of a damage function has been divided into two steps.

First, we defined the physical damage function or the environmental interaction function. Without any knowledge of this function, any further analysis of damage functions becomes meaningless. Therefore, it becomes a matter of utmost importance to get information on the interaction function. Such information is valuable in its own right too, because if it is impossible to assign monetary values to physical damage, the decision-maker has to rely on knowledge of the physical damage when he is making a decision.

Next, we defined the damage function for one individual as the compensating variation: that is, the amount with which the individual must be compensated in order not to be worse off than before the deterioration of the environment. It was shown that this definition included all the components that have been considered important in applied works with damage functions, but that it also included so-called psychic costs, that are seldom estimated.

When we then considered an economy with many individuals, we ran into several difficulties, because the definition of the damage function depends on the mechanisms that can be used to redistribute income. When lump sum transfers are feasible or when the decision-maker does not care about the income distribution, it was shown that the social damage function could in a reasonable way be defined as the sum of the individual damage functions. But when lump sum transfers are not feasible, it was concluded that one must know the methods that can be used to change the income distribution before it is possible to define the damage function.

It was also pointed out that instead of making the cost-benefit analysis in monetary terms, an analysis in welfare terms could be carried out. This topic was not discussed in detail, however.

Before ending this first part, one more point will be discussed briefly. So far we have assumed that the damage functions will be used in connection with general cost-benefit analysis. Assume now that the damage function will be used to determine the correct effluent charge to be used in environmental policy. Suppose we start with a situation in which the charge is zero. In this situation a certain income distribution has evolved, and the damage function has been estimated with this income distribution as a base. When we now impose effluent charges, this will, in general, change the income distribution, and thereby the damage function. As a consequence, the initial effluent charges may no longer be optimal but have to be adjusted, which in turn will change the income distribution. If the decision-maker has complete knowledge of all individual utility functions, he can obviously calculate an effluent charge in a way that takes all these repercussions into account. With limited information, however, this is not possible. It will be shown in the next part of the paper, that it is very difficult or impossible to obtain perfect estimates of damage functions, and that these damage functions will be based on aggregate data. Therefore, it is necessary to stress that before one uses the damage functions that can be estimated, one has to analyse very carefully possible repercussions on the income distribution that environmental policy measures based on such an estimate may have.

Before leaving this part of the paper it is necessary to decide which definition of a damage function shall be used in the next part. We shall use the definition given in (15) in 5.1. The reasons behind this choice are the following:

i)   if lump sum transfers are feasible, then (15) gives a perfectly reasonable definition of the damage function;

ii) if lump sum transfers are not feasible, but if the decision-maker is indifferent between different distributions of nominal income, then (15) is again a perfectly reasonable definition of the damage function;

iii) most damage functions actually estimated have had (15) at least implicitly as their starting point;

iv) there exist some possibilities of estimating the damage function defined in (15).

Admittedly, these are rather weak arguments.

Part II

THE ESTIMATION OF SOCIAL DAMAGE FUNCTIONS

7.   Introduction

As $Y_1, \ldots, Y_m$ are public goods, there are no markets in which the preferences of the individuals are revealed. For private goods we

238

saw that in section 3 it was possible to compute the expenditure function from a knowledge of the revealed demand functions. This opportunity does not exist in connection with public good, and it is this fact that makes it extremely difficult to estimate damage functions.

In order to estimate damage functions some ad hoc methods must be used. The following five general approaches have either been used or can be used.

a)   Evaluation of direct costs

In the example on the damage of a disease in section 4, we saw one case where direct costs could be estimated. These direct costs were the expenditures on medical care and the loss of wage income, which can be calculated on the basis of market prices. We will not discuss this method any further, because even if this method is extremely important from an applied point of view, it is not interesting from a theoretical point of view. A similar approach will be discussed in connection with methods in group d) below.

b)   Asking people about their willingness-to-pay

This method, which seems to be the most natural one, has the drawback that the individuals have in general incentives to distort their answers. We will discuss some of these incentives and how one might circumvent them.

c)   Voting

Voting is obviously the most practised way of obtaining information on what the individuals want their environment to look like. Voting is not a method of getting information on the social damage function, and we will not discuss it any further.

d)   A study of individual responses to environmental deterioration

It sometimes happens that a deterioration of the environment will cause individuals to respond in a certain way, and by studying these responses it may be possible to say something about the damage function. If, for example, one environmental quality is a perfect substitute for some private good, we can immediately draw inferences about an individual's marginal willingness to pay for this environmental quality by studying the price for the private substitute.

239

e) A study of market responses

It sometimes happens that the individual responses to changes in the environment will cause changes in market prices. A study of these prices may reveal the damage function.

Before entering a discussion of these approaches, one important difficulty must be touched upon. This difficulty arises from the fact that the quality of the environment may be described in many ways. When we measure environmental quality in applications we use technical terms as ambient concentrations of NO_x and SO_2, and dissolved oxygen deficit. These variables may be completely meaningless to the average individual. His perception of the environment and the environmental degradation must probably be described in quite different variables, and the difficulty arises when it comes to building a bridge between these two sets of variables.

8. Asking people about their willingness-to-pay

Already Wicksell (8) noticed that people may have incentives to conceal their true preferences about public good. If for example a public good is supplied free of charge and the supply is determined from the responses to the question of how much the individual is willing to pay, it is obviously in the interest of the individual to respond with a very high willingness-to-pay. On the other hand, if the individual has to pay the amount he responds with, he may have incentives to give a smaller response than the one he is actually willing to pay, hoping that the other individuals will respond with sufficiently high amounts.

There may exist methods by which it is possible to control these incentives, and to a certain extent counteract them. Let us study one special example.

Assume that it has been proposed to construct a dam that will destroy the scenic value of a river. We want to know how much citizens are willing to pay (or their compensating variation) for preservation of the scenic river.

Let $Y = \bar{Y}$ be the river without any dam, and let $Y = 0$ be the river with the dam. Let u^{-h} be individual h's utility in the original situation, that is when $Y = \bar{Y}$, and the consumer has not paid anything for the preservation alternative. Then the aggregate compensating variation can be written

$$(32) \qquad CV = \sum_{h=1}^{H} \left\{ m^h(p, 0, \bar{u}^{-h}) - m^h(p, \bar{Y}, \bar{u}^{-h}) \right\}$$

It is obvious that if the decision-maker asks the individuals for their maximum willingness-to-pay, they will have incentives to distort their responses. In order to analyse these incentives let us introduce the following notations:

δ^h is the response of consumer h;

$\bar{\delta}$ is the total response from all consumers except h, as perceived by h.

We assume that $\bar{\delta}$ is a random variable with density $g^h(\bar{\delta})$.

Assume further that if $\displaystyle\sum_{h=1}^{H} \delta^h$ (the sum of all responses)

exceeds C (the cost of not constructing the dam, i.e. the net revenue from the dam construction), the dam will not be constructed, while if the sum of the responses falls short of C, the dam will be constructed.

We will assume that the dam is constructed in connection with a hydro-electrical power station, so that if the dam is not constructed, the cost C will diffuse into the economy, primarily as increases in prices on electricity, if it is not covered in some other way. Assume now that the decision-maker, in order to counteract incentives to distort the answers, announces that each individual h has to pay the fraction α^h of the amount he has stated as his willingness-to-pay (that is the individual has to pay $\alpha^h \delta^h$ in case the dam is not constructed). This means that the costs will not be covered in case the dam is not constructed and there is a deficit

$$(33) \qquad D = C - \alpha^h \delta^h - \bar{\alpha}\,\bar{\delta}$$

where $\bar{\alpha}$ is a weighted average of the fractions of the responses the other consumers have to pay.

D is a random variable with a distribution given by

$$(34) \qquad Pr(D < \bar{D}) = \int_{0}^{C-\delta^h} g^h(\bar{\delta})d\bar{\delta} + \int_{\frac{1}{\bar{\alpha}}(C-\alpha^h\delta^h-\bar{D})}^{\infty} g^h(\bar{\delta})d\bar{\delta}$$

for $\bar{D} \geq 0$.

241

The deficit is financed by price increases on electricity and as a consequence the prices on other commodities will also rise. The deficit is thus diffused in the economy and the individual does not know exactly the burden that will fall on him. We assume, however, that he believes in a probability distribution over the fraction t^h of the deficit that will fall on him. In many cases this distribution will be concentrated to $t^h = 0$. Let the density of the distribution be $d^h(t^h)$. We assume that t^h is distributed independently of $\bar{\delta}$ (and therefore also of D). The mathematical expectation of t^h is denoted $\bar{t}^h$. Large consumers of electricity will probably have a higher $\bar{t}^h$ than small consumers. Define B^h by

$$(35) \qquad B^h = m^h(p, 0, \bar{u}^{-h}) - m^h(p, \bar{Y}, \bar{u}^{-h}),$$

that is B^h is the benefit accruing to individual h from preservation of the river.

We assume that the expected utility rule can be applied and that the elementary utility function is linear in money so that we can apply the expected utility rule directly on the compensating variation. This assumption means that the consumer acts as if he is maximizing

$$(36) \qquad E(CV) = I^h - m^h(p, \bar{Y}, \bar{u}^{-h}) \int_{C-\delta^h}^{\infty} g^h(\bar{\delta})d\bar{\delta} - m^h(p, 0, \bar{u}^{-h}) \int_{0}^{C-\delta^h} g^h(\bar{\delta})d\bar{\delta}$$

$$-\alpha^h \delta^h \int_{C-\delta^h}^{\infty} g^h(\bar{\delta})d\bar{\delta} - \bar{t}^h \int_{C-\delta^h}^{\infty} (C-\alpha^h \delta^h - \bar{\alpha})g(\bar{\delta}) d\bar{\delta}.$$

The first line in (36) gives the expected benefits, the first term on the second line gives the expected payment as a consequence of the response and the second term the expected burden from financing the deficit.

The first order condition for a maximum is

$$(37) \qquad B^h g^h(C-\delta^h) \qquad -\alpha^h \int_{C-\delta^h}^{\infty} g^h(\bar{\delta}) d\bar{\delta} - \alpha^h \delta^h g^h(C-\delta^h) -$$

$$-\bar{t}^h\left\{(C-\alpha^h\delta^h \ \ -\bar{\alpha} \ \ )\right\} \ g^h(C-\delta^h) \ -\alpha^h\int_{C-\delta^h}^{\infty}g^h(\bar{\delta})d\,\bar{\delta} \ \leq \ 0$$

with equality if $\delta^h > 0$.

In order to interpret this condition, let us assume that all individuals respond with a positive willingness-to-pay and that $\alpha^h = \bar{\alpha}$. Then one can rewrite (37) into

$$(38) \qquad B^h = \delta^h + (1-\bar{\alpha})(\bar{t}^hC-\delta^h) + (1-\bar{t}^h)\,\frac{\bar{\alpha}}{g^h(C-\delta^h)}\int_{C-\delta^h}^{\infty}g^h(\bar{\delta})d\,\bar{\delta},$$

or if we sum over all h

$$(39) \qquad \Sigma\, B^h - \Sigma\, \delta^h = (1-\bar{\alpha})(C\,\Sigma\,\bar{t}^h - \Sigma\,\delta^h) +$$

$$\Sigma\,(1-\bar{t}^h)\,\frac{\bar{\alpha}}{g^h(C-\delta^h)}\int_{C-\delta^h}^{\infty}g^h(\bar{\delta})d\,\bar{\delta}$$

From this expression it is seen that $\Sigma\,\delta^h$ may be an over estimate of $\Sigma\,B^h$ or an underestimate.

Let us assume that every $\bar{t}^h$ is small, so that $C\,\Sigma\,\bar{t}^h < \Sigma\,\delta^h$.

In particular, if $\bar{\alpha}$ is large enough, the first term will be small and dominated by the second term which is positive. In this case the responses will be smaller than the true benefits $\Sigma\,B^h$.

On the other hand, if $\bar{\alpha}$ is small enough, the responses will be greater than $\Sigma\,B^h$.

Although this exercise has not carried us far concerning the possibilities of obtaining information on the true benefits, it has given us some control on the incentives to distort the responses. It is for example, possible to create incentives to overstate the benefits by choosing the fraction α^h small, and it is possible to create incentives in the other direction by choosing the fraction α^h large.

This possibility to control the incentives to a certain degree may be used in a special way so as to solve decision problems. Peter Bohm (1) has suggested the following approach.

Choose two designs of the financial responsibilities, A and B, such that design A is known to induce over-estimates and B under-estimates of the true benefits. Choose two random samples from the population and confront the first sample with design A, and the second sample with design B. Associated with these two samples are two populations (consisting of the same individuals, but differing in the design of the financial responsibilities). It is now possible to test the hypothesis that $\Sigma \delta^h > C$ for the two populations, and if the tests go in the same direction in the two populations (that is the hypothesis is accepted in both populations or rejected in both), one has sufficient information to make a correct decision. If, however, the hypothesis is accepted in one population but not in the other, the results are not conclusive.

This approach seems very fruitful if it is possible to construct the financial responsibilities in such a way that the differences between the two populations become small; e.g., in such a way as to make the probability of conclusive results large. It is possible to discuss how the financial responsibilities should look, or how to choose the proportions α^h so as to increase the probability of conclusive results. We will not go into such a discussion here.

But, even if it were possible to discuss these problems at a theoretical level, it is very uncertain how relevant such a discussion really is. It is quite possible that all our assumptions about the behaviour of the individuals are far from realistic.

Moreover, it may be that the consumers do not believe in probability distributions of, for example, the other individuals' responses, in which case the analysis above becomes completely inadequate. But in this case we run into the problems of decision-making under uncertainty, and not very much can be said (see however (2), (5) and (6)).

The only way to get information on consumer behaviour is to perform experiments. The most important conclusion that can be drawn from this discussion is that there exist methods to control incentives to distort consumer responses, and that these methods must be tested in controlled experiments. It is, however, very difficult for private research groups to do such experiments, because they very often require participation of local or national governments.

9. Individual responses to changes in environment

It is sometimes possible to estimate the monetary damages from a study of how an individual or a group of individuals reacts to a change in environmental quality. We have already seen some examples of this, e. g. , our example of the monetary damage of getting a disease. In this example, one could not, however, estimate the total damage but only a part of it from a study of the individual behaviour. In some cases one can estimate the total cost from information of the responses of individuals.

The simplest case where this is possible is probably the one when it is known a priori that a certain environmental quality, say Y_1, is a perfect substitute for a private commodity, say c_1. By measuring Y_1 in the proper way, it is clear that we can attach the price p_1 to this variable, and it is thus possible to estimate the value of a change in Y_1. This approach has been used in studying the cost of air pollution by considering air conditioning as a perfect substitute for air pollution abatement.

Another simple case is when it is known a priori that a certain environmental quality is a perfect complement to a private good. If the demand function for the private good is known, it is possible to solve the Slutsky equations and obtain the expenditure function as a function of prices. By using the further information that the private good is a perfect complement to the environmental quality, it is possible to calculate the expenditure function also as a function of environmental quality.

This approach is not very interesting, however, because such a perfect complementarity is found very rarely. Perhaps it can be found in connection with certain recreational activities.

The assumption that a private good and an environmental quality are perfect complements is not necessary in order to perform the calculations mentioned above. It is sufficient to assume that there do not exist any option values, or that if the demand for some private good is zero, then so is the marginal willingness-to-pay for some environmental quality.

Let us aggregate all goods and services except the first one, to one composite good z, with price p_z, and denote the first good with x and let its price be p_x. Ignore all components in the vector Y except the first one which will be denoted by Y. The utility function of one individual can then be written

$$u(x, z, Y).$$

Our assumption above that there do not exist any option values can be formulated as the following requirement on the utility function

$$(40) \quad \frac{\partial\, u(0,\, z,\, Y)}{\partial\, Y} = 0.$$

It seems that this condition can be valid in many circumstances. If Y is the water quality in a certain stream and x is recreation activities in this stream, then the condition simply says that if you do not use the stream, you are indifferent to its quality. Another case in which (4) seems to be valid is the following.

Let Y be the air quality in a certain district, and let x be the demand for land in that district. If the demand is zero and the individual lives in another district, he will probably not be prepared to pay anything for an improvement in the air quality in the first district (as a matter of fact, (40) is basic to all estimates of damage costs based on property values).

Suppose now that we are interested in

$$CV = m\, (p_x,\, Y',\, \bar{u}) - m(p_x,\, \bar{Y},\, \bar{u}) \quad \text{for one individual.}$$

We can then write down the following identity:

$$CV = m(p_x,\, Y',\, \bar{u}) - m(p_x',\, Y',\, \bar{u})$$

$$+ \, m(p_x',\, Y',\, \bar{u}) - m(p_x',\, \bar{Y},\, \bar{u})$$

$$+ \, m(p_x',\, \bar{Y},\, \bar{u}) - m(p_x,\, \bar{Y},\, \bar{u}).$$

Let us choose p_x' so large that $x\, (p_x',\, Y',\, \bar{u}) = x\, (p_x',\, \bar{Y},\, \bar{u}) = 0$.

That means that the terms in the second row above will cancel according to (40). In the first and third differences, Y is held constant, so that it is possible to compute these differences from information on the demand function for x.

This has been a very brief exposition of the approach. For more details, the reader is referred to (4) and (5). The approach was first used by Joe Stevens in (12). He did not develop the theory behind the approach, however.

The approach is based on the following basic assumptions:

a) Condition (40) is satisfied. This seems to be a reasonable assumption.

b) It is possible to estimate the demand functions, not only as functions of prices and income, but also as functions of environmental quality. This may be impossible in many cases.

c) The conditions for complete integrability must be satisfied. This is clearly unrealistic, if the individuals are not homogeneous.

10. Market reactions to changes in environmental quality

If individuals respond to changes in environmental quality by changing their net demand, this will in general have effects on equilibrium prices. It may therefore be possible to say something about the monetary value of changes in environmental quality from information about these price changes. This idea has been used several times in connection with property values. The theory behind the approach was first developed by Robert Strotz in an unpublished mimeographed paper (Resources for the Future).

We shall consider here the most simple case, namely when the supply of the good to be considered is completely inelastic, the supply of land for residential use is usually considered to be constant. Our analysis can, therefore, be interpreted as an analysis of the land market, and we will baptize the variables according to this interpretation.

Assume that there are two districts, or regions, or pieces of land which are similar in all respects except some quality variable, for exemplé air quality. As long as the quality is constant, the consumers will regard these two districts as perfect substitutes, although the rate of substitution will not be unity because of quality differences. Let the supply of land in the two districts be L_1 and L_2, and let Y be the quality of the first district. The marginal rate of substitution between the two kinds of land is denoted by

(41) $MRS_{12} = B^h(Y)$

Since the two types of lands are perfect substitutes, this marginal rate of substitution is not a function of the consumption of land, but it is a function of the quality of the first district. An increase in the quality will, in general, increase B^h, and thus increase the demand for land in the first district.

Let x_1^h and x_2^h be the amounts of land demanded by consumer h in the two districts, and let c be an aggregate of all other goods and services with price p. The land prices in the two districts are denoted by p_1 and p_2.

We assume that the condition (40) is satisfied, which seems to be perfectly reasonable in this case. One can show (see chapter V in (5)) that this implies that the utility function can be written

$$(42) \qquad u^h(B^h(Y)x_1^h + x_2^h, \; c^h).$$

Utility maximization, subject to the budget constraint, gives the following conditions

$$u_1^h B^h - \alpha \, p_1 \leqq 0$$

$$(43) \qquad u_1^h \quad - \alpha \, p_2 \leqq 0$$

$$u_2^h \quad - \alpha \, p = 0,$$

where we have assumed that the composite good c always will be consumed in a positive amount.

As B^h does not depend on x_1^h, x_2^h, nor c^h, we can conclude that the amounts of land the consumer demands will be determined solely by the relation between B^h and the relative prices p_1/p_2.

If $\quad B^h > p_1/p_2, \quad x_1^h > 0 \quad$ and $\quad x_2^h = 0$

and if $\quad B^h < p_1/p_2, \quad x_1^h = 0 \quad$ and $\quad x_2^h > 0.$

Let us now make the very restrictive assumption that B^h is the same for all individuals. This assumption is not as restrictive as the assumption that all individuals have the same preferences, but it still

means that all individuals must be compensated with the same amount
of land for a unit decrease in the quality. The assumption is not necessary for the analysis, however. The only reason why we have introduced it is because it permits some simplification. If one drops this
assumption, one has to replace it with some other assumption on the
number of consumers.

It now follows immediately that equilibrium in the two land markets
require

$$(44) \qquad B^h(Y) = p_1/p_2.$$

Let us denote the relative price p_1/p_2 by n. This equilibrium
condition can then be written

$$(45) \qquad B(Y) = n.$$

By taking the logarithmic derivative of this condition with respect
to Y, we get

$$(46) \qquad \frac{1}{B} B' = \frac{1}{n} \frac{dn}{dY}.$$

It is easy to see that

$$(47) \qquad -\frac{\partial m^h}{\partial Y} = p \frac{\frac{\partial u^h}{\partial Y}}{\frac{\partial u^h}{\partial c}} = p \frac{u_1^h x_1^h B'}{u_2^h} = p \frac{u_1^h B}{u_2^h} \frac{x_1^h B'}{B}.$$

From (43) it is seen that the first factor is equal to p_1, and we
have just shown that the second factor is equal to

$$x_1^h \frac{1}{n} \frac{dn}{dY}.$$

We thus have

$$-\frac{\partial m^h}{\partial Y} = p_1 x_1^h \frac{1}{n} \frac{dn}{dY}$$

or by summing over all h

$$(48) \qquad -\frac{\partial m}{\partial Y} = p_1 L_1 \frac{1}{n} \frac{dn}{dY}.$$

If it is possible to estimate the relative land prices in the two districts as a function of quality, this formula can then be used to compute the damage function for air pollution in the first district.

The most important difficulty is probably the estimation of n as a function of Y. Usually there are so many factors determining property values and land prices, that it may be impossible to isolate one of these factors. Furthermore, this analysis is based on the implicit assumption that land and property markets are perfect. We know, however, that they are far from perfect and that, in particular, the adjustment toward an equilibrium is very slow. This obviously will depreciate the usefulness of this approach.

11. Summary of Part II

This part of the paper has been devoted to a discussion of some methods that have been or can be used in the estimation of damage functions.

We first considered estimation of direct costs which was quite straightforward. But such estimates will, in general, give damages which are lower than the true damages. These estimates can be used, however, in some instances, for example, as a control to insure that an ambient standard is not set too low. If the standard can be motivated by the direct damage, then it is clear that one should not try to lessen the standard.

We then went on to investigate the possibilities of asking the individuals concerned about their willingness-to-pay. Their answers will probably be distorted, due to certain incentives. In some cases it is, however, possible to control these incentives. The most important conclusion that can be drawn from that analysis is, presumably, that we should try to make experiments, from which we can learn how people react when they have to answer such questions.

The next approach we discussed was based on individual responses to changes in environment. By studying these responses we can get information on the monetary value of the changes. The main problems with this approach were estimation problems of demand functions, and aggregation problems. Furthermore, it may be that there are very few cases that can be analyzed with such an approach.

We concluded this part of the paper with a discussion of the connection between the marginal willingness-to-pay and the rate of change of land prices due to changes in the environment. If it is possible to isolate those changes in land prices that are due solely to changes in the environment, and if the land markets are perfect, then it is possible to estimate the monetary value of the changes in the environment. These assumptions were found to be unrealistic, however.

The general conclusion that can be drawn from these exercices is simply that we do not have any really reliable methods of estimating damage functions. We have some piecemeal information on different methods, but no approach which can be used in general.

REFERENCES

1. Bohm, P. A Note on the Problem of Estimating Benefits from Pollution Control. Problems of Environmental Economics, OECD, 1972.

2. Drèze, de La Vallé Poussin, A Tâtonnement Process for Public Goods, Review of Economic Studies, April 1971.

3. Graaf, Theoretical Welfare Economics, London, 1963.

4. Mäler, K.G. A Method of Estimating Social Benefits from Pollution Control, The Swedish Journal of Economics, Vol. 73, 1971.

5. Mäler, K.G., Studies in Environmental Economics, (forthcoming).

6. Malinvaud, E., A Planning Approach to the Public Good Problem, The Swedish Journal of Economics, Vol. 73, 1973, 1971.

7. Mishan, A Survey of Welfare Economics, Surveys in Economic Theory.

8. Musgrave, Peacock, eds. Classics in the Theory of Public Finance, New York 1959.

9. Niklasson, Consumers' surplus and related concepts, (mimeographed, Lund).

10. Samuelson, P.A., Social Indifference Curves, Quarterly Journal of Economics, 1956.

11. Samuelson, P.A., The Pure Theory of Public Expenditure and Taxation, Review of Economics and Statistics, 1954, pp. 387.

12. Stevens, J., Recreation Benefits from Water Pollution Control, Water Resources Research, Vol. 2, 1966.

DAMAGE FUNCTIONS FROM THE LEGAL PERSPECTIVE: JAPANESE LEGAL EXPERIENCE IN POLLUTION DAMAGES

by

Akio Morishima
Nagoya University, Nagoya,
Japan

THE CONCEPT OF DAMAGE

1. Legal Damages

In the field of law the term "damage" is differentiated from the term "damages". The term "damages" refers to compensation lawfully given to a victim, or to his inheritants in the case of death. All damage is not necessarily compensated. Damages must be proximate in terms of legal causation. Damages ordinarily must be caused by a negligent act of the wrongdoer, and so on. However, when we balance pollution abatement costs against damage costs, we must consider damage which cannot be compensated for in the courts. Let us take one example of a case involving death. If A is killed in an accident, the damages recovered by his next of kin are assessed basically upon A's income (1). But if societal loss is to be considered, personal loss to the victim represents only a part of this loss; societal loss also includes loss of surplus labour value to an employer, which is finally considered as a loss to the community-at-large. However, a loss to A's employer or community members is not included in legal damages, since such a loss is too remote in a legal framework. Therefore, legal damages do not adequately reflect social economic damage.

Nevertheless, looking into the question of measuring legal damages is very important as a first step in constructing damage functions.

2. Contribution to Economic Analysis

a) As we will see in the following chapter, the problem of causality is very important, but difficult when we speak of damage, particularly that caused by pollution: how can we decide upon the existence of a causal relationship between an activity and a damage (cause-in-fact)? What extent of consequences should be accounted for in determining damage (proximate cause) The latter problem is purely a matter of policy. In the legal field, mere disamenities have not been considered as damages to an individual person. However, in recent years, the question of whether or not environmental rights should be acknowledged in the courts has been discussed heatedly among Japanese lawyers. Some lawyers propose that we are entitled to enjoy a comfortable environment and that, if a factory trespasses upon our comfort, we have the right to ask for either damages or an injunction. Others oppose this idea, arguing that the right has no limit and, therefore, there is no trade-off point between freedom of commerce and freedom of an individual. Be it as it may, the scope of damages may change dependent upon the policy of the court. I believe that economists must confront the same questions. As a premise in the analysis of damage functions, they have to devise means of deciding causal relations and the scope of damage.

b)   The next point which should be stressed is concerned with the mechanism of internalisation of damage. Legal damages are enforced in legal institutions and, therefore, are internalised as costs without further devices. On the other hand, a mere loss to society has no motivation to be internalised as a business cost and, therefore, some type of incentive, such as charges or criminal punishment, should be utilized in order to make the wrongdoer bear the cost.

In this seminar, devices for internalising damage are not a matter of direct concern. However, in order to make economic theories of damage functions feasible, damage which has not been accounted for in the legal field should be carefully examined. If economists do not construct plausible theories, this sort of damage will be left out without internalisation.

3.   Purpose of this Paper

This paper introduces some Japanese examples which assess legal damages. The purpose is not to list all elements to be considered in damage functions, but to learn what kind of difficulties confront lawyers in assessing damages in pollution cases, and to what extent damage to society is estimated through established legal devices and how this estimation is carried out (2).

DAMAGES IN CIVIL POLLUTION CASES IN JAPAN

1. Trend of Cases of Damages

Recently many civil cases have been filed in the Japanese courts. Most of the cases treat damage to the health or life of people, and some of the cases deal with damage to agriculture. In noise cases, although the crucial issue is whether or not an injunction is to be allowed, the courts have often upheld nominal damages for mental suffering. In agricultural damage cases, decreases in crop yield are normally treated as damages, but in one case the costs of digging wells for irrigation water were allowed as damages. Although damage to fisheries has become a very serious social problem in Japan, only one case, a fishing industry case, has been reported. The determination of damages to fisheries is discussed below.

2. Damages to Human Health and Life

Among pollution cases in which human lives and health have been damaged, the itai-itai disease case, the Niigata Minamata disease case and the Yokkaichi asthma case should be mentioned particularly (3).

The itai-itai disease is called "itai-itai" (ouch-ouch) because the victims suffer serious and persistent bodily pains due to the fracture of bones. As a result of some research, the cause of the disease is presumed to be accumulated cadmium which had been included in effluents from the Mitsui Mining and Smelting Company. Cadmium is considered to have polluted the soil of the rice paddies in the area beside the river on which the factory has been located upstream over a long period. Well water had also been polluted. Since 1968 a total of 496 patients and family members of the dead brought eight lawsuits against the Company. The plaintiffs were inhabitants along the river who had eaten rice from the area and drank water from wells.

In the Niigata Minamata case, organic mercury was alleged to have caused serious disorders to the central nervous systems of persons who consumed large amounts of fish from a river along which a factory was located. Fish are considered to have been contaminated by the emission, from the factory, of effluents containing mercury. The number of persons affected amounted to more than one hundred (including 7 deaths). The first lawsuit was filed by 13 patients and by the time it was concluded in 1971 the number of plaintiffs had increased to 77.

The Yokkaichi case is an air pollution case in which six large factories, comprising a petroleum complex, were sued in 1967 on the grounds that their joint smoke emissions caused asthma to hundreds of neighbouring residents, including the 9 plaintiffs of this case.

255

a) "Cause-in-fact" of Damage

In these cases the most difficult question was to discover the "cause-in-fact" of the damage: whether a certain substance is a medical cause of a disease, and whether the substance is emitted from the defendant factory. Due to insufficient scientific information it is very difficult to decide upon the cause. Although careful investigations by the central or local governments resulted in hypotheses concerning causation, all defendants disclaimed these causal relations, arguing that the hypotheses had not been verified scientifically. However, the courts applied epidemiological methods to elucidate the causes, and did not require a detailed medical explanation. In court opinions, precise analysis of disease mechanism is not necessary for the legal purpose of allocating loss.

From our legal experiences we may infer that, in an economic analysis for damage functions, it is also vital for economists to construct a theory of procedure to decide causal relations between the activities of an individual industry and loss to a third party. Otherwise, the industries which are required to pay damage costs according to their activities will not agree to bear the burdens.

b) Measuring Damages

Let us move on to the question of measuring the damages in these cases. In the first two water pollution cases, the plaintiffs asked to be paid damages for mental suffering only. The theory behind the plaintiffs' demand is as follows. Since all victims suffered from the same disease, recoveries to all victims must be as uniform as possible. Only the seriousness of the illness should be a criterion for differentiating the amount of damages. In addition to that, due to the large number of plaintiffs, the introduction of complicated elements in measuring damages such as the expectancy of individual earnings would have caused a delay in court procedure. This pleading was quite different from ordinary cases in which the loss of expected individual incomes as well as mental sufferings is compensated. The courts supported the plaintiffs' argument.

In the itai-itai disease case, which was decided in a district court on June 30, 1971, the plaintiffs recovered 5 million yen for the dead patients and between 1-4 million yen for the injured, depending on the extent of the disease. The total amount of damages was 56 milllion yen for 31 patients and inheritants. Then the defendant company appealed to the Nagoya High Court. However, as a result of the appeal, the High Court, in the judgement of August 9th, 1972, increased the amount of damages by almost three times. Recovery for a dead person was

256

raised to 12 million yen and the total amount of damages to the 33 plaintiffs (one injured plaintiff died after the judgement of the first instance, and three inheritants succeeded) was increased to 146 million yen.

In the Niigata Minamata case, which was decided on October 19th, 1971, the court allowed 10 million yen for the dead and seriously injured, and from 1-8 million yen for the others, according to the degree of seriousness of the illness. The total amount of damages to the 77 plaintiffs, including inheritants was 249 million yen. The defendant abandoned the right to appeal fearing adverse public opinion.

These amounts of damages for mental suffering are very high in comparison with automobile accident cases where damages for mental suffering due to death is usually less than 4 million yen. And, even when we compare the total amount of damages given to a victim in these pollution cases with that given in an average accident case, it is rather high. In an accident case, the damages for expected earnings, as well as those for mental sufferings are claimed. Judges in these courts said that, on the one hand, industries were profiting from the emission of pollution and, on the other hand, people in the neighbourhood of industries have no way of avoiding injury. This conception has brought about changes in the traditional measure of damages. If victims recover enough from damages for mental suffering, there is no need for a complicated procedure to assess damages.

The trend was even strengthened in the Yokkaichi case. Here, the loss of expected earnings, as well as for mental suffering, was claimed as damages. Plaintiffs of the case thought it wise to ask also for damages from loss of income in order to raise the total amount of damages, since the amount of damages for mental suffering has limits. However, while the measure of damages seems to be traditional, the method of assessing damages for expected earnings differs from the normal one. In the Yokkaichi case, the assessment of damages for income, unlike ordinary accident cases, is not based upon individual actual income, but upon the statistical average of workers' wages. The theory is the same as that taken in the water pollution cases: a great number of victims, homogeneous sufferings, and the necessity for quick relief to all victims. As a result, in the judgement which was delivered on July 24th, 1972, the amount of damages to each plaintiff was increased. A hospitalized middle-aged fisherman was awarded more than 14 million yen and even a 78 year-old retired man got nearly 6 million yen. The total amount of damages for 9 plaintiffs was 192 million yen. The defendants of this case also decided against an appeal.

The reason for the rapid increase of the amount of damages from case to case is not a logical one, but rather, it is a reflection of change in public sentiment against environmental pollution.

Since there is no definite or absolute way of assessing the monetary value of human life and body, the limitation on amount of damages depends upon what people perceive as just. Therefore, in the case of pollution, we can hardly predict the actual amount of damages for bodily injuries while the framework of legal rules for assessing physical damages in automobile accidents, for example, has been firmly established.

3.   Reaction to Court Pollution Cases

There was considerable reaction from industry and the government, as well as from the public, resulting from the decision of these cases, and the consequences have been serious.

After the Itai-itai case was decided in the high court, the defendant company, the Mitsui Mining and Smelting Company, decided to pay all damages to the 489 plaintiffs in other itai-itai lawsuits (only the first suit was decided in court), by the end of August, 1972. This amounted to about 1,350 million yen. In addition, local governments made claims against the company for the expenditure incurred by them concerning the disease. For example, the Toyama Prefecture decided to ask the company for reimbursement of the 128 million yen which it was forced to expend for the medical treatment of patients, scientific research to elucidate the cause of the disease and develop methods of treatment, and for constructing water supply systems. Other related cities and towns also claimed similar expenses amounting to 20 million yen. In addition to that, as a consequence of the decision, the company had to promise to reclaim agricultural land damaged by cadmium pollution. The total damages may be an enormous amount of money.

In the Niigata Minamata disease case, the defendant company, Showa Denko, was also forced, by a group of patients, to make a promise to pay damages (although the amounts are not yet settled) to all patients other than the plaintiffs of the case. The company agreed with the Agano River Fishery Co-operative Union on compensation for damages for loss of sales of contaminated fish. The amount of damages was assessed as 50 million yen.

Just after the decision of the Yokkaichi case, the government declared that it would reconsider industrial land-developing plans. Power plants throughout the nation have started planning to use much lower sulphur content oil and to develop more effective pollution control equipment. Upon hearing the favourable decision for the affected persons, more than one hundred additional asthma patients were encouraged to prepare a lawsuit against factories.

These cases present some good lessons for learning how damage costs are calculated. One might say that these consequences are too political, but they are facts which may appear anywhere. If economists do not realize the vague notion of cause and effect relations and the loose framework of damages, they cannot construct feasible theories for damage functions.

LAWS RELATING TO DAMAGE COSTS

In the preceding chapter, I have described the court cases in which the problem of damages caused by pollution was discussed. In Japan there are some laws which require factories to pay for damage costs. In the administration of these laws, we have also confronted similar difficulties to those in court cases: causation and scope of damage.

1. Law concerning the Entrepreneurs' Bearing of the Cost of Public Pollution Control Works

This law was enacted in 1970 in order to implement Sec. 22 of the Basic Law of Environmental Pollution Control which provided that industries had to pay for all or part of the costs spent by administrative organisations for pollution control: construction of green belts, dredging operations for decayed sediments caused by factory effluents, reclamation of polluted agricultural land, industrial sewage systems, and removal of residents away from factories. These are administrative activities specified in the law. Factories have to pay according to the degree of their being the cause of these costs. To date the law has been applied to only one dredging case. Tagonoura Port was polluted by effluents from paper mills and Shizuoka Prefecture decided to dredge deposits in the port. 120 million cubic meters of sediment was excavated at the cost of 500 million yen. However, pulp dregs were not considered as the sole cause of deposits. Natural deposits of sand from Mount Fuji and deposits from sewage also contributed to the deposits. In addition, dredging operations were considered to be necessary, not only for pollution prevention but also for maintenance of the port. Finally only 82% of the cost (410 million yen) was shared by 158 related industries in that area. Here again, the problem of cause and the concept of cost are essential to deciding the actual amounts to be paid. Many projects are now being planned: a dredging operation in Niigata (to remove mercury from the river bed), excavation of a new canal in Miyazaki (to reclaim a mercury polluted river), and reclamation of cadmium-polluted agricultural land in Gumma are examples. But the most debated problem in these projects is to what extent and by whom the costs should be borne. While, as a result of the above-mentioned court decisions, public opinion is becoming intolerant towards industry,

259

the administration is in a difficult situation in imposing all the costs on the polluters.

2. Law concerning Special Measures for the Relief of the Pollution-related Patients (4)

This law was promulgated in December 1969 upon the Basic Law of Environmental Pollution Control of 1967. The law provided for medical allowances and other relief for patients of designated diseases in polluted areas. A medical relief system, originally began in Yokkaichi by the city authority as a result of strong demands from residents suffering from diseases induced by air pollution. Since then, similar relief measures have been provided in other cities and towns. Through this law, relief services were transferred from local authorities to the central government. However, it is not applied to all air- or water-polluted areas. Only nine areas (3 water and 6 air pollution areas) are designated as areas where the relief system is to be applied. Types of diseases are also designated by the government for each area. Upon an application from a patient suffering from a designated disease, resident in or commuting to the designated polluted area for a prescribed period of time, the local medical commission (authorized for this particular purpose) decides whether or not the disease of the applicant was caused by the designated pollution. The total number of officially recognized patients as of March 1972 is 6,668. The number is increasing every year.

One of the reasons for the increase of patients is that the medical commissions have shown leniency in their confirming procedure in order to provide quick relief. Consequently, although a patient is provided only with total medical expenses (5,000 yen monthly medical allowances and 10,000 yen nursing allowances), the total costs of the relief system have been increasing rapidly. At the beginning of 1969 the costs were 6 million yen, in 1970 - 89 million yen and in 1971 - 355 million yen. In 1972 costs are expected to be 666 million yen. Half of the costs are paid by industries, a quarter by the central government and the rest by local governments. The principle for cost bearing is that damage caused by pollution should be paid by polluters. But, as causal relations and the polluter's negligence are difficult to prove, the administration shares costs to give prompt relief to victims of pollution. The greatest difficulty exists in the allocation of costs among industries. To overcome this difficulty, industries organised the Co-operative Foundation for Pollution Control within the Federation of Associations of Business Managers, and it collects voluntary contributions from large scale industries. However, since the amount of costs has been getting larger and larger, this system will be unworkable in the near future. And, another question which has been raised by industrial groups is that as air pollution is caused not only by industries, but also by automobiles and other sources, the degree of contribution to the pollution by each source must be clarified.

On the other hand, as mentioned in the preceding section, since the Yokkaichi decision elucidated to some extent the causal relationship between smoke from industrial stacks and asthma, industrial groups have been planning to establish voluntary medical relief foundations in the areas where the medical relief law is not applied. And, following the itai-itai decision, some local governments decided to ask the Mitsui Mining and Smelting Company to reimburse their expenditures for resident patients. Niigata and Yokkaichi have also followed this procedure.

3. Law Concerning Prevention of Harm Caused by Aircraft Noise Around Public Airport Areas

This law was promulgated in 1967 in order to regulate aircraft noise around airport areas. The law also provides for the government to compensate damage caused to property, fisheries or agriculture by aircraft noise. In Japan the central government is responsible for operating airports. Similar laws were enacted concerning Defence Air Forces and American Air Forces.

In addition, all or part of the costs for soundproofing buildings for schools or hospitals around the airport area are reimbursed by the government. The measure of compensation is the same as in the case of eminent domain. In the eminent domain, the extent of ordinary damage to be compensated is always arguable. In practice, not only the sale price of a property but also the loss of customers and moving costs are compensated. In the case of fisheries, the yearly income from fishing is considered to be a capital interest and the value of the capital is paid as the price of the fishing rights. Moreover, three years' income is paid in damages for a change of job. In the usual contract case, if a buyer pays the sale price to a property owner, he need not pay additional costs for moving or changing jobs. However, in an eminent domain case the government pays all these items since the seller is forced to sell his property.

This method of compensation can be applied to other pollution cases as in cases where residents in the neighbourhood of industries are forced to move because of pollution.

CONCLUSION

We have studied examples of compensation of pollution damages through legal devices. To date no legal device has taken mere dis-amenities into account. Unless the feelings of discomfort are serious enough to be legally considered as mental suffering, the sufferers have no recourse in law to recover damages. Therefore, noise which is common in the area, odour which can be tolerated by normal persons and interference with pleasant views, cannot be a matter of law. Even in the case where disamenities are severe enough to be considered a breach of rights, damages are not usually recovered.

In theory we can recover damages for increased laundry bills, for house repair costs and so on. But no one wants to file lawsuits for these small amounts of money. Besides, very often we cannot find out who caused the damage and to what extent. From the legal viewpoint, the increases in costs for recreation and transportation (in the case of moving out to suburban areas) are too remote. As stated in the preceding sections, economists should define "damage" from their own perspectives and define a procedure for deciding upon causal relations.

Then with regard to a damage which has not been compensated by legal devices, economists must design incentives to enforce polluters to bear the costs.

In my opinion it may be very difficult for such damage as dis-amenities to be built into a market system. The costs for assessing the damage and of allocating it to the individual polluter may be as great or greater than the disamenity costs themselves. In such a field, a collective decision which imposes direct controls on industries to prevent them from causing damage may work more effectively. I do not oppose the necessity of assessing disamenity damage to society as a whole, but we have to realize that minor damage can hardly be broken down as a cost to the individual polluters.

Finally, I would like to point out that, even if economically speaking the control costs are in line with damage costs, a policy-maker may not allocate costs considering the adverse effects on income redistri-bution among people.

1. Damages for his expected income are assessed as:

    $$D = \frac{I - C}{1 + r} + \frac{I - C}{1 + 2r} + \frac{I - C}{1 + 3r} + \ldots + \frac{I - C}{1 + nr}$$

    D = Total damages;

    I = A's income for the year in which he died;

    C = A's living costs (50% or less);

    r = Interest rate;

    n = A's Expected workable years.

    In other legal systems, a multiplier is used instead of the above formula.

2. Recently there have been some economic studies which estimated environmental damage in Japan. These are concerned with assessment of damage to agriculture, fisheries and households. In particular, the studies concerning household damage are very interesting. These economic studies are not discussed in this paper.

3. See the details of these cases in: Environment Agency: Pollution Related Disease and Relief Measures in Japan, May 1972. See also, Environment Agency: Water Pollution Control in Japan, pp. 6-8, May 1972; Environment Agency, Air Pollution Control in Japan, pp. 12-14, 42-45, May 1972. These papers are supplements to the National Report submitted in March 1971 to the United Nations Conference on the Human Environment.

4. For details, see Environment Agency: "Pollution Related Diseases and Relief Measures in Japan", pp. 23-25.

ASSESSMENT OF RISK OF DAMAGE
TO THE ENVIRONMENT

by

L. D. Hamilton*
St. Catherine's College Oxford, United Kingdom

INTRODUCTION

The uncomfortable awareness of the environmental hazards brought
about by the scientific and industrial revolutions of the last two centuries is accompanied by insufficient knowledge of the actual damage and
its cost. Priorities in solving these environmental problems must be
set from quantitative assessment of the biological damage. Prediction
of the expected damage involves assessment of the risk of damage.
The logical and coherent analysis of such risks and assessment of the
biomedical and environmental costs would permit decision-makers in
environmental policy to set realistic priorities for control, aid in
weighing the advantages of one technology over another, and increase
public understanding of the biological costs of contemporary technologies thereby decreasing the difficulties of decision-makers.

RADIATION AS A MODEL ENVIRONMENTAL POLLUTANT

Solution of the problems surrounding the calculation of the risk of
the induction of late effects by radiation should serve as a model for
the critical evaluation of the relationship to be established between other
types of environmental pollutants and the risk of specific biological
damage.

Measurement of radiation has the advantage over that of many
other environmental pollutants in that it can be accurately measured
down to very low doses. Like some other environmental pollutants,
there exists a background of radiation from natural sources (1) (Table 1),
a natural background of a pollutant that must be taken into consideration
in assessing the additional risk of damage to be accrued from an additional

---

* Presently at the Brookhaven National Laboratory, Upton, L.I., N.Y., USA.

Table 1. DOSE RATES DUE TO INTERNAL AND EXTERNAL IRRADIATION FROM NATURAL SOURCES IN "NORMAL" AREAS (1)

SOURCE OF IRRADIATION	DOSE RATES (mrad Y^{-1})		
	GONADS	BONE-LINING CELLS	BONE MARROW
External irradiation			
Cosmic rays: ionizing component	28	28	28
neutron component	0.35	0.35	0.35
Terrestrial radiation (including) air	44	44	44
Internal irradiation			
H 3	0.001	0.001	0.001
C 14	0.7	0.8	0.7
K 40	19	15	15
Rb 87	0.3	0.6	0.6
Po 210	0.6	1.6	0.3
Rn 220	0.003	0.05	0.05
Rn 222	0.07	0.08	0.08
Ra 226	0.02	0.6	0.1
Ra 228	0.03	0.8	0.1
U 238	0.03	0.3	0.06
Rounded Total	93	92	89
Percentage from alpha particles + neutrons	1.2	4.1	1.2

NOTE : Average dose rates from natural sources in "normal" areas to tissues at risk: gonads (risk of genetic damage); bone-lining cells (bone tumours); bone marrow (leukaemia). Internal irradiation from radioisotopes naturally in the body.

pollutant. One such additional world-wide source of radiation has been fall-out from nuclear tests. The doses to be accumulated by the tissues at risk from all nuclear tests carried out before 1971 to the year 2000 — the dose commitments — are given in Table 2 (1). They can be compared with those from natural background and it can be seen that they are roughly equivalent to the radiation given by 2 years natural background.

Table 2. DOSE COMMITMENTS FROM NUCLEAR TESTS CARRIED OUT BEFORE 1971 (1)

SOURCE OF RADIATION	DOSE COMMITMENTS (mrad)								
	FOR THE NORTH TEMPERATE ZONE			FOR THE SOUTH TEMPERATE ZONE			TO THE WORLD POPULATION		
	GONADS	BONE-LINING CELLS	BONE MARROW	GONADS	BONE-LINING CELLS	BONE MARROW	GONADS	BONE-LINING CELLS	BONE MARROW
External									
Short-lived ..	65	65	65	19	19	19	44	44	44
Cs 137	59	59	59	16	16	16	40	40	40
Kr 85	2×10^{-4}	2×10^{-4}	2×10^{-4}	2×10^{-4}	2×10^{-4}	2×10^{-4}	2×10^{-4}	2×10^{-4}	2×10^{-4}
Internal									
H 3	4	4	4	1	1	1	4	4	4
C 14	12	15	12	12	15	12	12	15	12
Fe 55	1	1	0.6	0.3	0.3	0.2	0.7	0.7	0.4
Sr 90		85	62		23	17		57	42
Cs 137	26	26	26	7	7	7	18	18	18
Pu 239		0.2			0.05			0.1	
Total.........	170	260	230	55	81	72	120	180	160

NOTE: Dose commitments from nuclear tests carried out before 1971. Figures are the average total doses to be accumulated by the tissues at risk up to the year 2000. Totals have been rounded off to two significant figures. The total dose commitment to the gonads and bone marrow is about 140 mrad; it is about 170 mrad to cells lining bone surfaces.

266

Table 3. PROBABLE DOSE FROM NUCLEAR POWER STATION (2)

	mrem/year
At boundary of station	5
Population within 6 miles of station	0. 6
Eating fish and shellfish 50 gm/day caught at exit of condenser discharge canal	2. 5
Swimming 3 hr/day 120 day/yr in effluent condenser discharge canal	0. 03
Swimming 3 hr/day 120 day/yr at shore areas either side nuclear power station	0. 006
Average Natural Background in US	105

NOTE :   Probable whole-body doses from a nuclear power station; doses calculated for Millstone Point, Connecticut — a station containing two reactors about 1 300 MW electrical -- on the north shore of Long Island Sound. Doses at the boundary of the station and to the population within 6 miles are doses accumulated by individuals remaining for 24 hours/day and 365 days/year at the boundary or in the open within 6 miles of the station.

Table 3 gives the probable whole-body doses from a typical nuclear power plant situated on a sea shore. In the United States the upper limit of the dose on the boundary of nuclear power stations has now been limited to a maximum of 5 mrem/year (Appendix I to Chapter 10 of the Code of Federal Regulation, Part 50, covering licensing of nuclear power plants). Since nuclear power stations are point-sources of radiation, this would limit the dose to the population within 6 miles of nuclear power plants to 0. 6 mrem/year and within 50 miles to 0. 01 mrem/year (2).

There is thus no risk of acute radiation damage from normal operational releases of nuclear power plants since acute effects arise after doses hundreds of times higher than these, and would be likely only after a disastrous accident. Late damage may be somatic or genetic. Late somatic damage consists largely of an increase in cancer individually indistinguishable from those arising spontaneously in the population. Genetic damage affects the gene-cells of those irradiated, and by definition will eventually result in various hereditary diseases.

RISK OF INDUCTION OF CANCER BY IRRADIATION

Although it was clear since shortly after the discovery of X-rays that radiation induces cancer in man, it is only in the last decade or so that data have become available that permit quantitative risk estimations (1). From the Japanese atom-bomb survivors and from English patients treated for ankylosing spondylitis (a rheumatic disease of the spine) with therapeutic doses of radiation (3), data are available on the induction of leukaemia and other malignancies in man from largely high doses of radiation given at high dose rates. At Hiroshima and Nagasaki, mortality records in the Atomic Bomb Casualty Commission Life Span Study Sample have been collected until the end of 1970, 25 years after the bombings; the spondylitics have been followed fully for 24 years and, in part only, for an additional three years. The results on the survivors apply to the general population (41% male; 20%   10 years at time of bombing) irradiated with a pulse of mixed radiation (a much larger neutron component at Hiroshima); those on the spondylitics to a largely (84%) male, adult population affected by a specific disease irradiated with fractionated X-rays over long time periods. As widely appreciated by scientists and laymen there must still be large uncertainties in the estimates of the doses of radiation received by survivors although several revisions of the estimates have improved the accuracy of dose-effect relationships.

Among the survivors the incidence of leukaemia - based on mortality or morbidity data - appears to rise linearly with dose up to a few hundred rads. A significant excess of leukaemia is seen at Hiroshima after a mean population dose corresponding to 50 rads (Figure 1). The risk estimate from mortality is between 1-2 cases of leukaemia per million per year per rad over 20 years. This agrees with that derived from the spondylitic patients (Figure 2). Since in both the survivors and the spondylitics the risk after 20 years has returned to that in the general population, the overall risk estimate is between 20-40 cases per million per rad for single and fractionated irradiation, either whole-body or part.

Others cancers among the survivors for which dose-effect relationships can be made and hence tentative risk estimates given include lung cancer (bronchi and trachea) 1.5-3 cases per million per year per rad, breast cancer among women 0.2-0.4 cases per million per year per rad, thyroid cancer 1-2 cases per million per year per rad in males and 2-4 cases in females (1). Unlike the risk of leukaemia, there is no way to determine whether the increased risk of these tumors will continue in the future or will decrease. In the spondylitics the excess risk of tumors in heavily irradiated sites rose during the additional 3 years of observation, and has continued to rise (Table 4). Thus, estimates

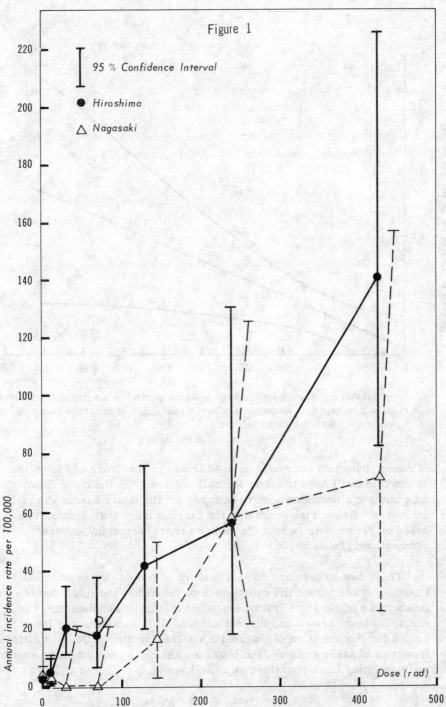

Figure 1

95 % Confidence Interval

● Hiroshima

△ Nagasaki

Annual incidence rate per 100,000

Dose (rad)

Annual incidence rate of leukaemia (all forms) per 100,000 atomic-bomb survivors in Atomic Bomb Casualty Commission (ABCC) master sample as a function of exposure at Hiroshima and Nagasaki, October 1950 - September 1966. (1,4)

Figure 2

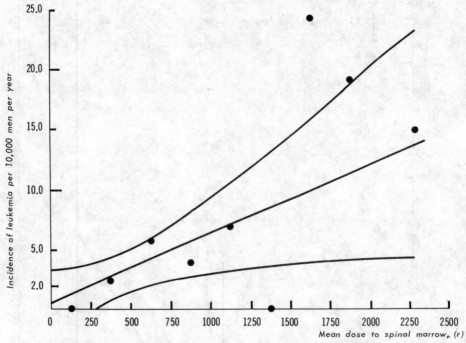

Annual incidence rate of leukemia (all forms) per 10,000 men in-patients with ankylosing spondylitis as a function of the mean spinal marrow dose with the 95 per cent probability limits of the value of the regression line shown by the straight line (cf. 3).

of cancer induction currently derived from the survivors and from the spondylitics will have to be periodically revised. In the meanwhile, approximate allowances need to be made for the future cancers in risk estimates. These risk estimates for cancers other than leukaemia are based on recent data (within the last two years) and many arbitrary assumptions (Table 5) (1).

These human data are compatible with a simple proportional dose-response — the higher the radiation dose the higher the incidence of leukaemia and, in some instances, other malignant neoplasms — for example, lung, breast and thyroid cancer. It is clear that the latent period for the induction of leukaemia and the duration of the risk differs from that of other cancers, the latter appearing to take longer to appear and persisting later than the risk of leukaemia.

Table 4. RATE OF INCIDENCE OF LEUKAEMIA COMPARED WITH THE RATE FOR OTHER CANCER OF HEAVILY IRRADIATED SITES (3)

YEARS AFTER FIRST TREATMENT	MAN-YEARS AT RISK	EXCESS LEUKAEMIAS		EXCESS OTHER CANCERS	
		CASES	RATE PER MAN-YEAR x 10^{-4}	CASES	RATE PER MAN-YEAR x 10^{-4}
0-2 ..	35,453	5. 9	1. 7	10. 5	3. 0
3-5 ..	40,746	17. 5	4. 3	2. 8	0. 7
6-8 ..	37,363	14. 4	3. 9	13. 5	3. 6
9-11 ..	27,082	8. 7	3. 2	34. 5	12. 7
12-14 ..	15,221	6. 2	4. 1	25. 7	16. 9
15-27 ..	9,766	0. 5	0. 5	19. 3	19. 8

NOTE: Rate of incidence of leukaemia compared with the rate for other malignant neoplasms of the heavily irradiated sites in the ankylosing spondylitis patients at different years after first treatment. Note that the latent period for the induction of leukaemia differs from that for the induction of other cancers; the latter taking longer to appear and persisting later than the leukaemias.

EXTRAPOLATION TO LOW DOSES AND LOW DOSE RATES

The very low doses and dose rates given by natural background radiation in the environment and the considerably lower doses that would be given at low dose rates by nuclear power stations are obviously very much lower than those for which there are data on tumor induction. However, to get a crude idea of risk, one assumes that the linear proportional relationship between dose and tumor induction observed at much higher doses and dose rates can be extrapolated down to the lowest doses (i. e. absence of a threshold dose) and at all dose rates. This assumption implies several additional important assumptions: (1) that a dose delivered over a long time is as biologically damaging as the same dose given over a short time. This assumption is known to be incorrect since there is some repair of radiation damage. The presence of a repair mechanism means that doses spread over a long period are less damaging than doses spread over a short period. Thus, an estimate that ignores the repair mechanism — for which a quantitative relationship cannot now be stated — is likely to be higher than the actual, but unknown, risk. So the assumption of linear proportionality down to the lowest doses and dose rates favors safety;

271

Table 5. SUMMARY OF RISK ESTIMATES (1)

IRRADIATED POPULATION[a]	RADIATION QUALITY[b]	MEAN DOSE OR DOSE RANGE (RAD)	OBSERVATION PERIOD[c]	TYPE OF DATA[d]	SEX	AGE AT EXPOSURE[e]	RISK PER 10^6 Y RAD[f]
				Leukaemia			
H	GN	60	5-25	Mt	MF	AC	0.7
H	GN	400	5-25	Mt	MF	AC	2.0
N	G	10-400	5-21	Mb	MF	AC	1.6
S	X	300-1,500	(5.5)	Mt	M	A	1.2
P_1	X	0.2-20	0-10	Mt	MF	F	10
P_2	GN[g]	25	0-10	Mt	MF	F	NF[f]
				Thyroid cancer			
HN	GN[g]	25-200	5-20	Mb	M	AC	1.2
HN	GN	25-200	5-20	Mb	F	AC	2.4
I	X	50-600	(16)	Mb	MF	C	2.5
				Breast cancer			
HN	GN[g]	150	13-21	Mb	F	AC	2.4
H	GN	60	5-25	Mt	F	AC	0.3
H	GN	400	5-25	Mt	F	AC	1.0
N	G	20-400	5-25	Mt	F	AC	0.7[h]
T	X	600-3,000	(17.5)	Mb	F	AC	1.6

Table 5. (Cont'd)

Lung cancer

H	GN	30	5–25	Mt	MF	AC	2.3
H	GN	260	5–25	Mt	MF	AC	0.6
N	G	20–400	5–25	Mt	MF	AC	NSE[i]
S	X	80	(10.5)	Mt	M	A	3

Other types of cancer

H	GN	30	5–25	Mt	MF	AC	NE
H	GN	260	5–25	Mt	MF	AC	2.5
N	G	20–400	5–25	Mt	MF	AC	NSE
P$_1$	X	0.2–20	0–10	Mt	MF	F	10
P$_2$	GN[g]	25	0–10	Mt	MF	F	NE

a. H = Hiroshima survivors; N = Nagasaki survivors; S = ankylosing spondylitis patients; P$_1$ = children irradiated pre-natally for medical reasons; P$_2$ = children exposed while in utero to A-bomb radiation; I = infants irradiated in the cervical region; T = tuberculosis patients.

b. G = gamma rays; N = neutrons; X = X-rays; GN = mixed radiation,

c. Years elapsed between exposure and beginning and end of follow-up period or, in brackets, average duration (years) of follow-up.

d. Mt = mortality; Mb = morbidity.

e. A = adults; C = children; F = fœtuses.

f. NE = no excess.

g. No neutron RBE applied to calculate dose.

h. Based on the over-all excess among those exposed to known doses > 10 rad (average 113 rad).

i. NSE = no statistically significant excess.

(2) doses to individuals can be totalled and then divided by the number of individuals exposed thereby giving the mean population dose which, multiplied by the rate of cancer induction, gives the statistical risk per individual (cf. Table 5).

CALCULATION OF THE RISK

With these assumptions, one can calculate the expected number of cancers in a population after radiation exposure. These risk estimates can then be used for comparison with other causes of death. Table 6 gives the chance of death per year for an individual for accidental death: 57 out of 100,000, death in a motor vehicle 26.7 out of 100,000, death from heart disease 364 out of 100,000, death from cancer 157 out of 100,000, death from all spontaneous leukaemias 67 out of 100,000.

Table 6. CHANCE OF DEATH - PER YEAR FOR AN INDIVIDUAL (2)

	CHANCE	PROBABILITY
Accidental Death	57 out of 100,000	0.00057
Death in Motor Vehicle	26.7 out of 100,000	0.00027
Death from Heart Disease ..	364 out of 100,000	0.00364
Death from Cancer	157 out of 100,000	0.00157
Death from all Spontaneous Leukaemias	67 out of 1 million	0.000067
Leukaemia after 1,000 mrem WBR	1 out of 1 million	0.000001
Leukaemia after natural rad. (35 years)	3.7 out of 1 million	0.0000037
Leukaemia after power reactors (35 years at boundary site eat fish and swimming)	2.6 out of 10 million	0.00000026
Leukaemia after power reactors (35 years - general population within 6 miles of site)	2.1 out of 100 million	0.000000021

NOTE: Chance of death per year for an individual in the United States (data from 1970 Statistical Abstract of the United States). Risk of leukaemia, given below the line, represents an additional risk of death to be added to that from all spontaneous leukaemias. Similarly, risk of death from all additional cancers that would be about 5 times that of the additional leukaemia risk would be in addition to the spontaneous risk of cancer 157 out of 100,000.

These figures have been taken from the 1970 <u>Statistical Abstract of the United States</u>. They can be compared with leukaemia after 1,000 millirem whole body radiation given at high dose rate, leukaemia after natural background radiation calculated on the basis of 35 years exposure 3.7 out of 1,000,000, leukaemia after 35 years exposure to reactor station assuming the individual remained on the boundary of the reactor site in the direction of prevailing winds for one year, obtained his protein from fish caught at the exit of the condensor discharge canal, swam for three hours a day for 120 days a year in the effluent of the condensor discharge canal; finally the risk of leukaemia after 35 years exposure to a nuclear power station for the average population within a six-mile radius, i.e., 0.6 millirem/year, plus swimming (2).

As seen from this table, autos are 1,000 times each year riskier than death from leukaemia under the uppermost limits of radiation after 35 years' exposure from the nuclear power station. After 35 years exposure, the risk of death from leukaemia under the average conditions of the population within six miles of the reactor, i.e., the population at the greatest risk, is one ten-thousandth that of being killed in an auto, i.e., after 35 years one would have had 350,000 times greater chance of being killed in a motor vehicle than of developing leukaemia. Since the total induction of all kinds of tumors from radiation is approximately 5 times that of the incidence of leukaemia, it can be seen that the total risk of dying from cancer at these doses is still infinitesimal. Moreover, even taking into account that the fœtus may be approximately ten times more susceptible to the oncogenic effects of radiation than the average members of the population, one appreciates that the fœtus normally remains <u>in utero</u> for less than one year. Thus, the risk to the fœtus will be approximately 1/3 lower than that calculated for the general population after a 35 year exposure.

CALCULATION OF GENETIC RISKS

Finally: genetic hazards. There are no direct quantitative data available for man, but it is not unreasonable to assume that since the genetic material DNA and protein is similar in man and mouse, one can extrapolate mouse data. (The spontaneous mutation rate in the mouse is widely accepted as 0.75×10^{-5} per locus, per generation, and the increase per rad in this rate in the mouse is now estimated as 17×10^{-8} per locus, per generation). The spontaneous mutation rate in man is estimated as 1×10^{-5} per locus, per generation. If one assumes that the induction of mutations by radiation is the same as in the mouse, one rem would produce a 1.7% increase in the mutation rate, making no allowance for repair of genetic damage at low dose rates.

Thus 3 rems accumulated from natural background radiation over
30 years would be responsible for 5. 1% of the spontaneous mutation
rate in man, not allowing for repair. Estimates on the contribution of
natural background radiation to the spontaneous mutation rate in man
range from 4 to 10%. If one accepts that 3 rem over 30 years may be
responsible for 5. 1% of the spontaneous mutation rate, exposure of the
population within six miles of the reactor will give only 18 millirem in
30 years, giving rise in this population to a 0. 031% increase in the
mutation rate, not allowing for repair. To the general population
within 50 miles of the reactor, the corresponding dose would be much
smaller and the increase in rate negligible (0. 0005%), again making no
allowance for repair.

For practical purposes, one concludes that the contribution of
nuclear power stations to the irradiation of the population — directly
or indirectly, by individuals swimming or eating food which has ingested
radioactive material - presents no significant hazard to the health of
the population, assuming accident-free operations. Far higher doses
of radiation are given unnecessarily by improper medical use of X-rays;
a reduction of only 5% in the population dose from medical X-rays in
the United States would more than compensate for present and projected
doses to the year 2000 from nuclear power plants.

RADIATION RISKS: ASSESSMENT OF THE COST PER MANRAD

On the assumption of linear proportionality down to the lowest
doses and dose rates, one estimates that the upper limit of the overall
cancer risk for a radiation dose of one rad is 200 per million (i. e. , if
a population of one million were given an average dose of one rad, there
would be at most 200 additional cancer deaths). If one arbitrarily
estimates that the dollar equivalent of one productive adult = $ 500,000,
then the somatic risk-cost would be $ 100/manrad — a figure obviously
applying only to developed countries. Calculation of the genetic risk-
cost per manrad involves more assumptions. Lederberg (5) has estimated that at equilibrium, a one percent increase in the mutation rate
of the US population will generate an estimated economic loss of about
$ 1 billion per year (measured in 1970 economy of US), but taking at
least 10 generations (assuming a generation to be 30 years) to approach
full impact. This calculation assumes:

1. that mutations account for half the health load;

2. that this is $ 200 billion per year:
   $ 85 billion direct medical;
   $ 15 billion gross lost time;

276

$ 100 billion reduction of efficiency in life and work attribut-
able to less than perfect health (judged by standard of
the healthiest genetypes).

On the assumption that one manrad to the population will increase
the mutation rate one percent, this calculation works out to an eventual
genetic health bill of $ 500 per manrad. Since this is paid many gen-
erations after exposure and one would need a complicated analysis of
the relevant discount rate to compute its present value, Lederberg has
suggested a genetic risk-cost of $ 100/manrad. Thus the combined
somatic and genetic risk-cost would be $ 200/manrad. A similar
figure has been derived somewhat differently by Hedgran and Lindell (6).
Although this assessment like theirs is open to criticism regarding the
assumptions, there is little doubt that the result of such an assessment
will fall within the range of $ 10 < 1,000 per manrad.

PERCEPTION OF THE RISK BY THE PUBLIC

Much has been made of the public's perception of damage. This
has been especially true in the tremendous increase in the public's
appreciation of the biological costs associated with the production and
utilization of energy and especially with the radiation hazard. While
there is little evidence that this new awareness has diminished the
demand for energy, it is increasing the difficulty government agencies
and utilities are finding in approving and constructing facilities to meet
this demand. The problem is that the public has not been given clear-
cut estimates of risk and that information about biological damage is
not readily available. Where quantitative information is on hand, albeit
with considerable reservation - as recently holds true for radiation - there
has been inadequate dissemination and understanding of the information.
Considerations of risk frequently use gambling as an analogy; many in
the public react to this by feeling they are not gamblers and this concept
then does not apply to them. Much has been made of the difference
between voluntary and involuntary risks; that voluntary activities have
an accident or fatality level about 1,000 times greater than the involuntary. But the real issue is probably an inadequate comprehension of
risk by the public. The car driver believes that he is in control of
his car and the risks apply to others and not to him. The difficulties
in persuading people to fasten seat belts or stop smoking all point to
an inadequate understanding of risk. An important objective of biomedical and environmental cost research, then , is to see to it that the
public is alerted to the results: dissemination and understanding of the
conclusions of such research are an essential part of the program. As
with the automobile and smoking, at least the choice is then up to an
informed public.

This survey of radiation as an environmental model has not included consideration of the full biomedical and environmental costs of all stages of nuclear energy production, although this type of calculation would apply to the radiation hazard at all stages.   The environmental decision-maker would need similar information on the biological costs of alternative energy sources in weighing the advantages of one source of energy over another.

NOTES

1. Ionizing Radiation: Levels and Effects. A report of the United Nations Scientific Committee on the Effects of Atomic Radiation to the General Assembly, with Annexes. Vol. 1, Levels p. 197; Vol. 2: Effects, p. 249, United Nations, New York, 1972.

2. Hamilton, L. D. : Biological Significance of Environmental Radiation: Calculation of the Risk. Presented at the American Physical Society Symposium on Biological Significance of Environmental Radiation, Washington, D. C. , April 1971.

3. Court Brown, W. M. and R. Doll: Mortality from Cancer and Other Causes after Radiography for Ankylosing Spondylitis, Brit. Med. Journal, 2, 1327-1332, 1965.

4. Ishimaru, R. , et al. : Leukaemia in Atomic Bomb Survivors, Hiroshima and Nagasaki, Radioact. Res. , 45, 216-233, 1971.

5. Lederberg, J. : Affidavit Petition of Vermont Yankee Nuclear Power Corporation, Public Service Board Docket No. 3445, Washington County, State of Vermont, September 8, 1970.

6. A. Hedgran and B. Lindell: "PQR - A Possible Way of Thinking", Acta Radiologica, Supp. 310, 163-172, 1971. An attempt to assess the cost society is willing to spend to abate one manrad based on questionnaires to experts in health physics.

Further References

- G. C. Butler et al. : "Assessment and Control of Environmental Contamination: Experience with Artificial Radioactivity", Biological Conservation, 4, 177-184, 1972. A somewhat formal analysis of the principles of assessing and controlling radioactive contamination of the environment as a possible model for other contaminants -

concerned more with concepts and terminology than with actual calculation of risks.

- C. W. Dolphin and W. G. Marley: "Risk Evaluation in Relation to the Protection of the Public in the Event of Accidents at Nuclear Installations", UK Atomic Energy Authority, AHSB(RP)R93, Report (Harwell, Didcot), 1969, p. 21. Some risk coefficients need revision in light of recent Japanese survivor data - nevertheless useful review of data and methodology.

- E. J. List: "Energy Use in California: Implications for the Environment", Environmental Quality Laboratory, Cal. Tech. (Pasadena, California), Report no. 3, 1971, pp. 58. Cogent analysis of growth versus technological abatement on a regional basis for California.

- W. L. Russell: "Studies in Mammalian Radiation Genetics", Nucleonics, 23, 53-62, 1965. A clear presentation of effect of dose-rate on mutation rate in mouse and possible significance for man.

*

*   *

Reports of the United Nations Scientific Committee on the Effects of Atomic Radiation (UNSCEAR) present full reviews of original literature, with references, and depict evolution of thinking in the radiation field; some duplication and some variation in quality, but invaluably comprehensive:

- UNSCEAR 1958 A/3838 General Assembly, Official records, 13th sess. Suppl. No. 17, pp. 228.

- UNSCEAR 1962 A/5216, G. A. Official records, 17th sess. Suppl. No. 16, pp. 442.

- UNSCEAR 1964 A/5814, G. A. Official records, 19th sess. Suppl. No. 14, pp. 120.

- UNSCEAR 1966 A/6314, G. A. Official records, 21st sess. Suppl. No. 14, pp. 153.

- UNSCEAR 1969 A/7613, G. A. Official records, 24th sess. Suppl. No. 13, pp. 165.

- UNSCEAR 1972, op. cit.

*

*   *

Publications of International Commission on Radiological Protection (ICRP) concerned with recommendations on establishment on radiation limits at international level; non-binding criteria documents:

- ICRP No. 9 - Recommendations of the ICRP, Pergamon Press, London, 1966, pp. 27.

- ICRP No. 7 - Principles of environmental monitoring related to handling of radioactive materials, Pergamon Press, London, 1966, pp. 11.

- ICRP No. 14 - Radiosensitivity and Spatial Distribution of Dose, Pergamon Press, London, 1969, pp. 118.

*
* *

- US National Academy of Sciences - National Research Council 1972. The effects on populations of exposure to low levels of ionizing radiation. Report of the Advisory Committee on the Biological Effects of Ionizing Radiation (The BEIR Report) Division of Medical Sciences. Comprehensive reviews of the genetic and somatic risks of radiation with special reference to "information relevant to an evaluation of present radiation protection guides". Will be available from NAS-NRC Publications Office, 2101 Constitution Avenue, Washington, D.C.

COSTS, REAL AND PERCEIVED,
EXAMINED IN A RISK-BENEFIT DECISION FRAMEWORK

by

Carl O. Muehlhause
Office of Science and Technology
Executive Office of the President, Washington, D. C.
United States

INTRODUCTION

The extent to which individuals and society are willing to assume risk to their health and safety in the pursuit of certain goals or benefits is vital in determining what the optimum balance between risks, benefits, and costs should be. Though neither the data base nor the method currently allow much quantitative analysis of risk-benefit problems, it nevertheless is the aim of "risk-benefit analysis" to reveal what the proper trade-off between risks and benefits should be in the public interest.

One of the key stumbling blocks to the development of a method or even a conceptual framework within which risk-benefit analysis may be performed is the one needed to relate risk of health and safety to the economic entities of cost, utilitarian value, and pecuniary measure. Another way of posing this problem is to ask in what way risk-benefit is an extension of cost-benefit analysis. Until this is clear one not only lacks the structural form for data utilization, but also the means for identifying the data required. Accordingly, clarification of this point will be attempted in this paper first, with explicit derivations given in the appendix.

It should be clear from the outset that, lacking a fundamental theory of human behaviour capable of predicting human choice regarding utility and risk, any method requires that the analyst go to the people, either directly or to an informed surrogate group to gain the public's revealed choice. A question of some import in this regard is whether or not it is possible to confine the decision-making process to research, survey, and expert analysis. If not, the ultimate decisions which must be made regarding social risks and benefits spreads to a much larger and more pedestrian political arena. This paper ignores that eventuality; instead, it examines the method of "analysis", which is to say a method which might be pursued by analysts internal to the system, but charged with and relied upon to make the relevant decisions on behalf of the public.

In pursuit of the stated aim of the first portion of this paper, focus is directed to the market place, an arena in which benefits are exchanged for pecuniary measure and in which exposure to product hazards is often assumed by the participating consumers. It is also in this arena that the hard realities of engineering and other costs condition price and therefore choice among the products of variable utility and risk. In general the analyst is interested in determining what relationship should prevail among risks, benefits, and costs in order that what might be agreed upon would constitute the "net public benefit" is optimized - at least to "first order".

The discussion of the market place, more explicitly developed in the appendix, begins with an ideal producer-consumer system of fully informed participants. By this it is meant they are able to assess for themselves both utility and risk. How this is done, and how risks, benefits, and costs could come into a socially acceptable equilibrium when informed sovereign choice is operative is examined. From this basic situation a certain generalization of the concept of cost-benefit is proposed which it is believed, constitutes a suitable one for the inclusion of risk. From this, a modification of the basic ground rule of cost-benefit optimization is shown to yield a more appropriate account of human decision-making regarding the taking of risk.

Next to be considered, also more fully in the appendix, is the case when the consumer and/or producer inadequately assesses the hazard associated with their product. This kind of market failure constitutes one of two principal reasons for interference in the free market by a third party, e. g. a regulatory agency. What information and authority are to be injected into the market system by this third party, still in the interest of optimizing the net public benefit, is then discussed. This, in effect, defines the role of a hypothetical regulator who, as a decision-maker, sets standards on the basis of risk-benefit analysis. The modified cost-benefit ground rule for optimization is shown to be further modified in order to account for the public's misperception of the risk. Its implications and a free interpretation of it are given.

The role of uncertainty and how much additional knowledge is "worth" after a product has been released is briefly discussed in the text; and this primarily to indicate how, in principle, uncertainty can be included within the risk-benefit analytical framework.

Finally, the application of the ideas developed for the "simple" case of consumer product hazard is extended to the more complex one of environmental pollution. The general case of a polluting plant is considered, and some final commentary is given regarding "damage costs", real and imaginary.

THE CLOSE-COUPLED IDEAL MARKET

In order to concentrate on the key issue of how informed consumers evaluate and account for risk it is well to begin by stripping the case down to as few complications as possible. Consider then a hypothetical situation in which a certain product having various utility to consumers is offered on the market place in which also the consumers perceive a hazard in its use. Assume that if this product were bought and used the consumer would be its sole beneficiary and in the case of an accident, its sole victim. This assumption avoids a collective social problem of consumer interference wherein the taking of risk by one member of the public poses a hazard to others. Assume too that the consumer is able adequately to assess both the utility, and the risk which exposure to the product generates. In this initial case it is also well to avoid consideration of live-saving or pain relieving products e. g. , efficacious drugs, so as to restrict consideration to only one life-vital element at a time, namely the issue of safety itself or risk to personal health. We assume then that the product, though not vital, has definite utility to which consumers assign various dollar measures, or "willingness to pay" for said product. Assume too that each consumer is able also to assess accurately the frequency and severity of the risk to which he is exposed in utilizing the product. This latter assumption in effect means that in analysing the various use modes of his product-interaction the consumer is able to assess his statistical failure rate. His analysis of use serves to assess both his utilitarian value assignment, i. e. , measure of benefit, as well as his level of risk via failure analysis. Having assigned a pecuniary measure to the product's benefit, say V_p, what value or what modified decision does the consumer face regarding the disutility of the risk? If the consumer could also translate his risk assessment into a pecuniary measure, say V_r, he would have effected the so-called "trade-off" between risks and benefits in his particular instance. This is to say he is a candidate for active participation in the market place provided the price, P, is such that:

(1) $$P \leqslant V_p - V_r$$

If all consumers made such informed value assignments their distribution of values would determine the market demand or rate schedule for the product as a function of risk level.

However a consumer would make his particular pecuniary assignment to risk taking, the resulting value V_r, is what the economist would term as that consumers "compensating variation" for assuming the risk. This, in effect, states that the dollar amount, V_r, is what that consumer would pay to avoid the risk. Conversely there exists a compensating variation, V_r, which would make that particular consumer "indifferent" to the insult of exposure to risk level, R. If in fact the consumer, knowing of the risk voluntarily enters the market for said product the economist must assume the consumer did so because he believed the benefits net of risk and other costs to be positive.

What are the items of statistical damage for which the consumer would require compensation? They are at least the following: 1) the effort to pay special attention to safety in utilizing the product, 2) time lost in pursuit of normal living should an accident occur, 3) medical expense and income lost during recovery from an accident, 4) other lost value due to his family or others for whom he feels responsible, and 5) so-called "pain and suffering". The first four items cited are statistical losses which are paid for by insurance and/or out-of-pocket on the occasion of actual events. Not to account for these items would constitute a give away and is something which a reasonable and informed consumer would not countenance. A fundamental problem arises, however, when one considers pain, suffering, and possibly death.

In the case of the first four items, the informed consumer could coldly "calculate" his compensating variation on the basis of the costs of the events in question, should they occur, by multiplying them by his estimate of the probability of their occurrence. The latter he has already inferred from his assessment of his own state-of-risk. That one can be made indifferent to the risk of pain, suffering, and death via pecuniary compensation, however, is of doubtful validity. One knows from a casual observation of the market place that in utilizing certain products the risk of pain, etc. is real and often voluntarily assumed; however, one does not know that the risk taking decisions were wholly governed by pecuniary value assignments. For example, enquiries which have attempted to determine a "value of life" suitable for multiplication by a risk probability as is done in the case of the first four items, ostensibly to obtain that part of V_r which would account for death, have so far failed to elicit a comprehensible response. The reason for this may be that no sensible pecuniary value can be given to these life-vital elements. It is perhaps more appropriate to regard that a non-pecuniary type of boundary condition governs peoples behaviour and decision-making in this fundamental regard. Clearly, if the risk is sufficiently great, the consumer rejects the product out of hand. This could come about because he had reached either a state of true alarm or one of strict principle. In his original assessment of product engagement he sought to determine if the projected operation in the use of the product fell within his capability of good management. If it did not or if otherwise his estimate of the risk exceeded his standard for acceptable risk taking, he would have rejected that product out of hand, and not simply on the basis that some probability multiplied by a "life-value" generated an expectation value which was in excess of his product value. While it is true that the pecuniary part of V_r, originating from the first four items cited earlier, if in excess of product value, V_p, would be cause for rejection of the product, the product would also have been rejected independently of this condition if the consumer's particular non-pecuniary demand for safety had not been met. The latter demand could, in turn, have been determined by a host of complex personal factors including at least the following: 1) his talent and ability to manage the operation of the product in question, 2) his past experience and success of similar undertakings, and 3) his natural propensity or aversion for assuming risks. A reasonable consumer accepts his fallibility but does not necessarily assume risk for a price where otherwise the projected product engagement fails to meet his living criteria for acceptable acts of choice. Such a choice would be non-compensatory. In other words, the pecuniary part of V_r could be less than V_p but the consumer would nevertheless remove himself from the market place if his non-pecuniary demand for acceptable risk taking had not been met. At least it would seem presumptious on the part of any risk-benefit analytical formulation to regard that all aspects of V_r must have pecuniary measure. It is this particular point that is overlooked by those who appear bound to the idea that because risks are assumed there must have been an implicit value placed upon mortality or morbidity. Such an idea could well be false resulting from too narrow an extension of the concept of cost-benefit to that of risk-benefit analysis.

The above point concerning non-pecuniary demand is important for two fundamental reasons. These are: 1) it alters the structure of any ensuing risk-benefit formulation, and 2) it alters the enquiry into human choice necessary to acquire the required data base for a given product. A spectrum or distribution of risk taking levels, independent of price and acceptable to a knowledgeable and sovereign consuming public would be vital to a description of market demand and related economic functions. The production engineer, seeking to incorporate that level of safety into a product most favourable to the public interest, would have to reckon with this non-pecuniary factor of acceptability, as well as with the pecuniary one, also assigned by the consumer.

On the assumption then that the consumer needs no surrogate decision-maker to assess either product utility or product risk, two sets of double questions would constitute the proper enquiry or market type survey necessary to describe consumer demand and ultimately to optimize the net public benefit. To a suitable sample of the consuming public the following two stylised questions must be put: 1) "Neglecting risk, at what rate would you purchase this product, and what pecuniary value do you place upon its utility?" and 2) "Neglecting utility, would you consider using this product and if so what compensating variation would you charge to assume the risk?" The first of these questions is meant to constitute the usual market survey and the second the appropriate enquiry into safety. Note the symmetry between the two questions sets.

The above ideas can be readily formulated into a quantitative description of consumer demand as a function of price and state-of-risk. On the assumption that the producer assesses the state-of-risk in a like and true manner as does the consumer, i.e. by a suitable public enquiry into a series of products having constant utility and variable state-of-risk, he is able to analyse the relevant economic functions by adding his own special knowledge of the engineering costs vs. state-of-risk. The quantity or function which economists for the most part agree should be optimized is the so-called "net public benefit" or sum of values net of all costs. The latter include those incurred in production as well as those assigned by consumers (i.e. V_r). The reader is referred to the appendix for these results. In addition to the classic condition that marginal cost with respect to production be set equal to price, there exists an additional optimizing condition which sets all marginal costs with respect to safety equal to the marginal change in non-pecuniary acceptance times the so-called "consumer surplus". It is this latter condition which expresses the sought for trade-off condition between risks and benefits. In effect it formally states that if improvements in safety are desirable in order to increase the flow of beneficial goods to the public, the excess value over price which the consumer attaches to the benefits can be tapped to improve safety up to the point where safety engineering costs are now so great that acceptance by the consuming public declines too rapidly on the basis of price relative to utilitarian value. Thus, when the risk is too high, people refuse to "trade" themselves for utilitarian benefits; rather they choose to abandon the market altogether. On the other hand, if risks have been reduced at too high a cost, then too many people again remove themselves from the market place, but now on the basis of price alone. There thus exists a balance which maximizes the net public benefit. This balance which is achieved is not a crass "materialistic" one which some might assume. This is because the non-pecuniary demand works to limit consumption always to acceptable people-product engagements.

In a system in which the producer correctly reads the consumer's interest with respect to risk and wherein the latter correctly assesses his own state-of-risk the optimum level of safety is ultimately and automatically embodied in the product, with no need for assistance from a third party. Included in this final equilibrium are both pecuniary and non-pecuniary factors, the ultimate balance involving not only risks, benefits, and costs, but the proper people-participation as well. This participation is governed by both price and the non-pecuniary demand for safety.

Symbolically, we have for an increase in safety - ΔR, the following optimum balance between the changes in cost per unit product:

$$(2) \qquad \Delta C_E + \Delta C_A = \Delta p \cdot \overline{(CS)}_{max}$$

$$+ \qquad\qquad - \qquad\qquad +$$

where for a decrease in risk, or gain in safety the direction of change in engineered safety cost C_E and accident cost C_A, is indicated by + or -. $\overline{(CS)}_{max}$ is the consumer surplus per product and Δp the change in acceptance probability resulting from the change in R. If the non-pecuniary conditioned factor on the right-hand side of this balance could have been expressed in all pecuniary terms, e.g., $V_L \Delta R$ where V_L would be the so-called "value of life" other than the expenses already recognized in V_r, it could then have been brought to the left-hand side of the equation and combined simply with V_r.* The broader interpretation or allowance in decision-making put forth here is that such a transcendent value cannot be given in pecuniary terms but rather in direct people-participation, an exchange which obviously

---

* A common misperception is to regard that $\dfrac{\partial C_E}{\partial R} \simeq V_L$

is commensurate with <u>life value</u>. This point will be returned to in the next section which attempts to describe the imperfect market.

In time, sufficiently cheap ways may be found to so improve product safety that all consumers find the risk acceptable, i. e. , p → 1. Optimization of the net public benefit then reduces to the usual cost-benefit ground rule of minimizing the sum of all pecuniary cost terms, including V_r, the expense for risk assumption as assigned by the consumers themselves:

$$(3) \qquad \Delta C_E + \Delta C_A = 0$$

Society thus continues to make manoeuvres which lower the costs associated with the product even though the non-pecuniary or <u>gut issue</u> of safety is past. In effecting these manoeuvres transfers can in principle take place in either direction between engineering and consumer assigned costs as long as their sum declines.

THE IMPERFECT MARKET AND STANDARD SETTING

The example given above of how a perfect market would operate serves to guide the case of an imperfect one. It is only when the market system fails that a third party, such as a regulatory agency, may justifiably interfere with the free mechanism of exchange.

There are two principal reasons for interfering with the free market in the interest of establishing safety. One would be when a collective problem exists wherein the voluntary assumption of risk, even if informed, cannot be granted individual sovereign status if at the same time it poses a hazard to others. This type of problem is exemplified in the driving of motor vehicles and even more so in problems involving environmental pollution.

The second principal reason for third party interference results from a breakdown in the previously discussed perfect market. This comes about when the consumer and/or producer fail to assess the product hazard adequately. Both failures can occur simultaneously, but the latter occurs in particular when the product contains such highly technical features that the consumer's assessment capability is transcended. If products such as these are passed on to the consumer two basic questions arise. With limited consumer ability to assess product interaction how may it be possible for the analyst to: 1) assess the level of risk which will ensue, and 2) assess the consumer's pecuniary cost assignments and his non-pecuniary risk acceptability? Expertness and consumption are now separate so that if a method is to be followed, experts must now conduct the safety investigation previously achieved by the consumers themselves. It must be assumed that these experts are at least capable of performing this function for themselves, i.e., as if they were also the consumers. The task is yet more difficult, however, as it also requires that these surrogate analysts anticipate the hazard which the product poses to the less perceptive and more pedestrian consuming public.

A glib solution to this problem is to insist that such products either be taken off the market or so improved that misperception cannot take place. Neither of these guides constitute an optimum policy. In effect what is taking place is that for an actual state-of-risk, R, i.e. the outcome of product use, the public misinterprets its engagement with the product such that it believes the state-of-risk to be R^1, some level different from R. In general R^1 can be either greater or less than R.

The effect of this misperception is twofold: 1) certain members of the consuming public will accept the risk whereas if they had been fully informed they would have rejected it, and vice versa; and 2) an incorrect pecuniary cost assignment will be utilized by them in determining acceptable price or demand quantity. The knowledge which the regulator must have if he is to best correct this situation concerns both the true and misperceived states-of-risk. This information could in part come from the same two survey questions cited earlier, but it must come also from expert psycho-physical and/or psycho-chemical analysis, plus whatever epidemiological evidence is available. Armed with adequate knowledge of this sort, the analyst is in a position to best optimize the net public benefit. Though the regulator cannot force the public to demand according to R rather than R^1 it can set up modified demand and net benefit functions which allow for the correct V_r rather than the incorrect one, V_r^1. To do so further presumes, however, that the analyst can anticipate at least an appropriate average V_r based on statistical costs of anticipated injury rates, i.e. true damage functions. In principle, the misperceived demand and utilitarian value distributions can again be obtained by the same market type survey or enquiry cited earlier.

The formulation of this case is given in the appendix. Again two marginal conditions are obtained: one with respect to production and another with respect to safety. The latter appears much as before,

but differs in that the perceived consumer surplus is modified by a factor $\dfrac{\partial R^1}{\partial R}$ correlating perceived and true risk levels:

$$(4) \qquad \Delta c_E + \Delta c_A = \frac{\partial R^1}{\partial R}\left[\Delta p\,\overline{(CS)}_{max}\right]_{perceived}$$

The latter factor moderates or amplifies the strength of the consumer surplus bank available for improving engineered safety. If changes in real safety effect only small public response, this resource term is of little import in optimizing the net public benefit. Essentially one is then reduced to the standard cost-benefit ground rule of making minimization manoeuvres among real cost terms. If, on the other hand, changes in real safety elicit an exaggerated public response, the consumer surplus bank is very effective in optimizing the net public benefit. Should the public be so unaware of the hazard as to accept risks highly unacceptable to the surrogate analyst, the non-pecuniary term should be augmented to some minimal value. Equation (4) is better suited to the case of an overestimation by the public of the risk. A similar problem is encountered in the collective case to be discussed later in the paper.

Finally, it should be remarked that we have been discussing the marginal conditions for maximizing the net public benefit. These two conditions, one for production and one for safety, coupled with the demand schedule determine price, quantity and risk, optimum in first order of the public interest. A rather obvious additional condition should be stated: namely, that if this "solution" does not yield a net positive benefit the product should be withdrawn from the market place altogether. The marginal conditions by themselves only guarantee a least negative value.

FURTHER COMMENTARY AND EXTENSION

In summary of the previous two sections of this paper, the inclusion of risk in cost benefit analysis not only adds the obvious pecuniary consumer assigned cost term to production costs, but in addition a term proportional to the consumer perceived surplus multiplied by his non-pecuniary risk acceptance factor. This last term is further modified if the consumer's perception of risk deviates from his true or epidemiologically revealed risk. The existence of the additional non-pecuniary term alters the rule for optimization that would otherwise prevail if the problem were only a cost-benefit problem, which is to say if it were only one of manoeuvring among pecuniary cost terms. In the latter case, i.e. the all pecuniary one, the optimum engineering or production cost is set at that level at which further safety engineering costs would equal the savings effected in consumer assigned risk-associated costs. When the non-pecuniary acceptance term is added, the engineering or production costs optimal for net public benefit must be further increased. This is because by increasing them over the value which the simpler cost-benefit rule would dictate gains some additional people-participation in product use. How important this additional effect or term is depends on the magnitude of the consumer surplus bank and the sensitive perception of the public to the risk. If the public is not sensitive, then its consumer surplus bank or excess of utilitarian value over price is not available for further improvement in engineered safety; moreover, there is no way a regulator can make it so. He can only utilize this fact in his calculations, as well as the real rather than the misperceived pecuniary terms.

This somewhat extensive discussion was necessary to resolve the confusion and political difficulty of attempting to assign and directly utilize some "value of life" in the damage function itself. Basically, the analyst needs to learn and utilize the means by which informed persons make decisions about risk to life and not to preempt this via some recipe not derivable from human choice. Such a procedure is not only incorrect; it will not be tolerated. The prescription for the cure is not to expect to represent risk taking wholly in pecuniary terms, but to ask at what point this accountability fails and what levels of risk to life does life accept. Even if the reply is not well correlated with true risk, the public answer will condition the investment in engineered safety optimal of the net public benefit.

Many practical matters have thus far been excluded from the discussion and are still in need of being addressed and evaluated if the implied analytical procedures were to be carried out. These have to do primarily with the talent, institution, and cost needed to gain the information cited. It should be evident that these costs and talents are formidable, thus making it unclear at present just what effort, detailed analysis, and data gathering are appropriate to protect the public from consumer product hazard. It may, for example, only be possible to mandate certain generic type safety standards which would constitute "good engineering practice" and, at the same time, effect an economic and adverse reaction data gathering system that would reveal suspect cases in need of more detailed analysis. All of this is to say that there are administrative and information acquisition costs which must also be included in the optimization of the net public benefit. An important subsidiary of this has to do with the cost of uncertainty or its converse, the value of more accurate knowledge in making the required assessments.

In principle, uncertainty can be included in the net benefit calculation by utilizing probability distributions around each quantity that
enters the net benefit expression. To decide at what point it is no
longer profitable to acquire further knowledge, cost terms representing
knowledge acquisition must be included. Starting at some current
state-of-knowledge it is possible to calculate the risk level which
should be set to optimize the expected net public benefit. If this
expectation would increase with increased knowledge in spite of the
increased costs to gain that knowledge the acquisition of more
knowledge should be undertaken. At some acquisition point the
marginal net public benefit becomes null, at which time the best
revealed safety level is set and the product is released. If, after
release, epidemiological evidence is cheaper to obtain than pre-release
research was to perform it is gathered and analysed for the possibility
of resetting the risk level at some yet more optimum point in the public
interest.

As with the static risk-benefit analysis described earlier this yet
more sophisticated type of analysis is even more remote from achievement. However, the concept of uncertainty as opposed to risk is worthy
of comment. For this reason as well as the one to complete the risk-
benefit description it has been briefly discussed here. As a practical
matter uncertainty looms large in the estimate of every quantity
discussed in this section. A very rough way of hedging against it is to
modify an estimate in question, e.g. a risk probability R, by a "safety
factor", say Γ , so that one would now be willing to <u>act</u> on a decision
which utilized Γ R in place of R, i.e. as it would function in the
relevant analytical expressions. Without further elaborating these
logical points we pass on to consideration of certain problems involving
pollution and of the role of risk taking in some of them.

EXTENSION TO ENVIRONMENTAL POLLUTION PROBLEMS

The formalism developed in the previous sections of the paper, if
freely generalized and extended to the more complex and collective
problems of environmental pollution, can be used at least to interpret
these problems; i.e. to exhibit the terms which a hypothetical risk-
benefit decision-maker must consider. Regard once more then the
result expressed by equation (4). This relationship assumed that the
benefactor and victim were one and the same, namely a consumer able
to exercise choice. If, on the other hand, the "product" were
automobiles or stationary power plants emitting pollution that engulfed
consumer and non-consumer alike, the non-pecuniary dependent term
on the right-hand side of the equation would be zero, i.e. no choice

would exist with regard to the avoidance of the hazard. In such a case
the marginal condition with respect to "emissions" reduces to:

$$(5) \qquad \Delta C_E + \Delta C_D = 0$$

a simple cost-benefit condition wherein the total damage term, C_D, to
the environment plus health is substituted for the original one pertaining
to accidents alone. It therefore no longer matters what the public
thinks the risk and damages from pollution are. It remains in their
interest to allow the surrogate decision-maker to optimize the net
public benefit according to (5). However, as with the case for consumer products when (4) degenerated into (5), the surrogate analysts may
need to impose an ad hoc type of condition in place of (5). That is,
if condition (5), even though net beneficial, would still render a
collectively unacceptable non-pecuniary condition, a surrogate group
may need to consider same on behalf of the public. How the outcome of
such a collective decision with regard to non-pecuniary acceptance
differs from, for example, the average individual acceptance is not
known. If it should prove more restrictive than (5) it would need either
to be substituted for it or integrated with it, the result being determined
differently than from p(R) and not expressible by the concepts of this
paper. What in effect is at issue here is a forced reevaluation by
some members of society of what constitutes for them acceptable risk-
taking. The realization that a new and inescapable level of pollution
must augment their acceptable level of risk-taking leads to a reevaluation
of that acceptable level. How this is achieved and how such is collectively compromised is of course beyond the scope of this paper.

Another situation, commonly encountered, but one of less demographic extent, is characterized by the introduction into a community of
a plant which produces a product harmless in itself, but which pollutes
the near environment. In such a case the hazard, rather than residing
in the product, stems from the production process itself. The threat
to human health reaches man from the source via an environmental
pathway. Those living in the pathway may or may not also be
beneficiaries of the process. Unlike the case just discussed a choice
now exists for those in the pathway to exit from it should they decide
living there is intolerable. This case is treated in the appendix also,
the incremental conditions with respect to residuals now being:

$$(6) \qquad \Delta C_E + \Delta C_D = \frac{\partial R^1}{\partial R} \left[NpCp(\Delta p^1) \right]$$

perceived

The result is perhaps evident from all that has been stated before. The incremental investment in engineered residuals must compensate not only for the actual damages to the health of those in the pathway as well as damage to the environmental pathway itself, but it must also account for the turnover expense of those dissatisfied with the threat to their health and safety.

Without attempting more examples, it should be clear that the general marginal condition with respect to engineered pollution residuals is given in the form:

$$(7) \qquad \Delta c_E + \Delta c_D = s c_o \Delta p$$

where C_E and C_D are true (i. e. expert as opposed to pedestrian) estimates of the cost to control residuals and the cost of damages, respectively. s is a sensitivity factor relating the change in the public perception of a threat to its health and safety (risk) relative to a real change in this threat. C_o is some cost or value to be saved by continued exposure to the polluted environment, and Δp is the public response to the non-pecuniary aspect of this threat. If the hypothetical risk-benefit regulator can indeed estimate on a political scientific basis, e. g. via an ordered enquiry, this non-pecuniary perceived term he may improve on the usual cost-benefit estimate which does not take such into proper consideration, e. g. when estimating damage costs. In general this term augments Δc_E beyond the estimate of Δc_D and in an algebraic sense might appear as a component of Δc_D. That this view can lead to logical and political difficulties has been adequately pointed out, e. g. re the transcendent nature of risk to health and possibly, for some, a comparable value judgement concerning the quality of the environment.

SOME COMMENTARY REGARDING REGULATORY DECISION-MAKING AND DATA ACCESSIBILITY

In examining the three terms in equation (7) it can be more or less appreciated that the order of difficulty in obtaining information on each increases from left to right, i. e. from control, to damage, and finally to a non-pecuniary body-exchange term which also involves the public misperception of the threat to its safety. Obviously this is the most difficult term to evaluate. Whether it originated from a non-pecuniary probability factor, as in the case of consumer products, or whether it was separately assigned, it "appears" as another damage term in need of compensation by the engineering control term. In actuality it is a type of resource term, i. e. one representing value to be conserved; or better, a type of <u>bank</u> capable of supplying funds to the engineering control of residuals (safety). A cardinal point of this paper is that it is <u>not</u> a term containing a transcendent and therefore non-existent "life value". Such values are not directly available in pecuniary measure to drive economic processes. Rather they affect <u>decisions</u> on the part of <u>people</u> to engage or not engage in an environment or product. When people decide favourably to do so, some other, but real economic value, e. g. consumer surplus or moving expense, etc. , accompanies the decision and thereby alters the risk-cost-benefit marginal null condition.

If the regulator is not simply to rely on such heuristic guidelines as "as much as practical" or "as much as reasonable" he must at least obtain estimates of the damage costs. Knowing only that some risk is present and barely detectable is entirely inadequate for setting standards at the correspondingly low levels. Such policy undoubtedly disserves the public interest but will, for political reasons, prevail until such time as the regulator is in possession of reliable damage costs. The effort to obtain same should be worth a very great deal.

As a final and specific comment on one particular recurring but apparently troublesome type of damage cost, namely the loss to society of a worker who either becomes ill or dies, the author would like to offer the following:

1.   Out of work but alive:

To first order this would appear to be the loss of willingness to pay by the employer for the wage earner's services. Thus, if dp(S) is the differential probability that this value is S, then the loss is simply:

$$(8) \qquad \int_{\mathscr{S}}^{\infty} S\, dp(S) \; \Big/ \; \int_{\mathscr{S}}^{\infty} dp(S)$$

where $\mathscr{S}$ is the salary of the worker including fringe benefits. This expression would need be reduced if the worker managed to subsist on less than his salary during his illness.

2.   Dead:

Under this condition the loss would appear to be the employer's surplus or simply:

$$(9) \qquad \int_{S}^{\infty} Sdp(S) \Bigg/ \int_{S}^{\infty} dp(S) - S$$

Since these expressions can be sizable and quite different from, for example, simply S, or wages foregone, it is important to have them clarified for future use as a part of health damages. Accordingly, the author recommends that professional economists resolve this concept, if possible.

*

*   *

References

"The Life You Save May Be Your Own", T. Schelling, pp. 127-176, in S.B. Chase, ed. Problems in Public Expenditure Analysis, Brookings Institution, 1968.

"Evaluation of Life and Limb: A Theoretical Approach", E.J. Mishan, Journal of Political Economy, Vol. 79, para. 4, July/August 1971, pp. 687-706.

"The Inclusion of Risk in Cost-Benefit Analysis", C.O. Muehlhause, to be published, US National Bureau of Standards.

"Social Benefit vs. Technological Risk", C. Starr, Science, Vol. 165, pp. 1232-1238, September 19, 1969.

"Perspectives on Risk-Benefit Decision Making", Committee on Public Engineering Policy, (COPEP) National Academy of Engineering, 1972.

"The Cost of Accidents", G. Calibresi, Yale University Press, 1970.

Appendix A

THE CLOSE COUPLED MARKET WITH RISK

In this, as with the other appendices, it will be assumed one is in possession of the riskless demand schedule or spectrum of willable values which people place upon the product's utility. The latter is obtained from the former by differentiation to yield the probability distribution of apparent value as a function of value. The demand quantity, q, as a function of price, $\mathcal{P}$, can thus be written:

$$q = Q \int_{\mathcal{P}}^{\infty} dp\,(V_p)$$

where Q is the total potential demand quantity, i. e. for zero price, and $dp(V_p)$ is the differential probability of product value assignment, V_p.

Regard that the product also exhibits a risk distribution independent of V_p, and that this consists of two parts: a non-pecuniary probability $p(R)$ that the risk is acceptable and a pecuniary one that, if acceptable, a charge of compensating variation, V_r, is levied against the product with differential probability, $dp(V_r)$. The risk-modified demand quantity thus becomes:

$$q = Qp(R) \int_{\mathcal{P}}^{\infty} \int_{o}^{V_p - \mathcal{P}} dp(V_p) dp(V_r)$$

V_p and V_r may not be independent, but their correlation is ignored in this treatment.

The net public benefit, η, can now be expressed in these same terms:

$$\eta = Qp(R) \int_{\mathcal{P}}^{\infty} \int_{0}^{V_p - \mathcal{P}} (V_p - V_r)dp(V_p)dp(V_r) - C_E(q\,R)$$

where $C_E(q,R)$ represents engineering costs as a function of quantity, q, and state-of-risk, R.

The fact that risk is represented throughout by the same symbol implies it is knowledgeably and accurately assessed alike by both producer and consumer. Though the ultimate result can be obtained without reduction, we will reduce the double integral to a single one by utilizing a "suitable" average value of V_r. Then:

$$q = Qp(R) \int_{\mathcal{P} + \overline{V}_r}^{\infty} dP(V_p) \qquad \text{and:}$$

$$\eta = Qp(R) \int_{\mathcal{P} + V_r}^{\infty} (V_p - \overline{V}_r)\, dp(V_p) - C_E(q,R)$$

The quantity η can be maximized subject to the demand constraint utilizing the method of Lagrange multipliers. When this is done two conditions result:

$$\frac{\partial C_E}{\partial q} = \mathcal{P} \qquad \text{and}$$

$$\frac{\partial C_E}{\partial R} + q\frac{d\overline{V}_r}{dR} = \frac{dp}{dR} \cdot (CS)_{max}$$

299

where $(CS)_{max}$ is the so-called "consumer surplus" accruing to the flow of q products and full acceptance. That is:

$$(CS)_{max} = Q \int_{\mathcal{P} + V_r}^{\infty} (V_p - \bar{V}_r) dp(V_p) - Q\mathcal{P} \int_{\mathcal{P} + \bar{V}_r}^{\infty} dp(V_p)$$

or the maximum possible excess value over price which this number of products "benefits" the public.

Appendix B

THE IMPERFECT MARKET WITH RISK

In this it will be assumed that a regulator operates to "best correct" an imperfect market situation in which the public acts imperfectly through a misperception of the state-of-risk. The regulator's view of the risk is presumed to be "correct" or at least hedged to permit decisions, and that this same view has been communicated to the producer. Two views of the state-of-risk must be reckoned with: the correct one, R, and the public's misperceived one, R^1. The regulator's job is made particularly difficult due to the need to relate R^1 and R, i. e. to include a new constraint condition, namely:

$$R^1 = R^1(R)$$

The demand and net benefit functions now appear as follows:

$$q = Qp(R^1) \int_{\wp + \overline{V}_r 1}^{\infty} dp(V_p) \quad \text{and}$$

$$\eta = Qp(R^1) \int_{\wp + \overline{V}_r 1}^{\infty} (V_p - \overline{V}_r)dp(V_p) - C_E(q, R)$$

wherein the correct pecuniary $\overline{V}_r$ was used in place of $\overline{V}_r 1$ as a cost item, but wherein also the public exhibited its misperception in the demand and acceptance functions.

301

Maximizing η subject to the two constraints, q and R^1, can again be accomplished by the method of Lagrange multipliers. The two marginal conditions which result are:

$$\frac{\partial C_E}{\partial q} = \mathcal{P} + \overline{V}_{r'} - \overline{V}_r \qquad \text{and}$$

$$\frac{\partial C_E}{\partial R} + \frac{q d\overline{V}_r}{dR} = \frac{dR^1}{dR} \cdot \left[\frac{dp}{dR^1} (CS)_{max} \right]_{perceived} 1$$

which is similar to the result in Appendix A, but wherein the quantity on the right-hand side of the equation is the perceived value modified by a sensitivity factor between R^1 and R.

Appendix C

POLLUTION WITH LIMITED DEMOGRAPHY

In this it will be assumed that the plant in question produces a beneficial and harmless product, but that all persons, Np, residing in the pathway of the plant's emissions are exposed to some statistical damage from those residuals. Assume too, that the residuals emissions cause damage to the environmental pathway itself, and that the engineering cost can again be expressed as $C_E(q, R)$. Though R now stands for "residuals" it is assumed also to correlate with the state-of-risk.

Three additional cost items are incurred: 1) that to the pathway, 2) that to people in the pathway, and 3) that due to residential turnover of those no longer wishing to tolerate the pathway. Let the first two costs be combined and indicated as $C_D(R)$, and let the unit extra cost of turnover be C_o. Then the net public benefit, η, is:

$$\eta = Q \int_{\mathcal{P}}^{\infty} V_p \, dp(V_p) - C_E(q, R) - C_D(R) - \left[1 - p(R^1)\right] N_p C_o$$

Subject to: $q = Q \int_{\mathcal{P}}^{\infty} dp(V_p)$ and $R^1 = R^1(R)$

Maximising η, again yields two marginal conditions:

303

$$\frac{\partial C_E}{\partial q} = \wp \qquad \text{and:}$$

$$\frac{\partial C_E}{\partial R} + \frac{\partial C_D}{\partial R} = \frac{dR^1}{dR} N_p C_o \frac{dp}{dR^1}$$

i.e. $\quad \Delta C_E + \Delta C_D = \left(\dfrac{\partial R^1}{\partial R}\right) . N_p C_o \Delta p$

perceived

SOCIAL PERCEPTION AND SOCIAL DEMANDS IN ENVIRONMENTAL MATTERS

by

Lucien Nizard and Jean Tournon
Institut d'Etudes Politiques,
Université de Grenoble

INTRODUCTION

1. All life, even that of savages, causes some damage to the environment (for example, hunting, food collecting) but this is no more than "pseudo-damage" so long as the natural cycles correct almost immediately the slight changes which have occurred.

There are, it seems, two crucial stages in the history of human societies: the first when men begin to take certain resources from nature at a more rapid rate than nature can renew them (1), and the second when they begin to add to nature things or effects which nature (2) cannot absorb, eliminate or correct at the same rate as they take place.

These two stages occur far back in our history, and even our prehistory (mastery of fire, beginnings of metal-working and agriculture), but do not coincide either with the first harm that man caused to man and which is inseparable from the advantages of life in society, nor with the sudden upsurge of anxiety which in the last ten years has accompanied rapid industrial and urban growth.

2. The problem of the environment is therefore that of the wrong men do to each other by their use of nature at a time when this harm is seen to be both serious and avoidable.

I. THE PSYCHOLOGY OF HOMO POLLUTUS

3. Applying the term "damage to the environment" or "pollution" to phenomena such as smoke, noise, exhaust gases, waste, etc. , is not something which is automatically done. For a long time, and often

still today, the harmful aspects of these phenomena have passed unnoticed and are accepted as an integral part of a justified activity.

The "disamenities" which are closely linked with valued activities are difficult to perceive and still more difficult to condemn. The roar of the motor-cycle is part of the pleasure of motor-cycling, smells and smoke are part of the pleasure of woodfires, and the siren of the fire-engine is part of the speed with which the firemen arrive to deal with the fire. Group reactions are also marked by the propensity to vindicate one's likes and condemn one's dislikes. Thus, the unpleasant side-effects of industrial activity were constantly pointed out throughout the 19th century by persistent conservationists and lovers of the country-side. On the other hand, countries like France or Japan, which took until the 1960s to free themselves from their postwar habits of mind, only saw reassurance and hope in factories which smoked, vibrated, consumed vast quantities of raw materials, and spewed out masses of new products and masses of waste.

4.   There are two ways of becoming aware of a deterioration in the human environment:

a)   a concrete way, through direct sensations: breathing air which chokes one or makes one's eyes water; seeing smoke darkening the sky; jumping at noises of machines; feeling over-whelmed in front of a horrible building, eroded soil, etc;

b)   an abstract way, through measuring instruments or reasoning or calculations; finding out how much of a certain toxic gas the air contains; forecasting the depletion of a certain resource; determining the water-heating effect of a power station, etc.

5.   But no matter whether the perception is abstract or concrete, it still only leads to a subjective estimate of the unpleasantness or danger. Nothing more. For an individual the concept of damage undergone or risk incurred can only be understood in a subjective sense. Even when confronted by scientifically calculated data, individual reactions differ. That is why it is always possible to find volunteers for dangerous work, usually without having to pay them excessive amounts for doing it.

For all of us and for all activities termed "harmful" there are certain levels at which the harm is negligible and the term "disamenity" has no internalised meaning; but there are other levels at which the same phenomena are intolerable. It looks very much as if these critical levels vary for different individuals, vary over time for the same individual, and vary over time for the average individual in a given collectivity.

6. Brief list of factors affecting perception and contributing to the toleration of or resistance to damage to the environment.

6. 1. The value put on the activity in question: The higher the value put on the activity, the more its liability to do harm is minimized (cf. paragraph 3); the existence of an underlying dislike will however make people hyper-sensitive to its "disamenity" potential.

6. 2. Awareness of a disamenity or a risk: Various factors come into play here, depending on whether the risks affect oneself or others, and whether they are immediate or future.

	For oneself	For others
Immediate		
Future		

The following are a few of the factors which seem on the face of it to play a part, and which could be the subject of more detailed study:

a) Cultural factors:
   - attitudes with regard to illness;
   - aesthetic considerations;
   - sense of responsibility towards subsequent generations;
   - recognition of the rights of the individual to certain living conditions and fulfilment.

b) Personal factors:
   - feeling of insecurity, of a threat to one's person, or, on the other hand, of invulnerability;
   - from a Freudian point of view: importance of the anal stage (obsession with cleanliness, purity).

c) Information factors:
   - existence of "scientific" measurements;
   - existence of pollution-harm causal relationships established by scientists;
   - publication of these data by the educational system and/or the media;
   - general attitude of the media towards the environment;

307

- action of "pro-environment" groups among the public.

d) Social stratification factors:
    - (see especially 6.3 and 6.4 below).

6.3.   Feeling of being able to act or not in the face of this disamenity or risk: The feeling of helplessness or of having ultimately to resign oneself to a particular damage to the environment reacts on the perceptive faculty itself: awareness is damped down or smothered in order to diminish its anxiety-generating effects. It must be remembered that fatalism has long been the rule in this sphere and that it is far from having been dispelled (while other forms of resignation which would have astonished our ancestors prevail on other questions).

6.4.   Taking into account the effects of possible action: Action to protect the environment is often, in its turn, the source of

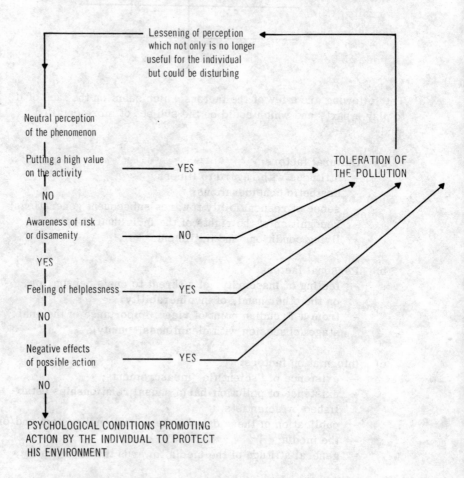

308

disamenities or risks which, being foreseeable and feared, tend
to induce a readiness to compromise with the activity in question,
and to react by revising one's perception of the danger involved.
For example, introduction of new constraints; paying higher prices
for products; living further away from one's place of work; what
would be the effects of a policy of rationing national resources to
ensure mankind's survival for one or more centuries ahead?

II. SOCIAL PERCEPTION OF DAMAGE

A. Social communications and conflicts of perception

a) Face-to-face communications

7. Bilateral relationships between the causer and the victim of damage
can result in a friendly settlement. B considers that A has caused him
a certain damage; A agrees and they agree on a certain compensation.
It is important to know whether A has promised not to do it again, or
whether he can do it again subject to further compensation, or whether
he has made no commitment as to the future.

In the case of successive friendly settlements, the compensation
curve is particularly interesting, since the damage is often cumulative
(poisoning, persistent disamenity, etc.). To begin with, the compensation may approximate to the "material" cost (repair of the damage);
subsequently the compensation must include an increasing element for
the disamenity caused; then comes the time when B no longer wants
compensation but wants the action complained of to cease. If A does
not wish to stop the activity which causes the damage, the situation
now becomes political: inevitable resort to violence or to an arbiter
possessing a power of constraint, usually a judge or public legislator.

8. The group of victims: face-to-face, informal groupings of victims
certainly exist (think of conversations on smog, fishermen on the banks
of a polluted river on which the fish are floating by belly upwards, etc.)
but they only acquire social significance through representatives (for
example, one of them makes a protest at the Town Hall, or a journalist
writes an account of what is happening); sometimes one of these representatives attempts to organise the protest by getting the victims
together, circulating a petition, etc.

9. One highly interesting phenomenon is when the group of victims
tries to identify a group of culprits:

- The group of culprits thus sometimes becomes aware of harming
others and a reaction process begins to take shape: attempt to

diminish or abolish the disamenity; attempt to convince people that there is none, etc.

- The group of culprits designated by the victims (or a given group of victims) corresponds more or less to the group of culprits which other people involved (another group of victims, experts on the disamenity in question, for example) would designate. Then begins a process of adjustment of differing views on the same phenomenon.

Face-to-face relationships thus trigger off a socialization of the conflict. Groups become aware of similarities of attitude and possibilities of mutual support; alignments begin to take place; spokesmen (individual or collective) will emerge now that there is a base from which they can draw support.

b) The experts

10. Well before the concern about the environment became widespread, our societies included persons specializing in the study of questions central to this problem (for example doctors, particularly those specializing in occupational health, geographers, sanitary engineers).

Other specializations are more recent: planning experts, ecologists, etc. In general, environmental problems only constitute one compartment, often as narrow as it is recent, of their special field, and at the same time of course extend far beyond their special field.

It is possible to conceive of concentric circles of communication of increasing size: first between teams or schools in the same speciality, then between experts of various specialities (or disciplines) and between those experts and the rest of the world (their customers, their students, the administration, public opinion, etc.). However faulty such communications may be, they promote a social recognition of the problem, while not necessarily its uniform perception since divergencies among the experts become clear and remain considerable. The underlying reasons for such divergencies would warrant thorough study; but we shall here do no more than briefly describe the effects which the experts' fields of activity should have on their social and time horizons, and beyond these, on their scales of values.

11. The respective fields of investigation or practice of the experts determine their respective social and time horizons. A hypothetical illustration is provided by the following table (in which the social horizon refers to the number of persons affected or taken into account by the expert's activity):

	SOCIAL HORIZON	
	NARROW	BROAD
Health experts	Medical specialists (respiratory tracts, psychiatry, etc.)	Preventive medicine, Public health, Social security.
Production experts	Engineers, Managers, Micro-economy.	Macro-economy, Geographers, Economic planners.
Lifestyle experts	Architects, Artists.	Town planners, Sociologists, Social planners.
Experts on biological balance	Biologists.	Ecologists.

Other similarly brief considerations will indicate the huge differences between experts' time horizons: the doctor does not look beyond the recovery of his patient; the architect does not look beyond the completion of a building or complex; the public-works engineer may try to find out about the foreseeable road traffic between two towns in 3, 10 or 20 years' time; the government planner tries to anticipate the behaviour of economic transactors in a few years' time and sometimes wonders about the next generation or beyond; the ecologist or certain geographers have problems about what will happen in 30 or 100 years.

12. The Field of Activity of Experts Determines Their Scale of Values. There can of course be no identity of views between experts in a same special field, nor will experts from different fields invariably disagree, yet on the whole the type of work which is done appears conducive to a specific line of thought. Thus a survey carried out in British Columbia, Canada (3), shows that environmental quality ranked first among the problems of the province in the eyes of 32 public health officials out of 79, compared with 5 engineers out of 50. When asked what most concerned them in the matter of water quality, three-fourths of the public health officers mentioned the danger to health and three-fifths of the engineers the higher production costs.

Trite conclusion: experts, even in one and the same special field, do not constitute a homogeneous group providing unequivocal data and recommendations. Experts have great trouble in communicating with each other. "Science" speaks with many voices, and as far as the environment is concerned, increases rather than reduces the social uproar (4).

B. The persistence of subjectivism

13. The scientific evaluation of damages may only play a transitory role in the conflicts and policies concerning the environment, since the progress achieved in each field either switches interest to a new, more subjective aspect, of the field, or else, when the most obvious problems in that field are in process of being solved), to another where the part played by subjectivism seems bound to be greater.

To give a rough idea of what we mean, let us say there are:

- Three broad fields of social preoccupation (concern):

    1. life (preservation of life: protection of health),

    2. quality of life,

    3. the future.

- and three approaches:

    1. sensory (through the senses: referred to above as "concrete perception"),

    2. scientific (attempt at objective knowledge, measurement, simulation, etc.),

    3. sentimental (or attribution of values: value judgements, beliefs, etc.).

With these we can sketch out - still in the broadest of terms - the following chronological framework: the dominant preoccupation will have as its object first life, then the framework of life and finally, hypothetically, the future, it being understood that, with varying degrees of emphasis, the three preoccupations are present simultaneously and, obviously, interact one with another. Within each field of preoccupation the main approach will be first through the senses (5), then to some extent through the scientific method, and finally through sentiment (attribution of values).

At the present time the dominant concern - although it is on the decline - is with the protection of life, and the accent is on the scientific approach. There are still some fine days ahead of us for value confrontations as to the respect due to human life, to all human life.

The concern in the ascendant is that for the framework of life, mainly through a sensory approach, plus a few attempts to master the problem in scientific circles, and no more than a few muttered comments (6) on the plane of values.

At some later epoch will the future become our dominant concern? We don't know the answer. Our assumption is that the future will not become a concern on its own account, but as a prolongation, a deepening of the discussion of values in regard to the framework of life and its preservation further and further into the future.

LIFE

APPROACHES

Sensory
Scientific
Sentimental

QUALITY OF LIFE

Sensory
Scientific
Sentimental

FUTURE

Sensory
Scientific
Sentimental

Use of approach :   weak
strong
very strong
dominant
impossible

14. Whatever the improvements or refinements made to this model, it will still have to be used with caution. It is an attempt to represent graphically the following series of hypotheses.

Disputes about the protection of human life are likely on the one hand to be appeased by the transition from the sensory approach to the scientific approach, and on the other hand stirred up again by the transition to confrontation on the values' plane. In practice this means that the damages will be better identified, better explained and better forestalled or repaired, but violent conflicts of values will break out and polarize citizens and nations. For example, how is the cost of very rare or costly medical treatment to be shared? Is there justification for fixing thresholds (of pollution for example) which insufficiently protect the most vulnerable one hundredth or one thousandth of the population? Is a rich (and overfed) country devoid of responsibility for the ravages caused by a famine at the other end of the earth? And so on.

At the same time concern about the framework of life is growing. On this issue confrontations of values are involved from the start, and it does not seem as if scientific or technological knowledge can be of much help in finding solutions or in reconciling points of view (it is easier to decide how to protect life than to devise safeguards for resources which are being depleted or aesthetic pleasures which are being threatened).

Finally, assuming that social concern for future generations becomes widespread, it is difficult to imagine that scientific demand can do more than provide support for the allegedly altruistic desires and phobias of particular groups.

The conclusion must be therefore that the relative importance of immaterial considerations, non-measurable damage or benefits will inevitably increase. The calculations and stratagem of the scientists and technocrats will matter less and less, unless they yield to the temptation of orchestrating a general conditioning of the population or find new ways of holding an active dialogue with them. On the other hand the ideologies, affinities, perhaps even the credos of sects or artistic schools will come more and more to the forefront and feed the flames of controversies in which any compromise will seem out of question.

When a society cannot allow its members to quarrel among themselves indefinitely, one course remains possible: that of a political decision to define and impose limits on the liberties and responsibilities of each member of the community.

III. SOCIAL DEMANDS AND POLITICAL DECISION-MAKING
IN ENVIRONMENTAL MATTERS

15. Conditions are mostly unfavourable to the formation of vigorous pressure groups and to agreement between them as to joint action.

15.1.   Excessive diversity of the interest concerned:

a) diversity of types of damage (noise, waste, depletion of resources, various types of pollution);

314

b) diversity of sources of damage:
   - geographic diversity,
   - diversity of damaging activities (industrial, military, transport, leisure pursuits ...);

c) diversity of damage caused by one and the same source:

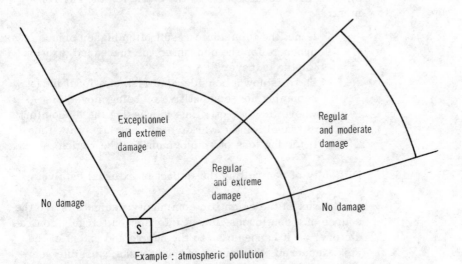

Example : atmospheric pollution

d) Heterogeneity of the dimensions of the damage:

   - small group of victims who can often obtain satisfaction at local level,
   - large group of victims (traffic pollution or chemical residues in food) only able to act at national or even international level,
   - ill-defined group among the population of the future (in 5, 10, 100 or more years) comprising the predictable victims of certain accumulations or certain harmful uses (depletion, non-treatment, etc.).

15. 2. Multiplicity of conflicts of interest - a factor tending to lessen the effectiveness of protest:

a) Everybody is polluted, everybody is a polluter'': the responsibilities are very unevenly divided but divided nevertheless (by his domestic heating, having a car, cigarette smoking, but above all and in general by his desire to maintain a certain style of life, the ordinary citizen is responsible for damage to the environment).

b)   Positive counterparts of activities damaging the environment: modern man cannot think of attacking those who damage the environment since they are the very people who are also its benefactors; he must act with circumspection, and this robs action of its impetus.

c)   Negative counterparts in the battle for the environment:

- is not the immediate result often higher prices of products for the consumer, or increased taxation for the taxpayer?
- there is now a considerable risk of a local industry becoming non-competitive or being moved elsewhere (further off, thus increasing the discomfort of travel for the worker; or very far away, thus involving loss of employment for the region).

15. 3.   Difficulty of controlling the impact of external catalysts.

a)   Impact of the scientific community: scientists are the source of a continuous flow of information (largely contradictory, as it happens) as to the nature and extent of the risks incurred, the causes of these risks, possible remedies, their cost, their possible advantages and disadvantages, etc. ;

b)   Impact of the mass media: the flow of information, even though incoherent, from the scientific community would only have a weak and gradual effect on opinion if it were not amplified and distorted by the press, radio and television: this combination of confused gropings or controversy in scientific circles with the sensationalism of journalists produces successive waves of interest, panic, incomprehension, indifference, anger, etc. ;

c)   Impact of the manipulative efforts of the administration and the government, which sometimes try to mobilize public opinion to obtain popular support for action against powerful vested interests, and sometimes seek to soothe public opinion when the proposed action threatens vested interests which it is desired to protect or exceeds the resources available at a particular time.

15. 4.   Inevitable extremism of certain elements, who

a)   transfer to environmental protection their hostility to modernization (industrialization) or to capitalism or socialism,

316

b)   suffer from a veritable ecological messianism according to which man is practically superfluous on earth,

c)   look for causes which lend themselves to demagogy.

This extremism can affect the forms and procedures of social demand and, often infecting those who would be prepared to play the most active roles, can give rise to problems of leadership, the most extreme leaders not being necessarily the best organisers and negotiators.

In the light of factors 1, 2, 3 and 4 above, it can be predicted that in spite of the universality of the damage (no one will escape one or other of its forms) and of the intolerable nature (physically or intellectually) of that damage for some people, it will be difficult to mobilize sufficient resources to organise and unite the many groups of interests concerned, and to carry on long-term campaigns and negotiations either vis-à-vis the authors of damage or vis-à-vis the public authorities.

The non-existence or ineffectiveness of ad hoc pressure groups makes it likely that the pro-environment interests will be taken over by organisations with more general objectives (political parties, trade unions, or possibly co-operative, consumer, or popular education movements) which are the only ones capable of pushing through the necessary compromises and organisation of structures; or they will be canalized by the public authorities into the formal systems of representation, unless perhaps they rally for a time around the banner of a charismatic leader or demagogue.

16.   Protection of the environment is a field of action which inevitably requires political decision-making but cannot be a field which the political authorities will spontaneously prefer.

16. 1.   Protection of the environment is par excellence a field which calls for political decisions (7); some of the reasons for this are as follows:

a)   conflicts of a similar nature occur repeatedly in various places, and it is logical to try to find a uniform solution for them: all the more logical because

b)   cases of damage to the environment are cumulative, and form a global problem for which groups demand global solutions (extending sometimes to international level), and because

317

c) to prevent market disturbances and to avoid creating additional dissatisfaction it is preferable to impose the same obligations on all those in the same situation;

d) The margin of ignorance or disagreement between experts as to the cause and extent of damage and the nature and foreseeable effects of policies for the environment prevents the experts from proposing a so-called exclusively technical solution to the problem;

e) furthermore, the designation of objectives cannot be left to the experts, the possibility of a return to a hypothetical natural state being ruled out;

f) equally, the choice of solutions cannot it seems be left to the protagonists involved, not only because of the general nature of the problem (cf. a, b, c), but also because of the inevitable absence of some of those concerned;

- in the first place, all those who are without knowing it the victims of damage to their environment (for example people who have not yet reached the critical threshold in the absorption of products harmful to health);
- in the second place, all those now living or not yet born who will be in the near or more distant future the victims of present harm done to the environment (for example, genetic risks, irreversible deterioration, depletion of reserves, etc);
- in the third place, all those who, fascinated by the positive aspects of this or that phenomenon, choose to tolerate negative aspects, including those which affect the environment (thus repeating the suicidal choice of some people in some of the most varied fields: food, alcoholism, car driving, etc.).

g) The intervention of a political authority seems particularly called for if a situation arises in which it is possible to impose a course of behaviour which, because it is initially unpleasant and costly, would not have been spontaneously adopted by the people concerned although it will ultimately be to their benefit (either because in the long run the benefits outweigh the costs, or because intangible satisfactions ultimately outweigh dissatisfactions), or if

h) the solutions which were originally intended to be purely technical result in an authoritarian redistribution of the rights or duties of certain social categories, or a re-allocation of resources within the society, both of which are recognized as falling within the competence of the public authority.

16.2.   Protection of the environment is a field of action in which the public authority is very reluctant to operate.   The main reasons for this are as follows:

a)   The instability of social demands in this field:

- because of the problems of leadership of the interest groups involved (see 15 above);
- because of the factors set out in support of hypothesis 15 above, in particular 15.3: impact of external catalysts (scientists, media), which are especially important since attention has only recently been drawn to these problems;
- because of the relationship at any given moment between the state of social perception of a non-specialized group, such as a social stratum, and its practice (and also the image it has of this through the organisations which represent it).   This practice, by mobilizing the group to work for a particular objective (which may even have no direct relationship with the environment) will evoke a certain number of pollution problems which are intellectually or symbolically connected with it, and modifies for a time the structuration of the field of its perception by bringing about a redistribution of the values it attributes to various disamenities.

b)   The unpredictability of the reaction of these social demands to a policy intended to give them satisfaction:

- in principle, the decision-maker believes he is dealing with a demand the satisfaction of which

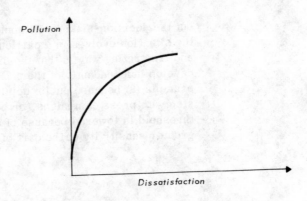

319

will pay him certain dividends (contentment of the
demanders, support for his action, favourable
votes, etc.): if he manages to diminish pollution,
the contentment of the demanders (though possibly
not of the polluters) will increase.

He will therefore pursue a policy aiming either at
reducing the pollution to a tolerable limit (so as to
remove this problem from the list of urgent claims),

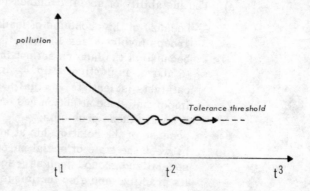

or at reducing the pollution well below the tolerance
threshold, so as to create significant well-being,
for which he hopes people will be grateful;

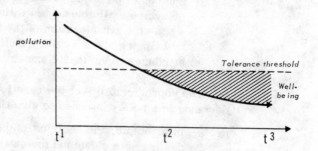

but the decision-maker will sometimes find that
the situation evolves in a particularly perverse
and frustrating way in that the dissatisfaction will
develop independently of the pollution, either for
example (8) because public opinion progresses in
step with press campaigns, or because the tolerance
threshold is lowered because of new information or
greater sensitivity on the part of the public:

320

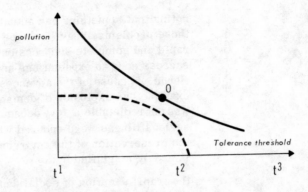

In the diagram above the policy initiated at time t^1 was directed at reducing the pollution level to the point O, after which it was expected that, the pollution now having come down to the tolerance threshold of the population, public opinion would now be satisfied; but when, at time t^2, the pollution level was brought down to the level aimed at, the tolerance threshold was already on the downward trend: the population is still dissatisfied, and, with the pollution level diminishing more slowly than the tolerance threshold level, dissatisfaction now increases; at time t^3, in spite of all that has been done, the feeling of well-being of the population has diminished... and the public authorities risk having to endure the consequences.

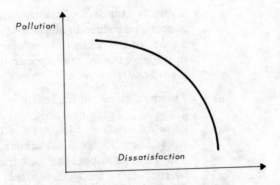

The situation represented in the above diagram is far from being an academic hypothesis in the 1970's. The combined effects of the interest and means of investigation of the scientists and the appetite of the media on these questions produces an increasing sensitivisation of at least part of public opinion which,

321

noting that something can actually be done about these problems, begins to hope for and demand the rapid and complete suppression of them. Every success adds to expectations and increases impatience: because of the advances in medicine, for example, an explosion of demand occurs which was unpredictable a few decades earlier when most serious illness were endured with resignation. In the preservation of the environment this phenomenon is unduly magnified by:

- the transformation of social demand: not only does a shift occur (see 13) in preoccupations and hence dissatisfactions from one field to another (as from biological imperatives to a quality of life bringing fulfilment), but the standards applicable to each field are constantly being revised. A few examples follow:

- First, the notion of risk, based on the probability of damage, is tending to be replaced by that of the integral rights of the human person - of every human person; the "weak concentrations" which a short while ago seemed desirable are now rejected, since they are now believed to have harmful effects even though it is hardly possible to measure them; any calculations which purport to show the economic irrationality of protecting the most vulnerable individuals are indignantly condemned.

- Secondly, the fact of taking future well-being into account introduced such a wildly erratic variable as that of the dates to be adopted: what is desirable in the short term may appear intolerable in the long term, and vice versa.

- Thirdly, since public health objectives are progressively being replaced by public happiness, a growing number of features of the present-day world begin to seem barbarous, unworthy, ugly - and if people begin to look for happiness and peace by respecting the environment, a new cycle of development opens up for mankind which is potentially as productive of drastic change as the "mastery of nature" cycle was.

- No political authority can relax in the face of the development of social demands to which neither the present instruments of measurement nor the good old political recipes of "a bone to gnaw at" type can be applied.

322

c) Both the arithmetic of democracy and that of oligarchy are ill-adapted to the treatment of socia demands in environmental matters.

The democratic way: Air, space, water are collective resources, and it is normal that the community should affirm its rights to manage the common heritage; but this poses serious problems: does the public (or, to put it very concretely, the electoral body) care sufficiently about the preservation of the environment a) to give solid support to the public authority which, when it takes appropriate action, provokes dissatisfaction among those who arrogate to themselves the right to use and abuse the community's resources? b) to accept for itself certain limitations to its rights or enjoyment? The dilemma for the political authority is the choice between the risk of giving the majority of the electors imperceptible and/or collective advantages which are outweighed by perceptible and/or individual disadvantages, and the risk of finding itself reproached by a majority of the electors (possibly somewhat hypocritically) with having managed the resources of the community badly.

Seen from this general angle, the problem of democratic government is either to devise environment policies which negatively affect only a small proportion of the population (hence no general increase in product prices, no generalized constraints, etc.) or else to find ways of mobilizing a large part of public opinion in favour of environmental objectives whilst remaining relatively assured that it will not provoke an explosion of expectations in this field (cf. above: transformation of demand).

But the problem can be seen from a more particular angle: that of the re-distribution, within the population, of certain advantages and disadvantages. What worries a democratic political authority is that, in the short and medium term, it seems that the advantages are distributed to a small number of people (those who were directly and consciously the victims) and the disadvantages to a large number of people (consumers and taxpayers who bear the brunt of the cost of the remedial action); obviously in the long run the advantages should become perceptible to a large number of people and the costs could in part be met out of savings in public health, etc., but in the long run the democratic leaders in power will have died.

323

Another cause for worry is the need to take account of the welfare of non-voters - the young (can one hope in this case to obtain some thanks from their parents?) and above all future generations. Is it possible, without going over to an authoritarian system, to limit the welfare or even the increase in welfare of the living for the benefit of those not yet born?

The democratic way would thus seem to take account of the following imperatives:

- making public opinion gradually more aware of the present harm being done to the environment and the improvements which have been and still remain to be made, at the same time staving off both short-term indifference and excessive expectations; this is more a matter for educational development than for publicity campaigns and rhetoric;
- choosing kinds of action which will penalize the smallest number and/or benefit the largest number of people possible, and conversely treating with the greatest suspicion types of remedial action which penalize too large a number of people for the benefit of too small a number;
- obtaining, when circumstances are propitious, a general mandate to protect the environment so as to ensure better conditions of existence for all citizens now living and yet to be born. On the strength of this mandate, the fundamental tasks of a specialized agency would be to:
  1) collect, process and criticize all available information, whether of a scientific or normative kind, and as necessary arrange for the production of indispensable but unavailable knowledge;
  2) promote, from its own standpoint, the consistency of official decision-making (by reconsidering energy, transport and other policies from the environmental policy aspect and by pointing out the possible consequences of environmental policy for public health, delinquency, tourism, etc.);
  3) conduct or organise specific actions which seem most urgently required and/or to best advantage;
  4) acquaint the public with fundamental options which can only be adopted by means of a political decision.

The oligarchic way: The brigades of ecological militants are still far from being able to seize the power which, at least in the near future, the electors will refuse to give them; even if they did seize it their internal dissensions and plans for the radical re-organisation of life on our planet would no doubt ensure that they would soon lose it again. The oligarchic prospect sketched out here therefore only assumes the possibility of the access of the "environmentalist" pressure groups to a polyarchic seat of power in the case where a certain number of groups agree among themselves (or through the intermediary of politicians) to take the main decisions.

The fundamental question is that of agreement with the economic interests: is it possible to find a basis for agreement by insisting on the short term (in which after all economic activity is not restricted but stimulated by a few constraints and the opening up of a new sector of activity) and on the long term (in which the survival of the system of production is at stake)? Or will the prospect of increasing subjection to a logic not compatible with their own drive producers into irreconcilable opposition to the guardians of the environment?

The support which the environmentalists could hope for should come from scientific circles (whose influence also makes itself felt on those responsible for running the economy) and public opinion; but their main source of weakness would probably be their internal disagreements, which would gravely handicap them in the continuous bargaining process which is an essential feature of a polyarchic system.

CONCLUSION

It is surely a worthy aim to become better acquainted with the cost of damage to the environment, or rather of the damage done to man through his environment. In its favour there is not only the usual scientist's argument that one should try to find out everything that can be known, but also the hope that, as a result, governments and public opinion will be alerted, and that this will in turn help to protect or restore the environment. However, to approach the question of damage to the environment from the standpoint of costs is to use a two-edged weapon. On the one hand, the revelation of a cost item provides a strong incentive for action (either to pass the cost on to the party responsible for it, or to urge investment designed to eradicate it); while on the other hand, the work of calculating the costs obliges one to accept the constraints and postulates of the methods available for the purpose, which may make one lose sight of the real significance of the problem.

Any change in a part, however tiny, of our planet and any repercussion of any act on the biological or psychic processes of a living being may, or may not, be described as "damage" (9), depending on the standards used by the observer, and his conception of damage will of course colour the assessment of its cost. All the approaches which claim to short-circuit these value judgements or simply pretend to be able to ignore them are delusions and, instead of trying to shed the light of reason and understanding on the clash of interests involved, they confuse the issue with their would-be socially neutral rulings untied to value standards. One could say much about those public health authorities who only see costs where there is a duly noted "disease" and about those welfare authorities who casually declare that they are not concerned with non-material welfare, and so on. However, it is certain economists who seem to be the worst victims of the illusion of ideological virginity and to be the most blind to the implications and consequences of their methodology, so that we shall conclude with some thoughts on their approach to the problem.

These economists, when faced with a social problem created by the way the market functions and by the clearly undesirable (and socially unsupportable) results of trying to satisfy individual desires, find nothing but the market and individual desires to use as tools and instruments for investigating and measuring.

The market, however, is man-made and if one uses it as the only instrument for trying to assess damage, one will inevitably come to reproduce the preferences and value judgements of the social groups who have succeeded in imposing their preferences on it. If one consults individuals regarding the money value they put on this or that damage to the environment, when they are very ignorant of the extent of the damage (10) and are also being continually goaded on by their need for additional money, one is making a short-sighted decision for a second time, but inexcusable this time as it is in a scientific study, such short-sighted decisions have brought present-day society so many agonizing problems.

An individual can only claim compensation for damage effects which he perceives (11) and suffers directly, but as a rule he is unaware of many of the damage effects (even the specialists rarely agree on them), or he is indifferent to the extent that he does not suffer them himself, or not at once. In practice, a person may have the impression

326

that a sum of money which, though small (say, a month's wages) is very desirable as marginal income in proper compensation for a disamenity which he considers to be of little importance. The economists will then put down this figure of a month's wages as being the damage cost, but the real damage will occur only gradually. Once this person's nervous or physiological balance has been upset, he will no longer work so well, he will be a greater accident risk and will cause disturbances around him (e. g. , his greater nervousness will cause family disputes). In the end, if there ever is an end, this person's difficulties will make society suffer considerable damage in the form of lower output, more accidents, greater tension and increased medical expenditures which, however, will be wasted because it cannot prevent the disamenity. There will also be problems of schooling or of juvenile delinquency due to difficulties on the father's side, in addition to which the person will be less inclined to assume his social responsibilities (as a school parent, in trade unions, and sports clubs, on local government boards, etc.). It is absurd to suppose that the accountable value of such a chain of damage is a month's wages.

To take another example, if the rents or prices of houses near a source of noise do not go down, economists will not consider that these houses suffer damage. The truth is that a source of noise is often at the same time a source of employment, in which case the occupants will have had to choose between two disamenities, namely, putting up with the noise, or living far from their work. As they will have chosen the lesser of the two evils, thereby keeping house rents and prices up at their previous level, economists are prepared to conclude that no damage has been done.

The following is a further example. If an open space has been made in an overcrowded area by pulling down buildings and one questions the surrounding population to find out whether they want this area made into a park, middle-class people will tend to strongly favour the planting of trees and flowers and the providing of children's playgrounds, and they will even agree to finance at least a part of the project. On the other hand, a population of immigrant workers will show no such enthusiasm, firstly because their aim is to save as much as possible for going back home or for supporting relatives in their home country, and secondly because they are afraid that the park project would lead to a rise in rents, so that sooner or later they would have to leave that part of town, which would then be taken over by middle-class people. However, economists are blissfully-ignorant of these social undercurrents and will conclude that, in identical circumstances, the park should be located in a middle-class quarter rather than in an immigrant workers' quarter. Meanwhile, if some other unspecified group expresses its readiness to pay more in order to turn the open space into a car park, this is the project which should be chosen. Nevertheless, there can be little doubt that the opposite order of priority will be followed, both in the interest of public welfare and for the sake of keeping down the costs which society will have to meet later, since it is the poorest section of the population which has most difficulty in finding compensation in the market-place for the low quality of its environment and which will pay the most to sickness, alcoholism, delinquency and general social maladjustment.

Furthermore, in addition to their ignorance of the social background, economists fail to take account of people's civic sense in certain countries. This civic sense makes nonsense of their approach, because these countries have for a long time had public institutions for settling problems which clearly could not be solved by individual initiative, including such things as street-lighting, street-cleaning, military protection, constructing water mains and minting coins. The citizens of these countries are accustomed to distinguish between the sphere of their private affairs in which they can reason like an "economic man" (but are far from always doing so for traditional, prestige or moral motives) and the sphere of public affairs in which they know that their personal points of view are unreliable because they do not cover all the interest involved. Without going so far as to say that all these citizens are imbued with Jean-Jacques Rousseau's ideas on the moral superiority of the public interest, one may at all events be sure that they would not take seriously anyone who tried to make them say whether a park, or a refuse incinerator, or a policeman was worth an increase in taxation of one or two per cent. They would consider that these were decisions to be taken at community level in the light of the community's overall requirements and of the most rational possible use of its resources.

It is surely a serious matter that economists who wish to guide public authorities in their efforts to correct the harmful effects of certain kinds of economic behaviour should be using a method which recognizes no yardstick except such economic behaviour and proceeds as if these public authorities did not exist.

NOTES

1. Including here their natural but artificially-accelerated renewal.

2. Even when assisted by human labour.

3. W. R. Derrick Sewell: Environmental Perceptives and Attitudes of Engineers and Public Health Officials, Environment and Behaviour, March 1971, pp. 23-59.

4. Sewell's above-mentioned study ends as follows: "Unless our present experts broaden their views and integrate their activities, they may well contribute more to the promotion of the environmental crisis than to its solution". (p. 58).

5. Except for the field of concern about the future.

6. This only applies to society; at the level of the individual we certainly have some values, which may be implicit, poorly defined and non-hierarchised, but values all the same as regards our environment.

7. The term political decision is used here to denote decisions not only by legislators but also by administrators or judges.

8. This situation resembles the one studied at Toronto where it seems that "the growth of public concern has followed closely the growth in newspaper coverage" (Auliciens and Burton: Perception and awareness of air pollution in Toronto).

9. Just as they may be called "goods" or "services".

10. "The immediately perceived sensations are merely the tip of the iceberg" - Coddington, Opschoor and Pearce: Some Limitations of Benefit-Cost Analysis in respect of Programmes with Environmental Consequences, in Problems of Environmental Economics, OECD, Paris, 1972.

11.   and his assessment will of course vary widely depending on the
       information he is given. He may be fobbed off with negligible
       compensation, or he may be alarmed so that instead of any kind
       of compensation he will demand a stop to the damage.

LIST OF PARTICIPANTS

Discussion Leader

M. Potier,
   Head, Central Analysis and Evaluation Unit,
   Environment Directorate,
   OECD, Paris.

Authors

Dr. Leonard Hamilton,
   St. Catherine's College, Oxford,
   United Kingdom.
(Currently at Brookhaven National Laboratory, Upton, L.I., New York,
   USA).

Prof. Robert Haveman,
   Department of Economics, University of Wisconsin,
   Madison 53706, Wisconsin,
   United States of America.

Prof. Serge Christophe Kolm,
   2, rue Henri-Heine, Paris 16°,
   France.

Prof. Karl-Göran Mäler,
   Department of Economics, University of Stockholm,
   Fack 104 05, Stockholm 50,
   Sweden.
(Currently Professor at the Economic Research Institute, Stockholm
   School of Economics, Sveavägen 65, Stockholm VA, Sweden).

Prof. Akio Morishima,
   Nagoya University, Nagoya,
   Japan.

Dr. Carl O. Muehlhause
   Office of Science and Technology, Executive Office of the President,
   Washington D.C. 20506,
   United States of America.

Prof. Gilberto Muraro,
   Università degli Studi di Padova, Facoltà di Scienze Statistiche,
   Padova,
   Italy.

Prof. Lucien Nizard,
   Institut d'Etudes politiques, Université de Grenoble,
   Cedex 17, 38000 Grenoble-Gare
   France.

Dr. Johannes B. Opschoor,
   Instituut voor Milieuvraagstukken, Vrije Universiteit, Amsterdam,
   Netherlands.

Prof. Jean Tournon,
   Institut d'Etudes politiques, Université de Grenoble,
   Cedex 17, 38000 Grenoble-Gare,
   France.

Dr. Ronald E. Wyzga,
   Environment Directorate, OECD, 2 rue André-Pascal,
   75775 Paris Cedex 16,
   France.

OECD Secretariat

J. Ph. Barde

W. Czerniejewicz

J. Doi

U. Luukko   Central Analysis and Evaluation Unit,
                             Environment Directorate, OECD.
G. Panella

H. Smets

R.E. Wyzga

Editor

R.E. Wyzga, OECD.